Water Wars

Water Wars

Coming Conflicts in the Middle East

JOHN BULLOCH

AND

ADEL DARWISH

VICTOR GOLLANCZ

LONDON

First published in Great Britain 1993
by Victor Gollancz
A Cassell imprint
Villiers House, 41/47 Strand, London WC2N 5JE

A catalogue record for this book is
available from the British Library

ISBN 0 575 05533 2

Photoset in Great Britain by
Rowland Phototypesetting Ltd, Bury St Edmunds, Suffolk
Printed in Great Britain by
St Edmundsbury Press Ltd, Bury St Edmunds, Suffolk

Contents

Authors' Note

No attempt has been made in this book to give a scholarly transliteration of Arabic or Iranian names of people or places. The style adopted is the one generally used in British or French newspapers, which it is thought would be most familiar to readers of this work in the English language.

Acknowledgements

The genesis of this book was the separate realization by the two authors that it was water, not oil, that was fast becoming the most divisive issue in the Middle East.

In 1991, as John Bulloch was researching his book *No Friend But the Mountains* on the plight of the Kurds, he gradually became aware that water was being used as a weapon, not only in the conflict between the Kurds and the Iraqis, but also by Turkey and Syria. In the same period, Adel Darwish had a number of conversations in Cairo with Dr Boutros Boutros-Ghali, the United Nations Secretary General who was then head of the Egyptian foreign service. Dr Boutros-Ghali has always been closely involved in the politics of water, and concerned at the effects which shortages might have in Africa and the Middle East. His ideas, as well as those of the team of very capable water specialists and diplomats he gathered around him in the Egyptian foreign ministry, inspired Darwish to carry out more detailed research.

Realizing that they were working in parallel, the two authors decided to pool the wealth of material they were accumulating and produce a joint book.

We are therefore grateful to Dr Boutros-Ghali for the impetus of his ideas, and to all the Egyptian officials whose perceptions forced us to reconsider old assumptions or re-think accepted wisdom.

The often heated debates in the Egyptian Parliament sparked other new assessments, and we are very grateful to Dr Hamdi el-Tahri for his advice and guidance, as well as for his interesting study 'Forthcoming Water Wars'.

We have decided to keep this book as free as possible of figures and statistics; these can be found by those who need them in more specialized works, some of which we list in the Bibliography. We have also avoided footnotes, acknowledging in the text wherever possible the sources of our information. Somewhat to our surprise, that was not always possible: in the Middle East water is now as sensitive a subject as arms, defence, or economic secrets; indeed, it is often linked with all those things. The result was that at the close of many interesting and useful discussions with ministers or officials, that dread phrase 'off the record' would be dropped in. That does not lessen our gratitude to those in Egypt, Ethiopia, Iraq, Israel, Jordan, Lebanon, Libya, Syria and Turkey who took us behind the public scenes of amity and good neighbourliness to reveal the fears they felt, the designs they had or the schemes they were determined to frustrate.

We discovered that a great mass of information was being published on our subject in many parts of the world, though it has so far made little impact; to keep track of all that material we were greatly helped by the staff of the library of the *Independent* in London: Justin Arundale, Gertrud Erbach, Ken Gresham, Brita Latham, Jeremy Turner, Giovanni Vasco, Barry Perkins, Stephen McEntee, Larry Lawrence and Jon Hall.

Other friends and colleagues who provided us with a steady flow of material included Pat Murray of Population Concern, Tariq el-Shami of Cairo Television, Samia Hosni of Reuters; Faried Abd el-Maguid, Amin el-Ghaffari, Aliyah Abd el-Azziz of Arab Research Centre; Dr Omar Al-Hassan of the Gulf Centre for Strategic Studies; officials of the Washington office of the World Bank; Tunisia's Minister of Environment Mohammed al-Mahdi Malika and the director of his office, Mme Zeineb Ben Youssef; Ibrahim el-Abed, the head of the Foreign Information Bureau of the United Arab Emirates; Salah Maaoui and Ezzeddine Besbes of Agence Tunisienne de Communication Exterieure; Helen Davis and her staff at the British–Israel Public Affairs Committee; Ahmed Ersoy at the Turkish Embassy in London; Dr John Dalton, formerly of the Food and Agriculture Organization in Addis Ababa; Ashraf Mohsen of the Egyptian foreign ministry; Duncan Snelling and Arlene Gorodensky; to all of them we are most grateful.

In addition to Dr Boutros-Ghali and Dr el-Tahri, other dis-

tinguished academics who helped us included Professor John Waterbury of Princeton University; Professor Tony Allan of London
University; Professor Ewan Anderson of Durham University; Professor Seyfi Tashan of Hacettepe University in Ankara, Professor
John Kolars of University of Michigan, Sana Bardawil of St Anthony's
College, Oxford. Natasha Beschorner, whose work was published in
the Adelphi papers series, discussed with us the result of her research,
giving new insight in many areas.

As always, we were greatly helped by Maryann Bird of the *Independent* Foreign Desk. John Parker, chief of the *Independent*'s copy
department, was of tremendous assistance in collating and organizing
the mass of material we gathered, while Ian Pecham's technical
expertise often saved our words from black holes in the computers.

Liz Knights, our publisher at Gollancz, suggested the idea of a book
on water in the Middle East, and has greatly improved the final result
by her careful and constructive editing.

We are grateful to all the many people who have helped us, but we
emphasize that the analysis, the conclusions, the inferences – and the
mistakes – are entirely our own.

John Bulloch and Adel Darwish
Oxford and London, July 1993

THE MIDDLE EAST

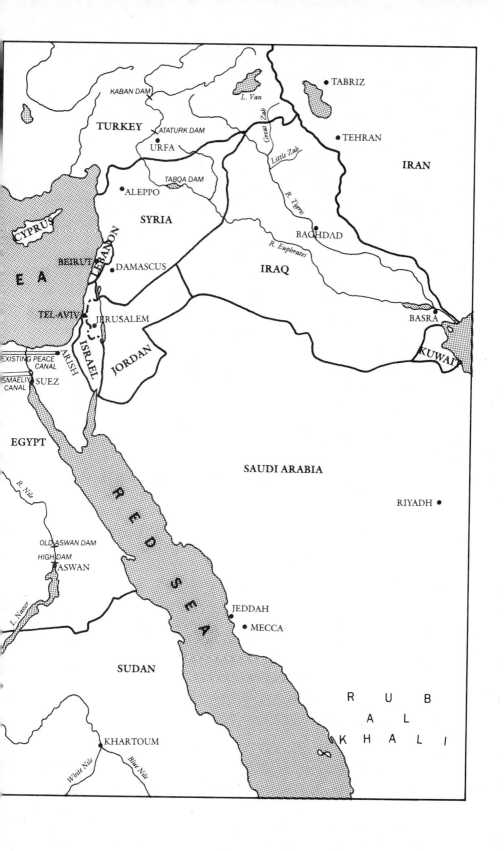

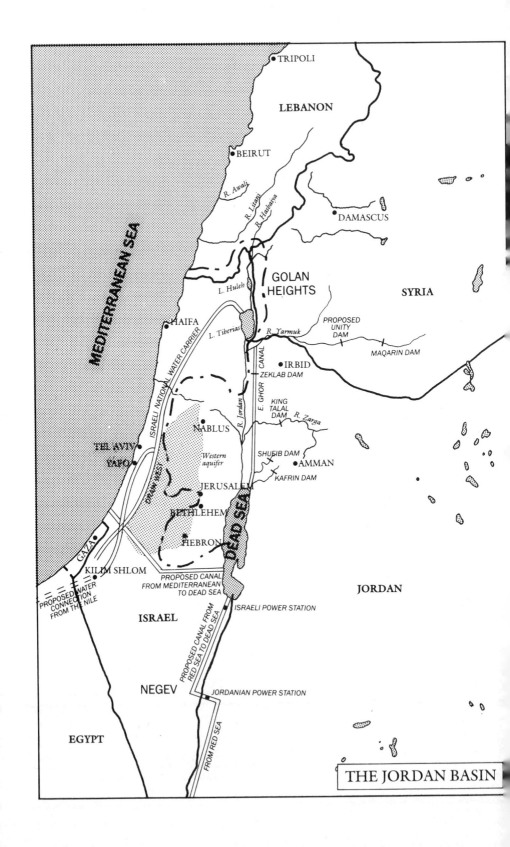

THE JORDAN BASIN

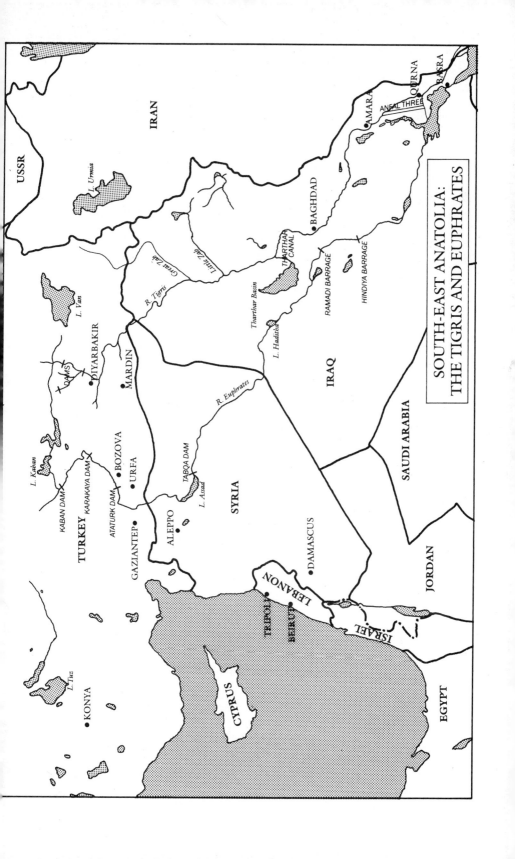

SOUTH-EAST ANATOLIA:
THE TIGRIS AND EUPHRATES

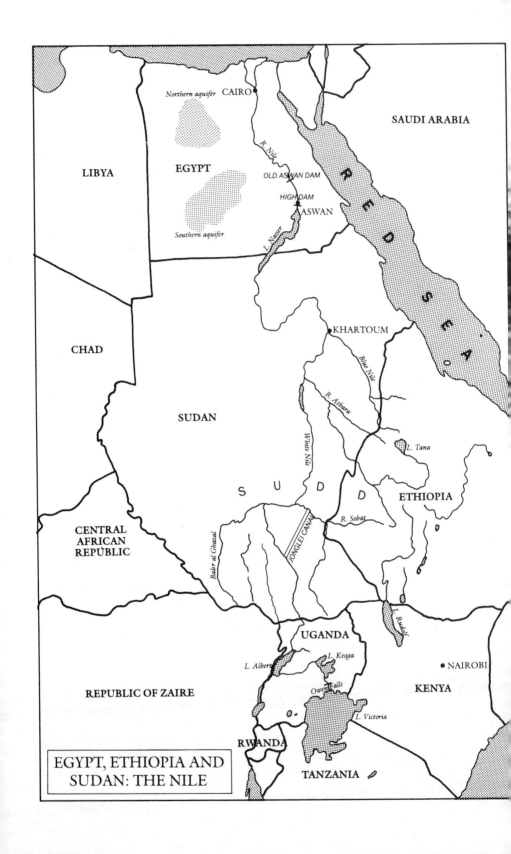

EGYPT, ETHIOPIA AND
SUDAN: THE NILE

1

Water: the Most Important Resource in the Middle East

From Turkey to the Gulf, through the heart of the turbulent Middle East, water is a vital factor in the politics of the region as well as the lives of its people. The lack of adequate supplies of water in the arid lands that form 80 per cent of the Middle East forces leaders into strange alliances and apparently pointless foreign adventures. In order to project power into areas where they seek either trade or influence, the few water-rich countries ostentatiously demonstrate the abundance they control. And in order to ensure their livelihoods, farmers take up arms to defend their land from their neighbours. Water is so vital in this most volatile of the world's troubled regions that it could be a force for peace, inducing old enemies to cooperate for the common good; but history and current events show that it is more likely to be a disruptive influence, a cause of conflict. Today, water can divide countries with similar political systems and a tradition of friendly cooperation, as in the case of Saudi Arabia and Jordan, or it can lead to cooperation between old enemies, as it has between Israel and Jordan, which have agreed an agenda for the discussion of their shared water problems.

Israelis and Arabs alike face vital questions over water, which will determine the future of their countries and their peoples. Both sides in the forty-year-old core conflict of the region know that finite resources and burgeoning populations, accompanied by urbanization and industrialization, are bound to lead to growing competition for the available water, if agreement cannot be reached. Already water has had a crucial influence in one major war, the Arab–Israeli conflict of 1967. As long ago as 1948 water shaped the policies of the early Zionists, as they tried to set the borders of their new state so as to have access to the then-plentiful supplies in Lebanon. More than thirty years later, the attraction of those rivers in Lebanon played a part in Israel's strategy as its armies swept into Lebanon to fight the Palestinians.

Now, the plentiful water supplies of Turkey are enabling that country to exert an influence on its Arab neighbours, and are a factor in the low-intensity war that has been going on for over a decade in south-eastern Anatolia between the Turkish forces and the Kurdish elements seeking greater autonomy. Egypt, almost totally dependent on the waters of the Nile, has always made the safety and continued flow of the great river the central concern of its policy: throughout history, Egypt has been as concerned with affairs in central Africa as it has with the actions of its immediate neighbours. The apparently profitless Libyan adventures in Uganda or Chad can be understood in the context of Colonel Muammar Gaddafi's efforts to influence Cairo, or to secure the source of his own 'Great Man-made River', a grandiose project to pipe water from the unpopulated south of the country to the urbanized north.

As the twentieth century nears its end, it is constant increases in population that put the greatest pressure on water resources, and force politicians to put water at the top of their agendas. A Central Intelligence Agency risk assessment paper for the United States government has estimated that in at least ten places in the world war could erupt over dwindling shared water resources. The majority of those potential crisis spots are in the Middle East; it was no accident that when, in 1992, the Pentagon undertook a drastic review of possible future conflicts that might call for American intervention, one of the first contingencies studied was a war between Syria and Turkey. For the fact is that disputes over water in the Middle East are bound to spill over into other areas: 85 per cent of the water coming into the rivers of Arab states* comes from non-Arab countries upstream.

* i.e. members of the Arab League, which includes all North African states plus Sudan, Mauritania and Somalia; all countries of the Levant and the Arabian Peninsula plus Iraq.

The fact that the USA remains vitally concerned with events in the Middle East, even though the rivalries of the cold war have ended, reflects the world's continued – and even increasing – dependence on Middle East oil. But water is in many cases now as important as oil in shaping the Arabs' development and relations with their neighbours. The outside world, and especially the developed nations led by the USA and in this context Japan, has to depend for its economic life on a continued steady supply of oil. Although at the time of writing there is a world oil glut, the predictions are that this will end before the turn of the century; after that, any interruption to Middle East oil would have serious consequences to the world economy. Outside powers therefore have an incentive to do what they can to ensure stability in the region. And to avoid disputes in the future, disputes that could spill over into conflict, the USA and its allies are eager to do what they can to help the countries of the region achieve their own solution to their own particular problems. Unlike the region's traditional border, ethnic or ideological disputes, which are normally defused with little or no military conflict or put on ice by bribes and pressure from external powers, the existing and coming water disputes make a large-scale military conflict very likely.

With the cold war won, and the USA the one remaining world superpower, Washington apparently feels that in 1991 it gave a sufficient demonstration of its capability for intervention when it expelled Iraq from Kuwait in the second Gulf war in a decade. The USA, though vitally concerned that the Middle East should remain stable and at peace, seems to have decided that it has little need to interfere in the day-to-day affairs of the region, even if it would move in again if the oilfields were at risk. The result is that the volatile states of the area are left to pursue their own quarrels and seek their own solutions.

The message coming out of the Middle East is that if tragedy is to be avoided there will have to be cooperation, but cooperation implies sharing, and sharing means that some countries will at times be worse off than they are now. At present, none of the countries involved seems willing to risk that. Egypt has always made it plain that any threat to the Nile waters would be a cause of war, an attitude echoed by Israel in modern times: Israel has threatened to attack Syria if any unilateral action is taken to build dams that would diminish the flow into the Sea of Galilee in northern Israel. Yet hydrologists in Israel, Syria and Jordan realize very well that dams are needed. What has not been worked out is who gets what, and who pays for it. Sooner rather than later that circle will have to be squared if there are not to be profound changes in water use in all three countries.

In the past, oil was the main cause of disputes among the countries of the Middle East, and access to oil drew the superpowers into involvement with events in the region. Today, sixty years after the first Arab oilwell was tapped, the rich countries of the Gulf have finally worked out an effective system with which to spread a small part of their wealth around to the poorer, non-oil countries by grants, loans and aid packages. This not only irons out disparities in national incomes, but also ensures that the rich countries receive help and support when they need it. Between 1973, when oil prices first began to rise, and 1989 the rich Arab states contributed almost US $100 billion to developing countries and multilateral aid agencies. Most was extended bilaterally, usually for general support, and 85 per cent was on concessionary terms. The main donors were the leading oil states – Kuwait, Qatar, Saudi Arabia and the United Arab Emirates between them provided more than 90 per cent of Arab aid. About 60 per cent of the money given went to Arab countries, thus defusing criticism based on jealousy and accepting the idea that Arab oil was the heritage of Arab League countries as a whole.

Naturally, the lack of water is a problem not only in the Middle East, although in general the lack of it is confined to the Third World and to the southern hemisphere, with the industrialized North better off. But it is in the Middle East that the problem is most acute, and most dangerous. While water is becoming scarce in other places, leading to a conflict of national interests, it is only in the Middle East that aggrieved countries have vast financial reserves, huge standing armies, air forces, bombs, rockets and, in some cases, nuclear capability. They also have a modern history of being willing to settle disputes by military means, a history of conflict, a common acceptance of the use of force to end quarrels.

Water: the Most Important Resource in the Middle East

A few years ago concerned scientists in all the countries of the region began uncoordinated but matching campaigns to force the politicians into awareness of the situation, and at least to begin discussing what should be done. Then in the winter of 1992 came one of the worst things that could have happened: after three years of the most severe drought the area had ever known, there were the best rains for years. Of course, it was an immediate boon to the water reserves, replenishing the reservoirs and aquifers, scouring river beds and rinsing land polluted by chemicals. But for the small but dedicated band of water engineers, academics and hydrologists of all the countries concerned, it was a set-back. As the land dried and cracked, as farmers saw their crops fail and industrialists had their supplies rationed, gradually the people and the politicians had been forced into understanding that they faced a crisis, that swift action was needed to avert disaster. Then the rains came, the earth greened, the desert flowers bloomed and the dire warnings of those who understood the situation were silenced by the welcome drumming of rain on the roof. The problem could be ignored for another year or two.

At one of the many water conferences arranged by the UN – in Dublin in 1992 – Dr Arcot Ramachandran, director of the UN Conference on Water and the Environment, described the 'profligate waste and degradation that has resulted from neglect of effective water resources management'. Water was no longer the cheap and plentiful resource that it was when today's giant cities were established, usually on the banks of free-flowing and pristine rivers that are now murky, sluggish streams of polluted waste. 'Lack of water will soon be seen to be at least as critical as lack of oil in conditioning the pace of national development,' Dr Ramachandran said.

Scientists estimate that by the year 2000 many countries will have only about half as much water as they had in 1975, yet demands for water may well have doubled. In the Middle East, with its sparse water resources, the situation will be worse than in many places: in 1989 the total population of the region was 314 million; with a growth rate of 2.8 per cent it will be 423 million by 2000, and will have doubled in twenty-five years' time. These figures alone mean that there will be a crisis, while other factors involved – wastage, national interests, traditional rivalries, urbanization and industrialization – mean that the crunch may come even sooner than the experts predict.

That a crisis point will be reached now seems certain, and scientists have worked out just when: the year 2050. At the mid-point of the next century, the world's population will have doubled to ten billion people, sharing the same quantity of water that is available today. The result, says Dr Haroldo Matteos de Lemos of the University of Rio de Janeiro, is that 40 per cent of the world's population will suffer from water shortages to one degree or another. Even then, the main effect is going to be felt in the deprived South, not the still affluent North.

Twenty-five years before the world reaches the crunch predicted by Matteos de Lemos, an earlier crisis point will be reached. In 2025, according to the UN, the world will have 8,000 million people to feed. The already large populations of Egypt and Sudan – 55 million and 26 million – will both double in twenty-four years at the present rate of increase of 2.9 per cent. In Syria, Oman and the West Bank population doubling time will be eighteen years. In Jordan, with an average increase of 4.1 per cent a year, the population will double in seventeen years. Even in ten years from now, the present world population of 5,000 million will have grown to 6,000 million. Land is limited, agricultural land is even scarcer, and new knowledge and understanding create pressure to leave untouched the primary forests that still remain, with the consequence that there is even less potential space to grow more food. But the teeming populations in the megacities of the future – urban sprawls of more than ten million people each – will have to have water. About 70 per cent of the human body is water, and it needs two litres a day to keep going. No one has yet worked out how it is to be supplied.

Today, 80 per cent of all disease and more than a third of deaths in developing countries are caused by contaminated water, and those who escape serious illness are usually affected by minor water-related complaints for a tenth of their lives. The situation is always worse in the teeming slums or shanty-towns that grow up on the edge of great cities, often as a result of migration from rural areas where life cannot be sustained. But it is these *barrios* and *bidonvilles* that provide the cheap labour on which the economy of many countries depends. UN studies show that money spent on improving facilities, and thus improving fitness and life expectancy, might prove an investment with a useful return.

The world has a total of 1.4 billion cubic kilometres of water, but almost 98 per cent of this is saline. Of the fresh water, more than half is permanently locked away in ice or is deep fossil water which cannot at present be reached. Demand for fresh water has increased eight-fold since the beginning of the twentieth century. It will double in the next fifty years. World water consumption now makes up one-tenth of the combined flow of all the world's rivers. Agriculture accounts for 73 per cent of global water consumption, but huge amounts are wasted as a result of primitive methods or inefficiency. Cultivable land, not all of it growing crops at present, comprises about 120 million hectares, or 0.5 hectares per head. According to UN guidelines, one acre in optimum condition could feed five people, so that the Arab lands could in theory be self-sufficient, if enough water could be found for irrigation. Arabs, who have a huge collective chip on their shoulder, always believe the world is conspiring against them: these figures, they claim, show that if enough water was available to them they could feed themselves and have a surplus for export. Outsiders in Europe and Israel conspire to prevent the Arab states from cultivating their 120 million hectares, they claim. The trouble is that although on paper the population of the Middle East looks reasonable, it is not spread out but concentrated into the small proportion of habitable land available. The fact is that 70 per cent of Arab lands are desert, with annual rainfall less than 100 millimetres. For the Arabs, the situation is made to look worse because the 'desert heart' of Arabia is embraced by two rain belts, the northern with a winter rainfall of 210–880 millimetres and the southern with a summer rainfall of 120–200 millimetres. Thus to the north and south the Arabs see areas with plentiful water, and abundant agriculture. This must certainly have had an influence in shaping the Muslim idea of paradise – oases with streams of running water – but has also made water a central factor in their policies over the centuries.

Politicians have not been unaware of the dangers. Boutros Boutros-Ghali, the Secretary General of the United Nations and for decades the effective head of the Egyptian diplomatic service, is not a man known for extreme rhetoric or scaremongering. Yet he has warned bluntly that the next war in the Middle East will be over water. King Hussein of Jordan, a ruler whose adroit footwork and ability to size up a situation have kept him in power since 1953, has said that he cannot imagine that his country would ever again go to war with Israel – except over water. President Hafez Assad of Syria, the man acknowledged by Henry Kissinger as the cleverest politician in an area in which politics is an art form, recognizes the vital part water must play in the development of his still-isolated country: when Syria and Lebanon concluded a treaty of friendship and cooperation in 1991, President Assad took the trouble to have a secret clause inserted ensuring that Syrian forces would guard and if necessary defend the source of the river Yarmouk, which rises in Lebanon before flowing into Syria.

In almost every water conference held since environmentalists forced the protection of natural resources on to the agenda, the argument has been advanced that subsidized irrigation makes farmers profligate in their use of water. Studies in Egypt have shown that the majority of farmers in one area were using 70 per cent more water than was needed, while experts are unanimous that the best practice is to use no more than necessary, as evaporating irrigation water leaves a residue of salts that will eventually poison the soil. Such contamination is on the increase all around the world, and restoration of land spoilt by salt is not always possible; when it is, it is expensive. More skilful irrigation techniques, of the kind practised in Israel – sprinklers, dripping and other methods to replace surface irrigation – can greatly reduce such damage by getting more growth for each litre, but they require skills and support mechanisms that most of the world's farmers do not possess. The most widely used system in the region is still surface irrigation, which has a 40–50 per cent efficiency rate. Sprinkler irrigation has a higher efficiency rate, of 65–75 per cent, and drip irrigation up to 90 per cent efficiency; both are widely used in Israel, Jordan and the Gulf states. But it is unrealistic to expect to see them in the huge irrigated areas of Egypt, Turkey or Iraq, as they are expensive to install and maintain and need to be operated by trained personnel. Equally, economists who argue that farmers should be made to pay more for irrigation, to encourage them to replace surface irrigation methods with more effective ones, ignore the fact that apart from Israel – whose agriculture was heavily subsidized by the Jewish Agency and other outside sources of finance for ideological reasons – very few nations in the region have the resources to make a huge switch in irrigation methods.

One way of paying for the improved methods that all agree are needed is to charge an economic price for water. The UN believed it had made something of a breakthrough when, in one of the preliminary meetings for the Rio Earth Summit of 1992, hydrologists from developed and developing countries alike agreed that water was an economic resource that should be treated like any other. From that base, hydro-economists argue that water is a commodity, capable of being traded. The gap between the value of a gallon of water to a farmer and to a thirsty townsman is enormous, and agriculture's use of water is so profligate, the theory goes, that deals can be struck. With regard to irrigation, wherever farmers draw their water from privately owned tubewells and thus pay something close to a true cost, as in Punjab, they irrigate more efficiently than where water comes from public supplies. 'If water is cheap it will be wasted,' argue the experts. 'Price it properly', they say, 'and people will treat it as the precious commodity it is.'

More than one-third of the world's total crop production is grown on less than 15 per cent of its irrigated arable land, but estimates are that 60 per cent of irrigation water is lost before it reaches a plant. FAO (Food and Agriculture Organization of the UN) statistics also show that irrigation is exacting an increasing toll: about 125,000 hectares of irrigated land become uncultivable each year owing to waterlogging and salinity. Particularly affected is the Euphrates basin in Iraq, but even in Saudi Arabia, perceived as merely a desert country by most, the salinity and degradation of arable land is a serious problem.

Two-thirds of all grain grown throughout the world goes to feed livestock. But four hectares used to grow cattlefeed produces only enough protein for two people; the same area used for vegetables will feed fifty people. Importing the world's surplus grain would make obvious economic sense for the oil-rich countries of the Middle East, but if they must have an agricultural sector they should concentrate on high-value, low-water-use crops. However, as a matter of policy, all the countries of the area are trying to increase food production and concentrating on cereals and such water-intensive crops as sugar cane or cotton. Yet for all the wasteful expenditure of money and often irreplaceable water, none has been able to keep pace with population increases.

To the UN experts meeting in cities of the north, where water is no problem, a proper pricing structure may seem a feasible solution. But where in the Middle East could such a policy be implemented? Egypt, in particular, has had experience of the effect of removing subsidies, with the government coming close to being overthrown when the sudden increase in the price of bread led to riots in Cairo in 1977. Governments might think that farmers would prove less effective than the urban poor, but in Egypt and Sudan action by farmers could disrupt the whole economy, and French farmers showed what can be done when they blockaded imports of cheap produce competing with their own, and so forced a change of policy.

In the Middle East, potential trouble spots are not confined to the three great river systems of the area, the Nile, the Tigris–Euphrates and the Jordan. Conflicts can also arise in places where people and countries are dependent on the sparser quantities of water stored in rock and sandstone aquifers. For example, the Hashemite Kingdom of Jordan and Saudi Arabia are traditional antagonists whose rivalry stems from the competition of their ruling families in the deserts long before oil transformed the wastes of the Arabian peninsula. In modern times, the real reason for their antipathy has more to do with Saudi Arabia's use of fossil water from the aquifer on the border between the two countries than with old enmities between their ruling families. The Jordanians accuse Saudi Arabia of 'stealing' water that, given Jordan's rising population and limited water resources, might eventually have to be used as a drinking supply for Amman.

This has been the usual pattern in the area, where in general the Arabs have traditionally relied on drawing water from the ground. The hydrology of the region is largely related to scarcity. There are few rivers: the Nile, Euphrates and Tigris are the three biggest, and seepage from these basins is the main contributor to the aquifers of the region. These aquifers are of two main types: the geologically young, quaternary, with underground water from non-perennial sources stored in sand and gravel, mainly in wadis; and the type that trap water in sandstone and limestone formations, especially in geologically stable zones. The first type has been exploited for centuries throughout the Middle East, on both sides of the Red Sea and the Persian Gulf, on the shores of the Arabian Sea and the Gulf of Aden and in north-east Africa. It was during digging for water above this type of aquifer in places like Kuwait, Qatar and Bahrain that oil was first noticed early in the twentieth century.

In the simmering dispute between Jordan and Saudi Arabia, as in other areas of the Middle East, agreement would seem easy between two states similar in so many ways; but underground aquifers do not lie neatly on one side or another of borders on the ground above, so compromise has proved impossible and resentment smoulders. Yet regional cooperation is imperative in the Middle East, as most countries depend directly on the three main river systems, and the others rely on them for the slow replenishment of their subterranean storage aquifers.

The Nile, the longest river in the world, has shaped the culture of Egypt over the millennia, and has come to epitomize the life-cycle, with its earth-renewing flood. The Nile's height at Aswan has been recorded from the earliest times and used as a basic indicator of the state of the whole country. Winston Churchill gave the best description of the map of the Nile. It was, he said in his book *The River War*, like a huge palm tree with its roots spread over central Africa – in Lakes Victoria, Albert and Keoga – a long trunk in Egypt and Sudan, and its crown in the delta in Northern Egypt. If the roots were to be reduced, then the crown would dry and the rest of the tree would eventually deteriorate and die.

The Nile affects life in nine countries, covers 35 degrees of latitude and stretches from Victoria Nyanza in Central Africa to the Mediterranean town of Rosetta 6,825 kilometres (4,266 miles) away. The Nile basin covers 2.9 million square kilometres (1,190,000 square miles) or about 10 per cent of the whole of Africa.

Egypt is the Nile and the Nile is Egypt, the saying goes, and it is true that without the Nile Egypt would be very different. The river has shaped the people, their beliefs and customs, and is a prime concern of every Egyptian government, making Cairo as concerned with affairs in the heart of Africa as it is with events in the Arab states. The High Dam at Aswan, built in 1971 by Gamal Abdel Nasser, was a political gesture as much as a means of defending the economy of the country, just as Anwar Sadat's offer of Nile water in return for Arab land in the negotiations at Camp David was an earnest of his good intentions. It may be that when Nile water does finally emerge in the Negev it will be the final proof that peace has come to the Middle East.

In most areas of the world, upstream countries can use water to control events in neighbouring states, by either diverting water or threatening to do so, as Turkey has done by implication. In the Middle East, Egypt is the main exception to the rule that it is the countries upstream that have their hands on the tap, and can thus exert power and influence lower down the waterway.

For thousands of years, until the beginning of the twentieth century, Egypt faced no real problem in dealing with the issue of Nile water. The situation that existed for generations and gave Egypt a privileged position was not the result of careful planning, international agreements or common laws; rather it was brought about by the economic and political weakness of upstream countries. The limited populations of the African countries through which the Nile flowed had also had other plentiful water resources not directly connected with the Nile, and so allowed the water of the great river to flow down to Egypt untapped.

In modern times, Egypt has maintained its privileged position by reason of its large population, its strategic position as a bridge between two worlds, its know-how and its military prowess. Not only has Egypt always been the dominant power in the Nile Basin, it has also carefully demonstrated its willingness to use its available force. Thus the military academy that Egypt established outside Khartoum to train Sudanese army officers was also home to an Egyptian tank brigade, and in addition to its teaching staff it housed combat units. A coup in Sudan had to have Egyptian acceptance if it was to succeed. Another telling example of the Egyptian military attitude is provided by the special Egyptian force called Al Sa'iqa (Thunderbolt), which includes units trained in jungle warfare. Egypt has no jungles.

In the West, Egypt is regarded as a moderate state, a bastion of security in the region, an ally of the USA second in importance only to Israel. But from 1948 to 1979, when President Sadat signed the peace treaty, Egypt was Israel's main antagonist, a potential conqueror. Since 1979 other countries – notably Iran, but also Libya – have regarded Egypt as an enemy and have therefore done what they can to cause trouble for Cairo; and every state eager to embarrass Egypt has seen the potential of threats to the Nile.

Today, Egypt is most concerned about events in Ethiopia as that country emerges from its bloody and costly civil war, made worse by famine. Ethiopia is still in a parlous economic condition, and needs financial and technical help to study its water needs and to develop water projects. That help is being offered, and the plans being made, which would be bound to diminish the flow of the Nile, are of growing concern in Cairo. Already it is clear that the flow of the White Nile will be diminished by the construction of new dams in Ethiopia, many planned and constructed with Israeli help; Israel has always had a policy of winning friends in Africa in any way it can, in order to win votes at the United Nations and to contribute when possible to the troubles of its potential Arab enemies. By helping Ethiopia it is neatly fulfilling both strands of that policy, which is still in existence despite all the 'cold peace' between Israel and Egypt.

As news has filtered out of Addis Ababa of what is being suggested for the future water needs of Ethiopia, there has been a noticeable increase in tension and concern in Cairo. The consensus among diplomats and Egyptian officials is that Ethiopia will be the next flashpoint. And the danger is that, rather than allowing things to drift on until development projects in Ethiopia begin to affect the Nile in Egypt, Cairo will precipitate a crisis by intervening militarily to stop some construction. The possibility of this happening has been aggravated by those in the Egyptian establishment who are alarmed – with some reason – by Israel's presence in the Horn of Africa and its ready agreement to Ethiopia's requests for Israeli agricultural and irrigation expertise. Many influential Egyptian officials are afraid that Israel will push Ethiopia to develop unnecessary projects on the Nile, which would affect the flow of the river down to Egypt. Pan-Arabists among Egyptians, as well as those in Libya and other countries that espouse Arab nationalism, argue that Israel is once again trying to keep Egypt tied up in Africa and too busy to come to the aid of Arab League Defence pact countries. It is unfortunate and destabilizing that the actions and policies of successive governments in Addis Ababa over the past twenty years, and the presence of Israeli military advisers as well as agriculture and irrigation experts, have strengthened the hands of those in Egypt calling for military action in Africa to secure the flow of the Nile.

The second river system of the area, the Jordan, is tiny compared to the Nile. It carries a flow equal to only 2 per cent of the Nile's, is no more than 340 kilometres long, and is an unimpressive, muddy brown stream compared to the serenely rolling river that spreads its wide expanse through the heart of Cairo. Yet the River Jordan makes its sluggish way through one of the most troubled parts of this crisis-torn area, and is one of the factors that could lead to conflict. It has already done so. The brief war of 1967 changed the landscape of the Middle East and laid the groundwork for today's bitter confrontation between Palestinians and Israelis. The Arab plan to divert the headwaters of the Jordan caused open warfare between Israel and Syria, and that in turn led in a straight line to Israel's devastating pre-emptive strikes against Syria and its ally Egypt. The decision by

King Hussein to join in the battle gave Israel the opportunity to break through into East Jerusalem and then to roll over the West Bank down to the river itself. Now, the continued Israeli occupation of the land captured in 1967 motivates young Palestinians to throw the stones which have become the symbols as well as the weapons of the *intifada*.

The dogged determination of Israeli politicians of both left and right to hold on to the occupied West Bank, or at least to maintain Israeli control of the area, has at times seemed a wilful, wanton obstruction of the elusive peace process that the United States finally forced on its reluctant ally. But examine geological maps of Israel and the West Bank, look at the figures for water consumption and watch the plane loads of immigrants arriving at Ben Gurion airport from the former Soviet Union, and things fall into place. Israel believes firmly that it needs the West Bank water, and is determined to retain access to it.

While the River Jordan was at one time the cause of a war, the increased demand on its waters from Israel, Jordan and Syria as they struggle to supply their growing populations may be an impetus to peace. That is a point understood by the officials taking part in the water negotiations which are part of the American-sponsored Middle East peace process. Water was one of five subjects chosen for inclusion in the talks, mainly in the hope that discussions between Israelis and Arabs, in the presence of many other countries, might build confidence between them. Other topics were refugees, the environment, arms control and economic development.

The third great river system on which the whole area depends brings other non-Arab players – and by that we mean non-members of the Arab States League, who have a number of defence and political pacts – into the equation. The Tigris–Euphrates basin is almost as big as that of the Nile, stretching from the snow-capped mountains of eastern Turkey to the warm waters of the Persian Gulf, and gives Ankara a decisive voice in the affairs of Syria and Iraq, and enables it to play a role in the politics of the whole Arabian peninsula. Because Turkey has an abundance of water, it is only comparatively recently that it has begun to exploit its riches, embarking on the

South-Eastern Anatolia Project (GAP), which will harness both the rivers through a series of dams, allowing Turkey to double its present hydroelectric capacity and to conserve or release water as it sees fit – or as it chooses for political reasons. Turkey's policies are guided by two considerations. While it has abundant water and a large population, it lacks what the Arab countries have in plenty: oil. So although Turkey proclaims itself a European country whose destiny lies in Brussels, not a Muslim country linked to its southern neighbours, it still has to maintain good relations with the Arab states and with Iran, its turbulent eastern neighbour. It also has to take into account what its neighbours can do to affect the situation inside Turkey by giving or withholding support for the Kurdish rebels conducting a violent campaign in eastern Anatolia, and this issue is at the heart of Turkey's relations with Syria.

To show its ability to influence its neighbours, Turkey went out of its way to demonstrate the power conferred by ownership of water resources. The Turks did this peacefully and quite subtly, and have of course firmly denied that their action had any political overtones. Everyone else accepts that when the Turks stopped the flow of the Euphrates river for more than three weeks in January 1990, they were making a point. Officially, the action was to allow the vast new Kemal Atatürk Dam to be filled, but that could have been done gradually and without stopping the river completely, as the downstream countries, Syria and Iraq, immediately realized. Turkey, aware of Syrian help to the Kurdish rebels, was showing what it could do.

Syria, always at odds with Iraq further downstream, wants the maximum flow of the Euphrates to lessen its dependence on the River Jordan and thus on Israel's goodwill, as Israel, although technically a downstream state, has made itself the dominant power in the Jordan basin through its military prowess. At the end of the Euphrates–Tigris system, Iraq needs all the water it can get for its programme of industrialization, including the production of armaments to back up its ruler's ambitions, and for its growing population.

Increasingly, modern Turkey is harking back to the glory days of the Ottoman Empire; secure in its present position, it no longer feels it has to be ashamed of its past. The Turkey of the 1990s is a strong and self-confident power, seizing its opportunities as they come – actively helping the USA and its allies during the war to free Kuwait, competing with Iran to exert its influence in the Muslim republics of the old Soviet Union, knocking on the door of the European Community and at the same time buttressing its links with its Arab neighbours, once its provinces. The 1990 decision to halt the flow of the Euphrates was not only a signal to the downstream countries, Syria and Iraq, that they had to be wary in their dealings with Turkey; it was also an affirmation by the new Turkey of the pivotal role it had taken for itself in the region.

The Tigris–Euphrates system, like the other two river basins of the Middle East, has potential conflicts all along its route to the sea. By building more dams on the two rivers and their tributaries as they rise in the mountains of Anatolia, Turkey plans to change this whole vast eastern area of its territory, transforming a barren region into productive land for agriculture and industry, and at the same time, the planners predict, making it impossible for the communist guerrillas of the Kurdish Workers' Party (PKK) to find allies among the local people, who will be more concerned with immediate prosperity than with eventual autonomy or political rights. But even if it succeeds in that aim, Turkey seems bound to build up antagonism in Syria, which will see its available water diminished. Iran, on Turkey's other flank, is worried by anything that affects Iraq, and is vying with Turkey for influence in the Muslim republics of the former Soviet Union.

Making the interconnection between the three river systems physical as well as political, there are now plans for pipelines or canals to take water from the Nile to the Negev, from Turkey to Cyprus, from Iran to Qatar, from the Tigris to the Euphrates, from the Euphrates to Jordan and, a revival of an old idea, from the Shatt al-Arab in Iraq, where the Tigris and Euphrates finally merge, to Kuwait. All these projects contain the seeds of conflict as well as the hope of peaceful cooperation, and it is being left to the states concerned to decide what the outcome will be.

Already, water has played its part in the major war between Israel and the Arabs in 1967; in the bloody civil war in Jordan in 1970; in the invasion of Lebanon in 1978 and 1982; in the continuing low-intensity operations in eastern Turkey from 1983 onwards; and in the north–south conflict that has racked Sudan for so long.

If, as seems all too likely, there are to be new wars over water, then they will be seen in the Middle East. Only cooperation can avoid confrontation; and on their past record, none of the states in the Middle East or on the periphery of the region has shown any genius for compromise. Even such political extremists as Rafael Eitan, the former Israeli chief of staff and agriculture minister, recognize that: cooperation between Israel and Jordan, at least, is vital, he warns. Academics, taking a broader view, go further, and Professor Elias Salameh of Jordan University sums it up: 'Water will determine the future of the Middle East.'

Severe shortages, which are all too possible, could mean there is no future for many.

2

The Jordan Basin

In 1951 Israel drained the Huleh lake and marshes in Upper Galilee to increase the flow of the Upper Jordan, the river formed by the Banias, the Hasbani and the Dan after they unite about six kilometres inside Israeli territory. The work spilled over into the demilitarized zone agreed with Syria in the 1949 armistice agreement which ended the 1948 Arab–Israeli war. The result was firefights between Israeli and Syrian troops, bombing raids by the Israeli air force, questions and debates at the UN and the involvement of the United States. Those first exchanges of shots between Arabs and Israelis in the spring of 1951, as the Arabs tried to prevent the expulsion of villagers from the demilitarized zone, while Israel sought to begin work on its vital 'national water carrier', made the Arabs focus on water problems, and by making them consider diverting the headwaters of the Jordan, led directly to the 1967 Arab–Israeli war.

The Huleh drainage drew the attention of the Arabs to the importance of water in their conflict with Israel and led to the realization that upstream countries had their hand on the water tap, and might be able to exploit this form of pressure. As the Jewish population of Israel built up daily through immigration, the Arabs saw that if they could limit Israel's water supplies, this would be bound to lead to a limitation on the number of people the country could support. Israel, with greater technical resources and ability, was determined to change the hydrological map so that it could control its own resources and ensure supplies for all the Jews who wanted to settle in Israel – the in-gathering that was one of the reasons for the founding of the state. So as Arabs and Israelis alike began to concentrate on schemes to increase their water resources, and to control the sources of supply, they always did so with an eye on the strategic effect any project might have on their neighbours. The result was that between 1951 and 1967, in addition to the hundreds of minor clashes between Arab villagers and Israeli engineers, Israeli and Syrian soldiers, and guerrillas of both sides, there were eleven identifiable incidents that might well have led to war, three of them so serious that they required international intervention to prevent a conflict. In the end, war could not be avoided; it was not about water alone, but the dispute over the Jordan certainly contributed to the conflict, and has caused many of the incidents since. Politicians and scientists alike are convinced that Israel's constant interest in Lebanon owes as much to concern about water supplies as it does to worries about guerrillas on its borders – Arab commandos have operated from both Jordan and Syria, but Israel has not invaded those countries or set up its own 'security zones' along their borders, as it has in Lebanon.

The 1967 war – the Six Day War – was caused largely by competition for the waters of the River Jordan, that short, muddy, brackish stream which forms the least impressive river basin in the Middle East, but has the greatest potential for conflict of all the three great river systems. It certainly played its part in causing the 1967 war, and may well cause another.

The statistics show just why: Israel is already using 95 per cent of its renewable water resources, and by the year 2000 need may exceed supply by 30 per cent. A former Director of the Agriculture Ministry, Meir Ben-Meir, set out the future in stark terms: 'This is a time-bomb, and if the peoples of the region are not clever enough to discuss a mutual solution for the problem of water scarcity, then war is unavoidable.' The idea of cooperation is regularly pushed by Israel, as a means of gaining access to new water resources without going to war. The Israeli agriculture minister, the extreme right-winger Rafael Eitan, who was a most hawkish chief of staff, said 'joint exploitation and sharing of water resources based on regional agreements will aid in postponing a water crisis for many years to come.' The minister seemed to imply that Israel would contribute technical expertise, and the others the raw material – water. But ex-generals think in military ways, and Eitan came up with a military solution: 'Just imagine how much we could change the face of the Middle East if we could transfer money from the arms race to the production of water. For the cost of a single F-15 fighter jet we could desalinate 17 million cubic metres of seawater,' he said. Yet even if some miraculous political breakthrough did come, the minister acknowledged, cooperation alone could not provide all the water needed. 'Cooperation between Israel and Jordan in solving the most immediate problems will postpone but not prevent a water crisis at the beginning of the next century,' Eitan believes, noting that consumption will be up 30 per cent by that time.

In Jordan, the predictions are that need will exceed supply by 20 per cent in the year 2000. Jordanian officials claim that the average Israeli already uses about 300 litres of water a day, on a par with Western Europe, while Jordanians consume only 80 litres. The Upper Jordan River is already fully developed, and though Jordan and Israel are the leading competitors for Jordan water, the Hashemite Kingdom may also face conflict with Syria over any plans to supplement the flow of the East Ghor canal, Jordan's national water carrier. Syria depends mainly on the Euphrates for its water, so that its chief concern is over its relations with Turkey. And it is a growing concern: water shortages are increasing, with rationing in Damascus and other major cities, so that all additional sources of supply are important. The Jordan, which provides only about 5 per cent of Syria's needs, is bound to seem ever more important to the planners in Damascus.

On the West Bank, water, the traditional lubricant, is a regular cause of friction between Israeli settlers and the native Palestinian inhabitants. The area's main water potential is already fully exploited, according to the West Bank Data Project, with Israel getting 95 per cent of it.

The Gaza Strip is the most horrifying case of all, the over-pumped aquifers bringing all the problems associated with low water quality and scarcity – water-borne diseases, alkalinity and salinity of the soil, the absence of proper sewage disposal, the impossibility of normal domestic hygiene. Surveys show that a new sewage system would have cost US $16 million at 1990 prices; Israel will certainly not put up that kind of money for an area which even the most fervent Zionists recognize as a drain on the state that should be off-loaded on to any Arab country willing to accept it.

As recently as May 1990, King Hussein delivered a solemn public warning to Israel, a country with which he has regularly held secret talks, and reached many a quiet understanding: 'The only issue that will bring Jordan into war is water,' he said. Today, the Jordan remains the likeliest of all the river systems of the Middle East to cause a new conflict, not only because it is shared by four mutually antagonistic states, with the Palestinians soon likely to form a fifth, but also because it is over-exploited, of low quality and capable of improvement only by complicated and extensive joint action.

The biggest problem of all is the competition between Israel and Jordan, as the river presents a zero-sum situation: if Israel gets more water from it, Jordan gets less, and vice versa. Add the facts that those two countries are using their few other water resources to the full, and that the populations of both are expanding rapidly by natural growth and immigration, and the situation becomes explosive. To make it worse still, Syria and Lebanon are also involved: Syria is painfully water-dependent on Turkey but dominates Lebanon, and so has a close interest in that country's relations with Israel. And though Lebanon is one of the few water-rich states of the area, it believes its own burgeoning population, rapid industrialization and intensive agriculture will mean that it will need all the water it can get within a few years. Israel disagrees, and notes that in south Lebanon the Litani and Hasbani rivers are under-utilized, and could well be tapped to increase Israel's reserves – according to UN reports, Israel has in fact already laid pipelines to extract some of the water in the area of south Lebanon it controls through its proxy militia, the South Lebanon Army, contrary to international law and the Geneva Conventions. Certainly the idea of using the Litani water is an old Zionist dream: when the state of Israel was first being discussed, Chaim Weizmann and his advisers wanted the northern border to be the Litani, not because it was a convenient natural frontier, but because even then they realized that water was going to be vital for the well-being of their fledgling state. As early as 1920, during Anglo-French discussions on the boundaries of what would be Mandated Palestine, Chaim Weizmann wrote to the British Foreign Secretary, Lord Curzon:

> Your Lordship realises the enormous importance of the Litani to Palestine. Even if the whole of the Jordan and the Yarmouk are included in Palestine it has insufficient water for its needs . . . The irrigation of Upper Galilee and the power necessary for even a limited industrial life must come from the Litani . . . If Palestine were cut off from the Litani, the Upper Jordan river and the Yarmouk she could not be economically independent.

Not surprisingly, from 1948 on, when the state of Israel was established, there was always a fear of Israeli expansion into Lebanon, not for any of the reasons sometimes given in Israel – defensible borders, the need to eliminate 'terrorist' bases, or biblical history – but because the Lebanese, like the Israelis, recognized the potential benefit to Israel of access to the Litani waters. The Litani and Hasbani rivers are only ten miles or so north of the border, and were bound to remain an attraction to the Israelis, the Lebanese believed. They were right. In 1978 and 1982 Israel invaded Lebanon, and though local resistance and international reaction eventually forced them to withdraw on both occasions, they held on to a so-called security zone which just happened to allow them access to both rivers.

It was Israel, too, which demonstrated to the people of the Middle East and the world the part water could play in twentieth-century warfare. During the 1982 invasion of Lebanon, Israeli forces swept north to besiege the city of Beirut, a modern capital of three million inhabitants, a place of crowded streets, tall apartment blocks, elegant shops and restaurants. The city was divided into two halves. To the east was the Christian zone, then run by allies of the Israelis, and thus an area that took no part in the war, but whose people often cooperated actively with the invaders. In the Muslim west of the city, the fighters of the Palestine Liberation Organization (PLO) put up makeshift barricades and began a stubborn defence, ensuring heavy – and unacceptable – casualties for the Israelis if they tried to storm the city. Israeli planners had prepared for this contingency: they had studied the situation in advance, and knew that west Beirut's water supply was fed from the main pumping station on the hill of Achrafiyeh, in the Christian zone. A small Israeli engineering unit went to the pumping station on a Sunday afternoon. The officer in charge had with him a copy of the plan of the water installation of the whole city. He and his men turned the wheel that closed the valve controlling the supply to west Beirut; then they removed the wheel and took it away with them. At the same time they cut off the electricity supplies and blocked all routes into the west of Beirut, turning their operation into a medieval-style siege designed to starve the inhabitants out, or to make them force the Palestinians to give up, as the only way of alleviating their own suffering.

In Beirut the deprivation, allied to constant bombardment, did finally achieve the Israeli objective. It also gave an up-to-date demonstration of what could be done by such means. A previous example involved a sophisticated force fighting a rag-tag army, but came from as long ago as 1961. Then, an Irish battalion of the UN force in the Congo was surrounded in its garrison at Jadotville by a unit of Katangese gendarmerie helped by mercenaries. The water supply to the garrison was cut off, and the Irish were forced to surrender.

Israeli sources have on a number of occasions said they would be prepared to withdraw from the self-proclaimed security zone inside Lebanon if they came to some understanding with the Lebanese over two issues: demilitarization and the use of water from the Litani. So far, no Israeli politicians have felt able to make this offer in public, though Labour Party ministers have said they would be willing to give up the Gaza Strip adjacent to Egypt. When the Zionist dream was realized in 1948 with the proclamation of the foundation of the state of Israel, immigration from all the countries of the world made Israel a melting-pot in which the new arrivals had nothing in common with which to establish a national identity except their shared religion. Weizmann added pride in the fighting forces of the new

38

country and an almost mystical belief in the land, in 'making the desert bloom', in self-sufficiency exemplified by the kibbutz movement. Agriculture was something that the craftsmen and businessmen of Central Europe who formed the bulk of the first waves of immigration could be taught quickly, though the growth in population could not be matched by any increase in the natural resources available, so to make Weizmann's vision become reality someone had to go without. Any gain by Israeli farmers was bound to become a loss for their neighbours – the Palestinians close at hand, the Lebanese, Jordanians and Syrians further afield.

Water became an imperative for both Israel and the Palestinians. It was no accident that when in 1965 a small party of guerrillas from al-Asifah – the Storm, the fighting arm of Yasser Arafat's Fatah group – infiltrated into Israel, the target they chose for the explosives they carried with them was a water pumping station. Israel dismissed the raid as of no importance, nothing more than an excuse to issue grandiloquent communiqués and boasts in Cairo, Amman and Beirut. But in private, Israeli military planners were concerned: they realized that the Palestinians had correctly identified an Israeli vulnerability, and worried that their enemies might continue to concentrate on it. The Palestinians may have wanted to do so, but have never had the ability to cause serious trouble. Rather, in that first raid the commandos were reflecting wider Arab efforts to use water to damage Israel, just as the Palestinians have been used by powerful Arab states ever since.

At their first summit conference, held in Cairo in January 1964, Arab kings, presidents, princes and prime ministers – all dominated by Nasser at the height of his Arab appeal – openly decided to use water as a weapon, not the first time that had happened but probably the first time such an august gathering had set out its intention so plainly, and sought to justify it in advance. The argument was the old one heard so often in the Middle East: the other side started it first. The Arabs held that they were merely reacting to Israeli attempts to divert the waters of the Jordan for their own use. The final communiqué of the conference said:

Believing in the just Palestinian cause and realizing its gravity, and with determination to return the stolen rights to its people, and considering the establishment of Israel as the main threat that the Arab nation has vowed to avert, and emanating from the actual participation in joint constructive efforts that would unite the Arabs, the first Arab summit expresses its satisfaction that its meetings have resulted in a consensus by Arab leaders to end their differences and clear the Arab atmosphere of all impurities, and halt all media campaigns.

The summit has decided that:

1 The establishment of Israel is a major threat that needs to be confronted politically, economically and by means of the media.

2 On the military side: the establishment of a United Leadership.

3 On the technical side: the establishment of an organization to exploit the Jordan River waters and its arteries.

4 On the financial side: investment in water projects through the contribution of Arab states.

In September 1964 Nasser called a second meeting, which endorsed the plan to divert the headwaters of the Jordan, and promised Arab troops to protect the work. In September 1965 a summit endorsed Arab investment in the Jordan River project – Egypt and Saudi Arabia had undertaken to foot the bill. In 1966 no meeting was held. In 1967, when the Arab leaders met in Khartoum, it was in the wake of their most crushing defeat of modern times, so that the Jordan project was not even mentioned.

Because it is relatively small, the Jordan basin lends itself much more than the other two major river systems of the area to manipulation and interference. The river itself is only about 320 kilometres long, and the basin no larger than 11,500 square kilometres, of which Jordan today has 54 per cent, Syria 29.5 per cent, Israel 10.5 per cent and Lebanon 6 per cent. Only 3 per cent lies within Israel's pre-1967 boundaries, the extra 7.5 per cent resulting from its occupation of the West Bank.

The Jordan has three headwaters: the Hasbani, which rises in Syria and Lebanon; the Banias, which comes from Syria; and the Dan, which is wholly within pre-1967 Israel. The only perennial tributary is the Yarmouk, which rises in Syria and forms the border successively between Jordan and Syria and Jordan and Israel. The Jordan itself forms the remaining boundary between Israel and Jordan, and further south between the West Bank and Jordan.

In theory, the upstream countries can dominate by control of a river's headwaters, but that depends on the power and technical ability of a country. Although it is downriver of eight other countries, Egypt has always dominated the Nile, and while the Orontes rises in Lebanon and flows through Syria and Turkey to the Mediterranean, no one would expect the weak and divided Lebanon to control its waters. A similar situation has developed over the Jordan, with the difference that Israel has actually used its superior military power to change the facts on the ground. Thus Syria and Lebanon were upstream of Israel in the Jordan valley, while Israel was upstream of Jordan. But in 1978 and 1982 Israel invaded Lebanon; on both occasions it was forced to withdraw, on the first occasion by international pressure, and on the second by a combination of determined resistance by guerrillas in Lebanon and dissent within Israel as well as by international pressure. But on neither occasion did Israel withdraw completely. In 1978 it established a zone about ten kilometres wide along its own border, and formed a Lebanese militia which it armed, paid, supplied and controlled, first under Major Saad Haddad, and after he died under Colonel Antoine Lahad. The United Nations, which set up the United Nations Interim Force in Lebanon (UNIFIL) to take over as the Israelis withdrew, was prevented from deploying right down to the border, and in addition Israel kept control of the so-called Marjayoun gap, ostensibly because it is the main Christian town of the area where the South Lebanon Army has its headquarters. Just as important, however, is the fact that the gap gives Israel access to the Hasbani and Litani rivers.

Intermittent fighting in South Lebanon, and strict control by Israel through its proxy militia, has made it difficult to be sure exactly what has been going on there, but reports by local farmers say Israel has built a tunnel from the Litani to the Hasbani, thus diverting water into the Jordan, from which Israel is able to transfer it to its national water carrier. According to some reports, Israel has gained an additional 500 million cubic metres a year in this way, a diversion of water – theft of water – illegal in international law and in contravention of articles of the Geneva Conventions governing the conduct of an occupying power. In an official report, the United Nations agreed that Israel had taken 'some' water from the Litani, but said that the amounts appeared small and were only of symbolic importance.

Many Arab commentators believe that a contributory cause of all Israel's wars from 1948 onwards has been its need for water. It cannot increase the amount available to it within its pre-1967 borders except by desalination of seawater or mineral-rich water, such as that of the Dead Sea, and that would be prohibitively expensive if Israel had to bear the cost on its own. One idea for the water negotiations at the general Middle East peace talks which began in 1991 was for the countries of the Jordan triangle, Israel, Jordan and Syria, to share the cost of new desalination plants. That was an idea that came from outside experts, not from those directly concerned, who were more intent on using water for political leverage.

The politics of the Arab–Israeli peace negotiations have taken all the headlines, but those involved say it is the practicalities of water that are causing the biggest headaches. The Lebanese delegation says that a fundamental difficulty is that all Zionist and Israeli-backed plans for Jordan basin water management have included the Litani in the river system. In the talks, Syria in particular at first used water to delay talks, as it was originally opposed to the whole process, and then used water as a bargaining counter – not its own water, as it has little, but the comparatively abundant supplies in Lebanon, which Syria now controls. Syria sought a promise that Israel would withdraw from occupied Arab lands, and in particular the Golan Heights, before it would even discuss water supplies. When it did agree to talk, it put the marking of the Syria–Israel border as the first condition, and an agreement on Palestinian water rights and exchange of hydrological data as the second. Syria also blames Israel for

Jordan's water shortage, arguing that it would be solved by the Unity dam on the Yarmouk, which Israel has vetoed.

Israeli sources have on a number of occasions said they would be prepared to withdraw from the self-proclaimed security zone inside Lebanon if they came to some understanding with the Lebanese over two issues: demilitarization and the use of water from the Litani. In 1992, Arab writers compared the attitude of Israeli cabinet ministers to Lebanon with their approach to the Gaza Strip, recalling that when the Health Minister, Haim Ramon, suggested unilateral Israeli withdrawal from Gaza he was supported by four other cabinet ministers. The critics noted that this had been Labour Alignment policy both in the coalition government with Likud and when ruling alone.

Syria and its client state Lebanon stayed away from the 1992 Vienna talks on regional water resources because Damascus refused to discuss water sharing or other multilateral issues before Israel formally committed itself to withdraw from the Arab territory it had occupied in the 1967 and 1973 wars, while Israel felt it could not compromise its vital security interests unless its Arab neighbours were prepared to conclude a comprehensive peace treaty.

According to many Arabs, the need to secure additional water supplies was one reason for Israel's seizure of the West Bank, and for the determination of the Likud government, at least, to hold on to the areas it called Judea and Samaria. During the 1988 elections in Israel, an official election publication of the Likud Party openly used the water argument to justify retention of the occupied territories. 'Judea and Samaria boast 40 per cent of Israel's available fresh water resources, and water is our life. It makes no sense to place it in the hands of those whose intentions towards us might not always be the kindest.' But Israel's heavy use of water, both domestically and for irrigation, is a costly business: about 40 per cent of all the energy Israel uses goes on pumping water to higher ground or through the national water carrier system, mainly for agricultural use.

In addition to the waters of the Jordan, which are stored in Lake Kinnaret (the Sea of Galilee or Lake Tiberias), Israel also draws on groundwater from two aquifers in Israel proper and two in the West

Bank, and on recycled water. Israel proper has a coastal aquifer extending from Mount Carmel to the Gaza Strip, varying in width from 10 kilometres in the north to 20 kilometres in the south. The maximum potential is estimated at 280 million cubic metres a year, and at present this aquifer provides water for over 1,000 wells. But it suffers increasingly from seawater incursion as it is over-used, and from pollution caused by salts from other ground sources.

The other main Israeli groundwater source is the Yarkon–Taninim aquifer, extending from Mount Carmel to Beer Shiva and from the mountains in the east down to the coastal plain in the west. The yield from this source is estimated at 290 million cubic metres of fresh water annually and 50 million cubic metres in saline water. Some 30 to 50 per cent of the water used by Israel originates as rainfall that replenishes the shared Yarkon–Taninim aquifer. While most of the water falls on the hills of the West Bank, it flows west-ward towards the Mediterranean and comes out in springs in the coastal plain within Israel's pre-1967 border. Palestinians argue that they should be the ones to control this 'Palestinian water' but Israelis point out that they have been using nearly 90 per cent of that source since long before the 1967 war. They claim a legal right to continue to do so based on the principle of established historical usage, just as Egypt does with regard to the 'Ethiopian waters' of the Nile.

Israel's other two groundwater sources are from aquifers in the West Bank, and it is reliance on these that has further exacerbated Israeli–Palestinian relations. One of the major causes of dissension is that in Middle Eastern terms, the West Bank is one of the few areas with adequate rainfall – varying from 700 mm a year in Ramallah to 100 mm at the Dead Sea. On the mountains, the average rainfall is 600 to 700 mm a year on the western slopes, and 450 mm decreasing to 250 mm a year on the eastern slopes and in the Jordan Valley. Average rainfall in the West Bank is 600 mm a year, and 70 per cent of the land surface receives more than 300 mm a year, the amount defined by UN authorities as the aridity threshold. According to Jeffrey Dillman, of Berkeley, California, the total water inventory of the West Bank is 850 million cubic metres a year, of which 620 million is easily usable. That is about half that of pre-1967 Israel.

Accurate statistics for the West Bank are difficult to find, with Israelis and Palestinians producing figures to support their own cases. Yet it does seem clear that Israel has been over-extracting West Bank water. Palestinian farmers say they have noticed a steady decline in the quality of the water they get from their wells, and believe this is owing to consistent over-exploitation by Israel over the past two decades, with an extraction rate exceeding the natural recharge rate, which allows salinity and pollution from fertilizers to lower water quality. A large increase in the amount of fertilizer used has also contributed to the problem.

Certainly the visual evidence supports the Palestinian case. In the new Israeli towns of the West Bank and in the settlements there is an almost profligate use of water. There are grassy areas for the children to play, quite often there are swimming pools, and many of the inhabitants cultivate gardens. The Arab villages from which the land for the towns and settlements was expropriated are usually near by. They are dusty places, where at all times of the day women trudge back and forth from the wells carrying buckets or tins of water. There is no grass and the only flowers to be seen may be a rare tin of geraniums kept alive by water previously used for washing.

Down in the Jordan Valley the farms of the settlers contrast just as sharply with those of the Palestinian farmers. The Israelis use trickle irrigation techniques, plastic sheeting to conserve moisture and the latest seed developed in Israeli laboratories. The Palestinians rely on the age-old methods of channel irrigation, if they can irrigate their crops at all. They take a realistic view: the main difference between them and the Jews, they say, is money, and that results from the ideological commitment of the Israeli government, which is not matched by any comparable Arab effort. Palestinian water experts recall that in the early 1960s, when the West Bank was under Jordanian rule, the Jordanian government undertook to pipe water from the Yarmouk river to the West Bank. The Israeli occupation put an end to that scheme, and though Jordan and many other Arab governments have continued to pour money into the area, this has gone on buying loyalty and not on improving water supplies. Jordan continued to pay the salaries of its officials, and other subsidies were given for building community halls, improving schools and other high-profile projects that would let the local people know they were not forgotten. There were even outright bribes to local officials to keep them in line. But there was nothing to improve the water availability because, the Arab governments argued, that would benefit Israel, not the local Palestinians.

The Israelis, particularly during the fifteen years of Likud rule, were totally committed to the establishment of settlements in the West Bank, and not only for the religious reasons advanced by the extremist settlers of the Gush Emunim movement: the commitment to Eretz Israel, Greater Israel as defined in biblical terms. Government policy on settlements was more hard-headed than that, and was defined in the attitude of General Ariel Sharon, at one time Minister of Agriculture and at another Minister of Housing, both positions giving him a major say in settlement policy. His idea was to create facts, to establish so many settlements and new towns in all the occupied territories that it would be impossible for the Palestinians ever to regain control of their own land. To carry out this policy the Israeli government offered substantial inducements to immigrants to make their homes in the Occupied Territories – though the USA, Israel's main backer, prohibited it from allowing Soviet Jews to move on to the West Bank. All others were offered mortgages at low interest rates, and various other subsidies. The result was not entirely as expected: instead of being settlers who would develop the land and put down roots, as the original kibbutzniks were, those who moved to the Occupied Territories were often middle-level workers who consciously decided that the risks and discomforts of living in the West Bank were outweighed by the financial benefits available. Usually, they commuted to work in Jerusalem or in towns within Israel proper, tilling no ground and putting down no roots. When a Middle East peace settlement is reached, there will be little difficulty in persuading such people that they will be better off elsewhere.

Many of the Jewish farmers of the Jordan Valley are regarded in a different light by their Palestinian neighbours, who believe they could coexist quite well if restrictions on Palestinian use of available water were lifted and all had the same opportunities and the same constraints. Many of those settlers take a similar view. They would be quite prepared to carry on farming under a Palestinian administration, they told us.

It is in the Gaza Strip that Israeli insensitivity to local problems can be seen at its most flagrant. The authorities have allowed a hotel to be built there, a luxury weekend resort complete with swimming pool, cocktail bar, and showers in every bedroom. It stands in the middle of one of the most crowded areas on earth, where 450,000 refugees are crammed into an area about 40 kilometres long and only 4 kilometres wide. Oranges used to be the main crop; now it is people, families dependent on UNWRA (United Nations Works and Relief Agency for Palestinian Refugees) for their livelihood, their rations, the education of their children. Heavy over-use of wells has led to a lowering of the water table, allowing seawater to encroach. The overcrowding has meant that the sewage system cannot cope, so that there is widespread pollution. New sewage systems would cost US$16 million at 1990 prices, which Israel is unlikely to provide. In Gaza, every water-related problem can be found: a serious lack of clean water for drinking or domestic use; inefficient or absent sewage disposal; rapid degradation of the quality of the water available; regular outbreaks of water-borne diseases such as dysentery and cholera; and the collapse of agriculture in many areas owing to salinity of the water and alkalization of the soil. And into this environment the Israelis have introduced not only a luxury hotel, but also some 3,000 settlers who farm their special enclaves behind perimeters of barbed wire studded with watch towers and patrolled by guards.

Syria is the most persistent of Israel's potential enemies, a country which has always made the Palestinian cause a central plank of its policy. It was Syria that would have been most concerned in the work of diverting the headwaters of the Jordan, it was Syrian gunners who regularly harassed Israeli engineers as they worked in the Huleh marshes, and it was Syria that came close to sweeping down to Haifa in the opening days of the 1973 war. Ruled by the ruthless, pragmatic and politically brilliant Hafez al Assad since 1970, Syria is a country which, like Israel, believes in relying on its own efforts and takes care to plan for the future. Concern at the course of events in

Lebanon induced President Assad to intervene there in 1975, when Syrian troops moved in to prevent the total defeat of the Christian forces by the left-wing, Muslim alliance. The real motive was to prevent the establishment of a regime in Beirut that might act so foolishly that it would involve Syria in a war with Israel at a time not of its own choosing. Soon afterwards, Syria changed sides, as the Christians allied themselves with Israel and it was the leftist–Palestinian alliance that was in trouble. Syrian policy was consistent: to maintain a balance in Lebanon and to make sure that it was the influence of Damascus that finally decided the way things would go in Beirut.

The policy succeeded. Often the most brutal means were used, demonstrated in the assassination of Lebanon's president-elect, Bashir Gemayel. In another display of Syrian power, when Amin Gemayel took over after his brother's murder and eventually agreed on a peace treaty with Israel, Syria prevented it from being signed. President Assad instead forced Gemayel and the Lebanese government to accept an ignominious treaty which gave Syria huge powers in their country. And in a secret protocol to that agreement, Lebanon was forced to agree that Syrian troops would always guard the sources of the Hasbani river, the Wazzani and Hasbieh springs, which are in Lebanese territory. As the Banias rises in Syria, the government in Damascus has thus ensured that it has control over two of the three most important sources of the Jordan, providing between 50 and 70 per cent of the discharge of the Upper Jordan river, the remainder coming from run-off after winter rainfall.

Syria is now limited in what it can do by the Israeli occupation of the Golan Heights, and was always inhibited by the threat of Israeli force. When the 1964 Arab summit decided to divert the headwaters of the Jordan, two possible methods were considered: the diversion of the Hasbani to the Litani and of the Banias to the Yarmouk, or the diversion of both the Hasbani and Banias to the Yarmouk in Jordanian territory. This second option was chosen, although according to independent assessments it was only marginally feasible. Because of the soil porosity and other factors, the whole scheme would have been technically extremely difficult, and certainly very expensive, though that was not such a consideration when Saudi Arabia agreed to foot most of the bill. Syria was closely involved, as the diverted waters were to be stored in the Mukheiba Dam in Syria. Israel estimated that if the plan went ahead it would have prevented Israel from extracting 35 per cent of the water it intended to take from the Jordan, to which it was entitled under the 1955 Johnston Plan. Work began on the scheme in 1965, despite a warning that Israel considered any attempt to divert the Jordan headwaters to be an infringement of its national rights. The Israelis were not bluffing, but it was difficult for them to act, as all the work was going on in Arab territory, though some of the land was disputed and had been made into demilitarized zones whose final status remained to be decided. It seems clear that the Israelis were looking for an excuse to act, and found one in what was presented as a prudent move to protect the third source of the Jordan, the Dan, which rises in one of the disputed areas. The springs that form the source of the Dan immediately formed a small lake, surrounded on three sides by Israeli territory, but with the Syrians at the northern end claiming sovereignty there. To establish control, the Israelis decided to build an embankment which would have the effect of enclosing the Dan headwaters and bringing them within Israel. The watching Syrians immediately realized the serious consequences of what was being done, and brought up armour and artillery. On 1 November 1964 they began shooting at the Israeli bulldozers, trucks and engineers. The Israeli forces responded, and a battle between tank guns, mortars and machine guns quickly followed, with the Syrians getting the better of the initial exchanges. Two days later the Israelis resumed work on the embankment and the Syrians once more tried to halt operations. The battle flared again, but this time the Israelis had brought in more armour and experienced gunners. They were far more effective this time, and did not confine themselves to the Syrian forces which were opposed to them. Just as the Syrians had tried to stop Israeli work on the damming of the Dan lake, so the Israelis targeted the army of Arab workmen building the canal that would carry water from the Banias to the Yarmouk, while in response the Syrian gunners ranged in on Kibbutz Dan and the Israeli air force was called in to strike deep inside Syria. It was the end of the Jordan River diversion scheme.

General Ariel Sharon, then Chief of Staff of Northern Command of the Israeli army, recognized that even without the provocation provided by the Syrian artillery attack on the Dan lake, Israel would have been bound to act.

> We could not have sat there much longer just watching the [Arab] canal make headway. Exactly when the government would have moved against the Syrians, or in what context they could have done so, I do not know. But with their assault in November, Syria started off a round of fighting that gave us the opportunity to put an end to their project. People generally regard 5 June 1967 as the day the Six Day War began. That is the official date. But in reality the Six Day War started two and a half years earlier, on the day Israel decided to act against the diversion of the Jordan.

At the same time that the Arabs were being prevented from carrying through their grandiose scheme to divert the Jordan, Israel quietly completed the first phase of its major enterprise, the 'national water carrier'. Planning for water needs had begun right after the country was founded following the 1948 war, though the opportunity to adopt a unified approach was not taken when it was provided by the negotiations that led to the 1949 armistice agreements. Instead, Israel and the other riparian states drew up their own plans in isolation. In 1951 Israel published its All-Israel Plan, which included the draining of the Huleh marshes, the diversion of the Jordan and the building of a carrier system to take water to the coastal plain and the Negev desert, which was judged to be fertile enough for agriculture if water could be provided. At the same time, Jordan was drawing up its own plans after studies by the British consultants Murdoch Macdonald and the American engineer M. E. Bunger in 1950. The favoured Jordanian plan called for a dam on the Yarmouk at Maqarin, with a second dam at Addassiyah providing gravity flow into the East Ghor canal along the Jordan Valley. This scheme would give hydroelectric power for both Syria and Jordan, and irrigate 60,000 dunums (about 20,000 acres) in Syria and five times that area in

Jordan. Jordan and Syria agreed on ways of sharing the waters, UNWRA was brought in to execute the Bunger Plan and work started in July 1953. Again Israel protested, arguing that its riparian rights in the Yarmouk had not been taken into account, though it had only a 10 kilometre frontage on that river, and even that was in a demilitarized zone of the so-called Yarmouk Triangle.

In the same month that engineers prepared to start work on the Maqarin dam – July 1953 – Israel began diverting the waters of the Jordan into its new national carrier at Jisr Banat Yaqub, again in a demilitarized zone awaiting final apportionment. It was a risky place for Israel to choose, but it had the advantage of having a lower salinity level than possible diversion points lower down the river, and it was also at an elevation sufficiently high to give a good gravity drop down to Lake Kinnaret. Now it was the Arabs' turn to protest, and in September Syria took the issue to the UN, just as it had done over the Israeli actions in the Huleh marshes. Then, Syrian protests had been brushed aside, but this time the Syrian case was accepted and Israel was ordered to stop work. Israel ignored that order, and only in November 1953, when the USA threatened to cut off aid funds, did it finally obey. It was forced to move the intake for its national carrier to Eshed Kinrot on Lake Tiberias, where salinity was higher and hydroelectric power had to be used to pump the water to the carrier.

Perhaps in an effort to show that it was even-handed, the United States then cut off funding for the Bunger Plan, forcing Jordan to abandon that project altogether. The ostensible reason was a complicated Israeli legal argument stemming from a British decision in 1926 to give a Jewish engineer, Pinhas Rutenberg, a seventy-year concession to use the Jordan and Yarmouk to produce hydroelectric power. Rutenberg formed the Palestine Electric Corporation, and it was that concession plus the failure of the Jews and Arabs to reach any basic understanding which for the next four decades prevented the formation of a single integrated water plan for the area.

When the Israeli national carrier was inaugurated in 1953, just as Jordan was being prevented from carrying out the Bunger Plan, President Eisenhower realized that the USA was becoming increasingly involved in the hydro-politics of the region, and so appointed Eric Johnston as a special ambassador with the task of mediating between the two sides and of hammering out a comprehensive plan for the development of the Jordan river system. The US idea, based on the success of the Marshall Plan in Europe, was to lessen the possibility of conflict in the region by promoting cooperation and economic stability. The first result was a competition between the Arab and Jewish sides to produce the most impressive plans to support their maximalist demands, with the Israelis pressing for the Litani waters to be included in the unified plan and the Arabs demanding that Israel should drop its idea of transporting water out of the Jordan basin area, that is, abandon what Israel saw as the vital need to use Jordan water to irrigate the Negev. Eventually, and after dozens of meetings, reports, technical papers and compromises, Ambassador Johnston produced a unified plan calling for a three-member Neutral Board to supervise water withdrawal, record keeping and control of building projects. Technical committees from both Israel and the Arab League accepted the plan, which was discussed by the Israeli Cabinet in July 1955, though no vote was taken at that time. The Arab Experts' Committee gave its approval in September of that year, and the plan was referred to the Arab League Council. On 11 October 1955, the Council voted against ratification, though the vote was not a total rejection of the plan and all the countries concerned quietly accepted the water share Johnston had recommended: 52 per cent to Jordan, 36 per cent to Israel, 9 per cent to Syria and 3 per cent to Lebanon. That tacit agreement has lasted to the present day, though water has continued to play a major role in the continuing conflict between all the parties concerned, particularly in comparatively recent times.

In the case of Israel, this was because after the 1967 war the country was in a much stronger position, its occupation of the Golan Heights preventing any new Arab attempt to divert the headwaters of the Jordan, and its presence in the West Bank giving it control of half the length of the Yarmouk, against the 10 kilometres it had previously. This improved position allowed Israel to make its boldest strategic use yet of water: it warned that it would completely destroy

Jordan's East Ghor Canal, the backbone of Jordan's water system, and would not allow it to be repaired if Jordan continued to allow Palestinian guerrillas to operate from its territory. That was in 1969. In 1970 King Hussein's Bedouin troops expelled the Palestinian guerrillas in the battles of Black September. The King kept his word. In return, the Israelis refrained from damaging the Jordan valley works, but did all they could to minimize the amount of water the Jordanians were able to extract from the Yarmouk for the East Ghor Canal.

The canal, 69 kilometres long, carries water from the Yarmouk along the Jordan Valley and is planned to be extended as far south as the Dead Sea. The first stage of the Great Yarmouk Project was to control the river inside Syria to prevent winter floods and even out water distribution during the summer. When work started, Syria was in control of the area; today, Israeli forces occupy the north bank of the river, and have a position directly opposite the intake tunnel for the canal. Israel can, and does, dictate what works the Jordanians can carry out there, and has prevented Jordanian engineers dredging the river to improve the intake flow. In 1976 Jordan had to get the Americans to persuade the Israelis to allow Jordanian workmen to remove rocks around a silt bar opposite the intake. Israel agreed to that under pressure, but would not then allow the Jordanians to bulldoze away the silt. In 1979 the same thing happened, and this time the Jordanians charged that Israel had replaced the rocks a few days after Jordan had removed them. On that occasion, Jordan moved its forces up to the Yarmouk and Israel mobilized its troops in the area. Again, American intervention was needed to avert a clash. Then in the drought year of 1984 Jordan said that the silting opposite the intake was seriously affecting the amount of water in the East Ghor Canal, and claimed that Israel was deliberately allowing it to happen so that it could increase the Yarmouk's flow downstream into Lake Tiberias, where Israel could increase its extraction rate. Israel has not kept to the letter of the secret agreement it reached with Jordan in the way King Hussein has done.

The East Ghor Canal was begun in 1957, and was to have been

the first phase of a much larger system than now exists. There should have been a 47 kilometre West Ghor Canal on the other side of the Jordan, with a siphon between the two, seven dams on side wadis and two major dams on the Yarmouk, as well as flood protection and drainage works. Only the East Ghor Canal and a few other minor works had been completed by the time of the Six Day War in 1967, and the two dams on the Yarmouk had not been begun. After the war, the new Israeli positions meant that nothing could be done, and in the absence of any agreement the project remains on the drawing board.

The Arab defeat in 1967 led to an increase in guerrilla activity by the PLO as the Palestinians tried to atone for the failure of the Arab armies. They regularly launched attacks into Israeli territory across the Jordan, which in turn caused clashes between the Israelis and the Jordanian and Iraqi army detachments stationed in the valley – Iraqi forces had been dispatched to Jordan in 1967 and remained there when the war ended.

Retaliation against the East Ghor Canal, which had revitalized the Jordanian side of the valley, was an obvious consideration for Israel, particularly as a number of PLO attacks were directed specifically against Israeli water installations. However, such a move might have brought retaliation against Israel's vulnerable national water carrier, and so attacks were resisted by the Israeli government for some time. Then in June 1969 the Israeli Cabinet revised its policy, partly at the insistence of the military, partly because of technical reports from water engineers: in April and May of that year the level of the Jordan fell well below the average for the period and there was a suspicion that Jordan was taking more than its fair share of the available water. Secret negotiations between Israel and Jordan, arranged by the USA, later showed that the decrease was owing to the severe drought and that there had been no over-pumping by Jordan. By the time that was established, it was too late: on 23 June and 10 August 1969, Israeli planes put most of the East Ghor Canal out of commission, preventing the irrigation of the banana and citrus plantations and so destroying not only the crops but also the livelihood of thousands of small farmers. Follow-up raids forced all but

5,000 of the 60,000 people living in the valley to join the hundreds of thousands of refugees who had streamed across the Jordan from the West Bank. The American diplomat Philip Habib was brought in to conduct the negotiations, which established that Jordan had been taking no more than its fair share of the waters. Once that was accepted, he was able to go on to extract Israel's promise to leave the East Ghor Canal alone in return for the expulsion of the Palestinians from Jordan.

Since that time there have been other secret agreements between Israel and Jordan, and complaints from one side or the other over water use or new works have usually been sorted out with American help. However, Jordanian plans to build the Maqarin Dam on the Yarmouk, the vital next link in the whole project, have been held up because Israel demanded a larger share of the Yarmouk water as the price of its consent and threatened to bomb the works if they went ahead without its permission. International funding for the joint Jordanian–Syrian Unity Dam to store the Yarmouk's winter flood waters has been blocked by the Israeli veto.

So desperate was the situation in the Jordan Valley, the most productive area of the country, that Crown Prince Hassan was put in charge of rehabilitating the area and in 1974 produced a new plan, which called for the establishment of a Jordan Valley Commission to oversee all aspects of the region. The East Ghor Canal, which had been silting up, was cleaned, new pressure pipes were installed to irrigate 300,000 dunums (100,000 acres) with water flowing in from the side wadis in the east, and new villages with modern amenities were planned to attract the people back. So far, the Commission – now the Jordan Valley Authority – has been remarkably successful. The King Talal Dam on the Zarqa river, on 18 kilometre extension of the canal and a north–south highway have rejuvenated the valley, while King Hussein's careful policies as well as secret US mediation have prevented any further clashes with Israel.

In 1973, King Hussein kept his country out of the war, earning the approval of the west, and the understanding of his own people and of the Arab world. In 1990, he was one of the very few Arab leaders to give a degree of support to Saddam Hussein after Iraq invaded Kuwait. For this, King Hussein was roundly condemned in both the Arab world and the West, though it was understood that, given the geography and the economy of his country, it was certainly to the advantage of Jordan to side with Iraq: throughout the Iran–Iraq war many of Iraq's imports went in through the Jordanian port of Aqaba and were transported overland to Baghdad, while Iraqi oil was taken in tankers to the same port for export. In 1990 an early action by Saudi Arabia – cutting off oil supplies to Jordan to punish King Hussein for his support of Saddam – made the country even more dependent on Baghdad. Oil tankers maintained a constant shuttle between the two countries throughout the crisis and afterwards, keeping Jordanian wheels turning and opening the border for Iraqi sanctions-busting. But according to one senior Jordanian minister, in 1990 there was another reason for King Hussein's decision to back Iraq: there is an agreement in principle between Baghdad and Amman for the pumping of Euphrates water to Jordan, and all the forecasts are that Iraqi water will be needed. Lack of finance means Jordan cannot build the desalination plants it obviously needs and no more water can be taken from the Jordan, but the population is expanding. According to the minister, King Hussein was heavily influenced in his decisions by the hydrological imperative: it was more important to ensure future Iraqi goodwill than current western or Arab approval.

Israel itself has not hesitated to use water as an instrument of policy, particularly in relation to the Arab population of Israel and the people living under Israeli occupation in the West Bank and Gaza. Its habit of severely restricting Palestinian use of water while allowing its own settlers to have much larger supplies is not merely a case of favouring its own; an unstated but well understood Israeli policy is to induce as many Palestinians as possible to leave their homes. The far right in Israel speaks openly of 'transfer', of forcing Palestinians out; the Likud did not acknowledge that this was its policy, but followed it in practice; Labour does not favour such a solution, but cannot always control all the soldiers and officials who administer the Occupied Territories.

Even in Israel itself water is used to try to force Palestinians out of 'Jewish' areas. An unofficial tribunal on water disputes set up in the Netherlands in 1992 by left-wing groups condemned Israel for refusing to supply drinking water via the national carrier to several dozen Israeli Arab villages. Appealing to the Tribunal on behalf of those affected, Arab health groups accused Israel of trying to subjugate its Arab citizens and 'Jewishize' land belonging to the villagers. Israeli government representatives argued that the villages were being denied water from the network merely because they were not recognized as municipalities. The Tribunal, not surprisingly, disagreed.

Given its chronic shortage of water, even the small saving gained by depriving some Arab villages helps Israel, and water also played its part in the remarkable Israeli offer to give the Gaza Strip back to the Arabs – if anyone could be found to take it. A senior Israeli minister made the suggestion at the end of 1992, after an upsurge of violence by Hamas, the Islamic movement. No Israeli minister, Likud or Labour, has ever suggested returning the West Bank. The difference between the two areas is plain: Gaza is desperately short of water, a liability, while the West Bank provides Israel with water. Without new alliances, new economies and better cooperation, Israel is going to suffer severe shortages in the near future. It looks to Turkey as well as its Arab neighbours to help it out.

3

The South-East Anatolia Project

President Turgut Özal and Prime Minister Süleyman Demirel sat a few feet apart, for once united in support of a project, even if they were still barely speaking to each other. Ministers from the newly independent republics of Central Asia sweltered in the 45 degree heat, an orchestra played, fireworks went off with minimum impact against the cloudless blue sky, and the thousands of local people 'encouraged' to be present queued up for the bottles of water imported at some cost from factories many miles away. It was Saturday, 25 July 1992, the day of the formal opening of the Atatürk Dam near Bozova in south-east Anatolia as an electric power generating plant. Speeches were made, flags unfurled, hot-air balloons drifted about and hang gliders swooped dramatically down from the huge dam wall as Turkey put into commission the central element of the South-East Anatolia Project (GAP), the largest integrated scheme in the country's history, a multi-billion irrigation and power generation complex designed to transform a backward province and to change for ever the social, economic and political make-up of the region. By 2015, hydroelectric turbines at the Atatürk Dam and its subsidiaries should be generating a fifth as much electricity as the whole country produces now. The water could also irrigate 20,000 square kilometres of land, an area almost as big as Israel and enough, in theory, to double Turkey's farm output.

On that same day, 25 July 1992, a fighting patrol of Turkish Army paratroops was making its cautious way along a dirt road near Cizre, not far from the point where the Turkish, Syrian and Iraqi borders all meet. There was a sudden burst of fire, and with the speed of long practice these elite troops instantly took up defensive positions and engaged the ambushers, as the lieutenant in charge radioed news of the 'contact'. Five soldiers and two guerrillas died in the battle that developed, while in other incidents across the south-east, two more guerrillas were killed, a village guard was murdered and police and troops came under fire, while in Diyarbakır Prison the security men went about their brutal daily task of extracting information from newly caught prisoners, information needed quickly and extracted swiftly by any means available.

A third element provided the direct link between the celebrations at Bozova and the regular routine of the low-intensity war that continued every day in the remoter areas of south-east Anatolia. In Ankara, officials of the Foreign Ministry stayed late at their desks preparing briefs for their minister, Hikmet Cetin, while in Damascus, Syrian advisers studied the latest reports from Turkey and drew up their own notes for the series of meetings planned for the following week.

The war in the badlands of Turkey's south-east was being waged by the PKK, the Kurdish Workers' Party, constantly armed and supported by Syria and occasionally helped by Iraq and Iran. It was President Hafez Assad's direct response to Turkey's decision to harness the abundant waters of the Tigris and Euphrates in a huge project bound to have effects far beyond the borders of the country. At present, the Euphrates carries about 7,000 billion gallons of water across the border into Syria every year. The South-East Anatolia Project is expected to divert as much as half of that into Turkish dams and irrigation canals. Much of the water will get back into the Euphrates, but after irrigating Turkish fields it will be saltier when it reaches the Syrian and Iraqi farms downstream. The most pessimistic forecasts in Damascus and Baghdad are that the GAP could cost Syria 40 per cent and Iraq 90 per cent of the Euphrates flow. Syria's own ambitious irrigation plans would take another 3,500 billion gallons or so of water a year out of the Euphrates at the expense of Iraq, where farmers have been using Euphrates water for irrigation for 6,000 years. In 1975, after Syria built its Thawrah Dam, the Iraqis claimed that the loss of water put the livelihood of three million Iraqi farmers at risk. The argument brought the two countries within an inch of war. Now that Iraq is weak and divided after the war over Kuwait it can do little, though it still hopes to make up for its loss of Euphrates water with more from the Tigris. Even so, it is worried: the growing salinity of the Euphrates has already ruined some Iraqi farming land around Basra.

President Assad, the most astute of all Middle East leaders, had decided much earlier that he needed something with which to bargain in his dealings with Turkey and other countries. So to have some extra cards in his hand, he invited representatives of dozens of different guerrilla factions, liberation movements and dissidents to set up their headquarters in Damascus. Among those who accepted the invitation to go to Damascus quietly put out by Syrian intelligence were young members of Dev Genc and Dev Sol, of the Turkish People's Liberation Army and other small factions of the revolutionary left. In Syria they were given the kind of welcome extended to all other potentially useful organizations: a small monthly stipend, places in a training camp and access to arms strictly controlled by the all-pervasive Syrian intelligence. Many of them returned to Turkey once they had completed their first courses in guerrilla warfare, and played their part in gradually turning Turkish cities into urban battlegrounds as they exploited the political paralysis caused by the parliamentary deadlock between Süleyman Demirel's Justice Party and Bülent Ecevit's Republican People's Party. As well as fighting, these young activists took care to spread their revolutionary gospel, and among those who heard it were members of the innocuous-sounding Democratic Patriotic Association for Higher Education, a Kurdish group at Ankara University in which Abdullah Ocalan was active. In 1978 Ocalan found the attentions of the Turkish police too pressing, and decided to follow his comrades to Damascus. Through a mixture of charm, charisma and efficiency he soon took over the leadership of the PKK. It was not much of a feat then: numbers were low, activities minimal and to their Syrian hosts the PKK was just one more among a proliferating array of exiled activists in which the mainstream Turkish factions were far more important. At that stage, it looked as though a revolutionary regime might actually win power in Ankara, so that the Turkish exiles were far more important to President Assad than any Kurds.

By 1978 Turkey was close to civil war, the police were divided and ineffectual, and only the army held the country together, waging a bitter war against the violent left and turning a blind eye to the rise of an equally violent right. Turkey's twelve million Kurds did not officially exist: they were 'mountain Turks who had forgotten their native language'. In practice, they were brutally suppressed in the eight Kurdish provinces of the south-east, and watched and discriminated against when they migrated to the relatively prosperous west of the country.

In 1980 the situation changed: General Kenan Evren, the calm, avuncular Turkish Army Chief of Staff, led a final military intervention which to the surprise of most people restored order to the lawless streets almost overnight. The squabbling politicians were banned as the army opted for direct rule, though Turgut Özal (who died in April 1993), a hydrological engineer reputed to be one of the best economists in Europe, was kept on as head of the State Planning Organization.

This rang the alarm bells in Damascus. The combination of Özal's background, his vision of a stronger and economically more powerful Turkey and his influence in various ministries made him an enthusiastic supporter of an ambitious scheme which had been formulated in the 1960s as a simple plan to irrigate the plain between Gazientep and Mardin along the border with Syria. With Özal's support, what had been intended merely to increase food production was escalated into a vast project to double Turkey's electric power potential, vastly increase water availability and transform the whole backward south-east corner of the country into an area of prosperity which would attract industry as well as develop agriculture, and in which the new wealth and modern infrastructure would induce the people to support the government and make it impossible for dissidents to operate.

The planners in Damascus saw the implications very clearly. Syria depends on the Tigris and Euphrates for the vast majority of its water supplies, and any interruption to them, any diminution in quantity or quality, could have a serious effect in a country where political balance was always precarious. The GAP could cost Syria 40 per cent and Iraq 90 per cent of the Euphrates flow. Yet Syria seemed to have no cards to play: certainly it had a large, battle-trained standing army, but it was preoccupied and increasingly bogged down in Lebanon, and its air force had twice been blasted out of the skies by Israel.

Hafez Assad was once described by Henry Kissinger as the kind of man who went into a poker game with a hand of twos and threes and came out scooping the pot. In a country like Syria, he needed that kind of guile. In the twenty years before Assad took over in 1970, Syria had suffered dozens of coups and changes of government. Three years earlier it had lost the Golan Heights to Israel, and months before he seized power in a bloodless coup, Assad had been forced to back down in a confrontation with Jordan. The country depended on Soviet experts and Soviet arms for its existence, while at home the powerful Sunni merchants were kept in line only by the threat of force from the security services and special army units of the minority Alawites, who controlled the country through their mafia-like network of family and friends in all-important posts.

Assad, a pilot and former air force commander, set out to restore his country's military might, and to give it the political clout he felt it deserved. East and West were played off against each other as long as the cold war continued, regional states were supported or ditched according to the advantage to be gained, the Palestinians were used to project Syrian power by proxy, and in that astute move typical of his concern for the future, President Assad had encouraged all those 'liberation groups' to make their headquarters in Syria.

In 1978 that foresight paid off. Assad realized he had a lever that could be used to force Turkey to take account of Syrian demands. Suddenly, the PKK was no longer an anonymous, unimportant group among many others. Senior Syrian intelligence officers arrived at the camp north of Damascus where the Kurds had their meagre headquarters. It had been decided at the highest level, they said, that the time had come for Syria to give full backing to the just aspirations of the Kurdish people. New instructors would be provided, more weapons, and better premises would be found; the PKK should step up its recruiting campaign. Abdullah Ocalan – Apo to his supporters – was not taken in for a moment by the protestations of the intelligence men. He understood very well that Syrian national interests were at stake, and that he and his men were to be used by Damascus as pawns in a game between two regional superpowers. Ocalan also understood the need to seize the moment, to take full advantage of any help offered, ignoring the reasons it was being given. Just as Assad had thought ahead soon after he took power in 1970, and had given a welcome to all the potentially useful freedom fighters, so Ocalan looked ahead and believed that he could transform his raggle-taggle army into a fighting force which could achieve a momentum of its own, and in time be able to operate independently of Syria. Just as Assad got it right, so did Ocalan.

From the camp shared with others north of Damascus the PKK was moved to the Masoum Korkmaz training base in the Bekaa Valley of Lebanon, part of the area under the control of the Syrian army. Ocalan and his senior lieutenants were given safe houses in Damascus – flats in high-rise blocks in the fashionable areas of the city, constantly guarded – or watched – by the ubiquitous intelligence services on which the Syrian regime depends. Bank accounts were opened, training stepped up, arms provided. And in August 1984 the go-ahead was given for the campaign that has been going on ever since.

As usual, the Syrians sought to distance themselves from what was being done and to muddy the waters by implicating others. Instead of allowing raids directly across the border the Syrians ordered the first teams of PKK guerrillas to move out of Syria into Iraq, and it was from that country that the initial attacks were launched into the Şemdinli area of the extreme south-east of Turkey, close to the frontier where Iraq and Iran meet. The Syrian aim was to cause trouble between Turkey and its other neighbours before acknowledging its own role and seeking its own advantage. The tactic worked at first, not least because other Kurdish groups had launched a few hit and run raids from Iraq. This time it was different: the attack was in force, with about 300 PKK guerrillas taking part, many of them young women. The targets were gendarmerie and police posts, public buildings in the small towns and villages of the area, and banks – like the IRA in Northern Ireland, the PKK wanted to be self-financing.

The Turkish response to these first attacks set the pattern for all that was to follow, and was in part responsible for the escalation of the insurgency. By this time Turgut Özal had become prime minister in the election that followed the military decision to return to barracks. He was not the candidate preferred by the generals, but they accepted the people's verdict in what was acknowledged to be a free and fair election. But on security matters the Turkish military have always made their own decisions and pursued their own policies, and in the face of this new threat their knee-jerk reaction was to respond with a huge show of force and a massive crack-down. Thousands of troops were drafted into the south-east, the borders with neighbouring countries were sealed, and a search and destroy operation was launched in the mountains, while in the towns and villages men from MIT, the Turkish intelligence service, moved in to identify and interrogate possible sympathizers. Their brutal methods did much to persuade the local people that cooperation with Ankara was useless, and that the only hope lay in armed revolt.

Between 1984 and 1993 some 5,000 people were killed as the revolt spread. South-east Anatolia became a battleground, with those trying to live peacefully caught between the hammer of the PKK and the anvil of Turkish security. If they refused to help the guerrillas, they were killed; if they gave them food or shelter, the army arrested them, imprisoned them and tortured them.

While the fighting went on, so did the engineering works: the bulldozers and earth movers were everywhere, armies of engineers and technicians swarmed over the south-eastern provinces, seminars were held, papers written, plans drawn and redrawn. The military were becoming involved too, as it was realized that Syria or Iraq might actually try to prevent work going ahead. In 1986, reports surfaced that Turkey had uncovered a Syrian plot to blow up the Atatürk Dam, but this was probably no more than a ploy by MIT to let Assad know they were aware of what he was doing. As the

Turkish engineers say, it would take an atom bomb to blow up the massive dam wall.

By this time, the GAP was no longer an irrigation scheme involving a few small dams, but a vast project absorbing a disproportionate amount of Turkey's skilled manpower, of its work force and engineering capacity, and of its revenues. The aim now was not merely to irrigate a part of the coastal plain, but to transform an area twice as big as the Netherlands, with a population of 5.2 million. When the GAP is complete – probably in about 2010 at current rates of progress – 1.7 million hectares of land will be irrigated and 27 billion kilowatt-hours of electricity will be generated each year. More than three million new jobs will be created across the whole country and the per capita income of the backward region will be doubled, according to the economists working full-time on the scheme. There will be twenty-two major dams, nineteen hydroelectric plants and dozens of subsidiary irrigation schemes. But given the continued violence in the region during the 1980s and 1990s, international lenders had no desire to get involved in financing the GAP: every lira had to be found by Turkey itself, at a time when inflation was running at 70 per cent and unemployment was rising as European countries took steps to 'persuade' Turkish guest workers to return home. Many Turkish economists blamed the GAP for much of the country's economic troubles, and believed that the priority given to the GAP was the result of an obsessive interest in it by Özal. In that they were wrong: Süleyman Demirel, banned from politics by the army in 1980, was rehabilitated, and in 1992 returned as prime minister at the head of a coalition government, just in time to officiate at the formal firing up of the first two generators powered by the Atatürk Dam. He was as committed to the GAP as Özal.

Syria and Iraq remained as wary as ever of what Turkey was doing, and on 13 January 1990 their worst fears were realized. The 169 metre high rock-fill dam wall, the ninth largest in the world, almost two kilometres long at its crest, was completed, and the reservoir behind it could be filled. That could have been done in two ways. The diversion channel could have been left partially open, so that some water would continue to flow on down to the Syrian border at Karkamis. A quicker way was to shut off the supply of water to Syria altogether; and that was the way the Turks chose, despite an informal agreement that Turkey would allow an average flow of 500 cubic metres per second into Syria. To the Iraqis and the Syrians, it was a message and a warning: Turkey, they believed, was flexing its muscles, showing that it had its hand on the tap and could starve them of water whenever it chose to do so. In fact, Turkey was also making its bid for recognition as a major player in the Middle East, having failed in its effort to turn towards Europe and to be accepted by the European Community. The effect was dramatic: Syria and Iraq, for years sworn enemies, suddenly united in denunciation of Ankara, and even went so far as to hold secret military talks to discuss what to do in case of future Turkish pressure. Syrian and Iraqi rivalries, stemming from the rule of the Baath party in both countries, each claiming legitimacy, were put aside. Editorials in Baghdad and Damascus were at one in denouncing Turkish 'water imperialism', while politicians hurried between capitals and made speeches. This was a salutary surprise for the Turks, who had not expected that the danger of the loss of their water lifeline would be enough to make the rival regimes in Baghdad and Damascus sink their differences and unite to face a common enemy. Through all the hubbub, Turkey put on a face of injured innocence. Adequate notice had been given to Iraq and Syria that the river would be diverted for a month while the reservoir was filled, the Turks said; it had even been arranged that the flow of the river should be increased for a while beforehand to allow the two neighbouring countries to fill their own reserve storage areas. What on earth was all the fuss about, they asked plaintively. The Turks, of course, knew very well; perhaps this time they were playing a little game and showing President Assad that he was not the only one who could dissimulate.

The one unplanned result was to precipitate the negotiations that both sides had come to realize to be necessary – talks that would have as their bottom line the exchange of water for peace. No one was crass enough to spell it out in such stark detail, but according to the Turks it was the Syrians who had first linked security and water. That was in 1986, when the Syrian prime minister paid an official visit to Ankara. According to the Turks, at that time the Syrians said they would sign the security protocol – a routine treaty governing customs matters, border controls and so on – only if Turkey entered into a formal water agreement. In 1987 that was done when the Turkish prime minister, Turgut Özal, visited Damascus and signed the security protocol, adding to it provisions on economic cooperation and a note setting out the Turkish commitment to maintaining a Euphrates flow of 500 cubic metres per second at the Syrian border. The security provisions of the protocol were general in character and made no mention of the PKK, so in April 1992 the Turkish diplomats set out to remedy that defect when the interior minister, Ismet Sezgin, met his Syrian counterpart, Muhammad Harbah, and also held talks with President Assad. The most significant exchange came when the Turkish delegation met the Syrian leader. 'Can I say when I go back to my country that the PKK problem will be solved?' asked the somewhat ingenuous Turkish minister. 'There will be cooperation to solve this problem,' Assad replied, much more enigmatically.

There was a marked difference in the official reports of the talks from each side. 'The two sides affirmed their concern for enhancing bilateral ties in the interest of achieving security and stability for the two countries and the region,' said the Syrian communiqué. 'During its stay in Syria, the Turkish delegation visited some archaeological and historic sites . . . Dr Muhammad Harbah accepted with gratitude an invitation to visit Turkey, on the understanding that a date would be arranged later'. Translated from diplomatic jargon, what the Syrians were saying was that nothing of any consequence had been decided, that it was a routine, relatively low-level visit concerned only with the sort of frontier questions any neighbouring countries would have, and no specific problems had been addressed.

The Turks took a very different view.

Turkey and Syria have agreed to fight terrorism together [said Turkish radio]. A conclusive document and the addenda prepared within the framework of the protocol on security and cooperation adopted by the two countries in 1987 were signed at the end of the official talks in Damascus. The issue of the PKK, which created interest and largely preoccupied the two sides, was included in the document after discussions that lasted six hours.

The Syrians disagreed: there was no protocol, only agreed minutes of the meetings. And a provision concerning 'the terrorist organization PKK was included at the request of the Turkish side'. The Syrians also talked about the 'stolen' province of Hatay (in Turkey). This was not exactly the meeting of minds that the Turkish minister had claimed. The reason was plain: no one had brought up the subject of water, and that was what the Syrians wanted, though, true to form, they would not spell it out themselves as that would be tipping their hand.

The message got through, and soon afterwards Turkey reaffirmed its promise to maintain an average flow of 500 cubic metres per second from the Euphrates into Syria. But it was a grudging promise, plainly made under pressure, and accompanied by a justification of Turkish water policies:

The Euphrates and Tigris watercourses constitute 28 per cent of potential water resources in Turkey and have significant importance for her. Iraq and Syria advocate sharing the water of the Tigris and Euphrates. However, under international law, transboundary watercourses cannot be shared, though they can be utilized in an equitable, reasonable and optimum manner. This is the definition under international law, which considers natural resources like water, oil, minerals etc. to be under the sovereignty of the countries concerned. However, Turkey has unilaterally committed itself to release 500 cubic metres a second to Syria and has always honoured its commitment.

The construction of dams on the Euphrates is designed to regulate the flow of water, generate electricity and irrigate the land. The function of regulating the flow of water of the dams of the Euphrates not only serves the interests of Turkey, but also contributes to the water needs of neighbouring countries, Syria and Iraq. The velocity of the Euphrates may fall as low as 100 cubic metres per second during the summer while it could reach a maximum of 7,000 cubic metres when the spring snows melt. The existence of the dams enables Turkey to provide a regular flow of 500 cubic metres to its neighbours throughout the year, even during the summers of 1989, 1990 and 1991 when three consecutive droughts were registered. Obviously, the main beneficiaries of this regular flow of water have been Syria and Iraq, who have been provided with enough water by Turkey not to have suffered the severe consequences of the drought.

However, it should be noted that Syria and Iraq have in no way contributed to the construction of the dams on the Euphrates but have even tried to prevent the establishment of these dams. Moreover, the entire water potential of the Tigris is used by Iraq by transferring its water to the Euphrates through the al-Tharthar canal.

The Turkish paper went on to note that the Orontes, which rises in Lebanon to flow through Syria and Turkey into the Mediterranean, had two dams constructed on it, one in Syria and one in Lebanon. Orontes water was also used for irrigation, so that during the summer the river dried up before it reached Turkey. Mention of the Orontes rang more alarm bells in Damascus: a general agreement with Turkey would have to cover the Orontes, but that would bring in the disputed province of Hatay, as the river runs through that corner of Turkey. The Syrians think the Turks would take an agreement on the Orontes as recognition of Hatay as Turkish.

The Turkish note went on: 'If a comparison is made between the utilization of the Orontes and the Euphrates, there is justified cause for Turkey to complain about how the water of the Orontes is completely consumed by Syria and Lebanon, while Turkey releases 500 cubic metres of water even when the velocity of the Euphrates falls to 100 cubic metres a second.'

Turkey went on to promise cooperation, while emphasizing that the Tigris and Euphrates came under Turkish sovereignty as long as they were within Turkish territory. Although it was not spelt out, it was also quite clear that Turkey had no intention of entering into any tripartite agreement with the other riparian states, though a fifteen-member technical committee had been established with Syrian, Turkish and Iraqi water engineers as long ago as 1980. It last met in 1990.

The Turkish foreign ministry claims that whether in a formal protocol or in agreed minutes, the fact is that in April 1992 Syria had accepted that the PKK was a terrorist organization, and that it would cooperate by arresting its members, preventing cross-border infiltration and closing any training camps. Of course, it did not go nearly as far as that, and never intended to do so, but merely ordered Ocalan and his men to be a little less visible, and made sure that all camps and bases were moved to the Bekaa Valley. Then, when Turkey again complained that Syria was tolerating and even encouraging the PKK, it was the Syrians' turn to look pained and to protest that there were no PKK men or PKK camps in Syria. If Turkey was concerned about activities in the Bekaa Valley, they said, then Ankara should address itself to the Lebanese government, as the Bekaa was obviously in Lebanese territory. That was certainly so, but what the Syrians did not say was that the Bekaa was also firmly under the control of the Syrian army, which had some 40,000 troops in Lebanon, most of them by this time withdrawn from Beirut to the east of the country.

The Turks decided to try again. Another visit was arranged, this time by the foreign minister, Hikmet Cetin, to emphasize that this was a question of international relations, not merely border co-operation. And though Turkey was careful not to make any threats, the visit was carefully timed for just one week after the ceremony to start the generators on the Atatürk Dam, an event to which the Syrian Irrigation Minister, Abdel Rahman al-Madani, was carefully invited. He sat stony-faced throughout the ceremony and speeches, then hurried off to the Syrian embassy in Ankara. The next day the ambassador, Abdul Aziz al-Rifai, went on the radio to emphasize Syrian 'sensitivity' on the water issue, and to call once again for a tripartite agreement on sharing Euphrates water. Questioned about Syrian support of the PKK, the ambassador denied that his government supported the PKK but admitted that there might be 'infiltrations' by groups he agreed were terrorists. 'Thousands of people cross the 900 kilometre border every day, some of whom carry both

Syrian and Turkish passports,' he said. 'It is very difficult to distinguish ordinary citizens from smugglers or terrorists.' As nobody suggested that the PKK guerrillas went about their business in civilian clothes or passed through border formalities, that hardly seemed important. Asked about the PKK camps in the Bekaa Valley, the ambassador fell back on the old argument of Lebanese sovereignty. On the same day, the Lebanese authorities passed the buck firmly back to the Syrians.

We asked senior officials of the Turkish foreign ministry what they would do if Syria continued to support the PKK while blaming Lebanon for allowing the camps to continue. The diplomats accepted that Syria was playing for time, and that the involvement of the Lebanese government was irrelevant. So what would they do? It was no easier to pin down the Turks than to get straight answers out of the Syrians:

> We shall continue to make diplomatic representations. We shall not make any threats, or mention water; that is quite a separate issue on which there is no outstanding problem. If we go on complaining about Syrian support of the PKK, it may be that eventually the Syrians will come to believe we are threatening them. That is up to them. All we expect is good neighbourly relations.

We asked a senior policy-maker of the Turkish foreign ministry if he accepted that Syria was using the PKK to put pressure on Turkey over water. 'It is true that Syria does have a habit of working through proxies. It was about 1980 that we started talking very seriously about expanding the GAP project, and it was about that time that Ocalan began getting help from Damascus. You could make a connection . . .'

So there were no specifics from the Turkish foreign ministry, but one question arose. They spoke of Syria 'playing for time'. Why? The answer to that came increasingly in the meagre information put out by the military authorities on the daily clashes with the PKK guerrillas. The location of the daily battles had gradually changed: the area from Mardin round to Şemdinli was no longer the most active theatre; instead, the action had moved north, into Van province. The indications were that the guerrillas had changed their bases, and were no longer launching attacks from Syria or Iraq but had set up camps in Iran.

Captured fighters confirmed this, and described how the shift had come about. The rear headquarters remained in the Bekaa, where Ocalan and his senior lieutenants conducted their planning sessions, and where new cadres were trained. Ocalan still had his flat in Damascus, but the forward camps from which operations were launched had been moved to Iran, under an agreement reached not with the government in Tehran but with the Revolutionary Guards, the Pasdaran, who still gave their allegiance to Ali Akbar Mohtashemi, the former interior minister and Iranian ambassador in Damascus who had been responsible for introducing the Pasdaran into Lebanon. The Iranian Revolutionary Guards were still occupying the Sheikh Abdullah barracks in Baalbeck while the PKK men trained nearby. Contact was established, and Mohtashemi, still fighting for power in Iran and too strong to be crushed by President Hashemi Rafsanjani, saw a useful tool in the PKK. He authorized his men to reach an agreement allowing the PKK to set up forward camps in areas of northern Iran under their control. Forced to adopt a low profile in Syria and regularly betrayed by the Kurdish Democratic Party (KDP) in northern Iraq, who wanted good relations with Turkey, Ocalan desperately needed the lifeline offered him by Mohtashemi. The new Iranian bases meant that operations could go ahead as regularly and violently as ever, and the Iranian extremists could be sure they had an ally in the future if either they or Ocalan should ever achieve power. Syria, anxious to placate Turkey as it sought better relations with the West, and with Turkey's ally the USA, was happy to encourage its one regional ally to take on the burden of support for the PKK. And even President Rafsanjani was not too concerned: Iran and Turkey were competing directly for influence in the newly independent republics of the old Soviet Union, and Turkey was winning; continued trouble in eastern Anatolia would preoccupy the Turks, and show them that Iran could be difficult if it chose.

Turkey has abundant water and it has people, but it lacks what the Arab countries have in plenty: oil. So it has to maintain good relations with the Arabs and with Iran. During the eight years of the first Gulf war, Ankara succeeded brilliantly in walking the tightrope, staying on correct terms with both Baghdad and Tehran, and was rewarded when Iraq doubled and trebled the capacity of its oil pipeline to the Mediterranean, paying Turkey handsome royalties in oil and cash for being allowed to do so. At the same time convoys of trucks were rolling east to provide munitions to Iran.

Turkey is vulnerable on two fronts, however. Although it was proclaimed a secular state when Kemal Atatürk became the first leader of the modern country in 1923, its people remain Muslims. Atatürk decreed in 1928 that the country had enough mosques and that no more should be built; it is the one edict he passed down which has been consistently ignored. And though religious parties have never gained more than 15 per cent of the popular vote, the politicians note that the return to Islam is strongest among the young, and that it is the brand of Islamic Revolution popularized by Ayatollah Khomeini in Iran that seems to have the greatest attraction. So Turkish policy is to avoid confrontation with any Islamic country and thus to avoid trouble at home, following an Atatürk dictum that is obeyed: peace in the world, peace at home.

The country's second concern is its Kurdish minority. Right up to 1990 Turkey denied the existence of the five million Kurds within its borders, describing them as mountain Turks who had forgotten their own language. Ankara's decision to throw in its lot with the Americans, and the events which followed the liberation of Kuwait, meant that the Kurds in Turkey had to be acknowledged. But that did not mean that they had to be accommodated. On the contrary, the war against the PKK was stepped up as a few minor reforms were announced for Kurds who undertook to give up violence.

Turkey's relations with its neighbours were made no better by the political discord at home. President Özal should have been above the fray, according to the Turkish constitution, but had no intention of accepting any such role. During the Gulf war he had run Turkish foreign policy almost single-handed, losing foreign ministers and a

73

chief of staff as a result. But that strengthened his position, and emboldened him to go on the same way even after his Motherland Party lost the general election to a combination of Demirel's True Path Party and the Social Democratic Populist Party of Erdal Inönü. President and prime minister were soon barely on speaking terms, and each was very ready to say or do things that would embarrass the other.

It was only the GAP that united them. Demirel started life as a water technician, and has a degree in hydrological engineering from Istanbul University. As Director of the State Hydraulic Works he became known as 'king of the dams', and during his first stint as prime minister in 1965 it was his government which obtained World Bank backing for the Keban Dam, the first link in the chain of dams that makes up the South-East Anatolia Project. Özal's links with the GAP went back just as far. He studied economics and electrical engineering in the USA and became deputy director of the Electrical Studies and Research Administration. It was then that he worked on the schemes to harness the hydroelectric power of the Euphrates. Yet Demirel, always the populist, the man who could draw the crowds, had little taste for the subtleties of riparian politics. On that sweltering July day when the generators were started, Demirel had packed the VIP stands with leaders from the central Asian republics; he was the architect of Turkey's successful drive to win friends and influence there. It was Özal who insisted on inviting Syrian and Iraqi ministers, though the Iraqis politely made their excuses. As it turned out, Özal and Demirel came close to doing a 'nice cop, tough cop' act, with both making unexceptionable speeches on the day, but Demirel setting out Turkey's hard-line attitude to its one great natural resource on the day before the opening. At a news conference, the prime minister was asked about the effect of the GAP on neighbouring states. Neither Iraq nor Syria should feel disturbed, he said, but immediately went on to worry them more than ever:

Neither Syria nor Iraq can lay claim to Turkey's rivers any more than Ankara could claim their oil. This is a matter of sovereignty. We have a right to do anything we like. The water resources are

Turkey's, the oil resources are theirs. We don't say we share their oil resources, and they cannot say they share our water resources.

This is strictly true, of course, but not what a politician bent on compromise and cooperation might say. This was Turkey in a tough mood, the expansionist, self-confident Turkey that its neighbours were learning to recognize and perhaps to fear.

There was a predictable and swift response in the Arab countries. Demirel's statement was against international law and justice, and incompatible with good and friendly ties, said a Cairo commentary, going on to admit that there was no legal barrier to Turkey using the Euphrates waters as it liked. 'But it is illegal to deny the peoples of the neighbouring countries the water resources they have been using for centuries. Turkey's tight rein on water shows there is no end to its regional ambitions.' Syria, unusually, was more reasoned: 'Syria calls for a fair sharing of the Euphrates and Tigris waters, so as not to deny Syrians drinking water and water to irrigate their land,' said the government newspaper *Tishreen*. 'Nobody has the right to divert these rivers and subject Syrians to a catastrophe. If every country started to divert rivers claiming they were on their lands then the whole world would be subject to grave dangers.'

Instead of letting all the controversy die down, Turkey chose to fuel the blaze, and demonstrated that when it came to national issues, Turkey was united. Kamran Inan, a member of the opposition Motherland Party who had been the minister responsible for GAP, endorsed Demirel's stand. If Iraq and Syria wanted to make claims on Turkish water, then Turkey might make claims on their oil, he threatened. Instead of complaining about the GAP, the two Arab countries should contribute to its cost.

Ilnur Cevik, a columnist friend of the prime minister, chose to attack Egypt for rushing to the help of Syria and Iraq. 'The Egyptians are too busy trying to be a regional power to look into the facts,' said Demirel through Cevik. 'Instead of trying to play the role of a regional power, Egypt should concentrate on putting its own house in order. We have seen too many paper tigers in the past who tried to dictate to us. Egypt should not be one of them.'

Only in the calmer havens of universities in Turkey and the Arab countries were the issues debated more rationally and objectively. In Turkey, opinion was divided. Many economists felt that too great a proportion of Turkey's resources was being poured into the GAP, and that even if the basic idea was good and the project worthwhile, construction should be spread over a much longer period. They noted that construction of the Atatürk Dam had been completed a year behind schedule not through any fault of the Turkish contractors, but because of lack of money, which was also the cause of a five-year slippage in the expected date of completion of the whole project, now put at 2005. The determination to push ahead as quickly as possible was put down to political rather than economic imperatives, and was blamed for 70 per cent of Turkey's inflation, then running at 60 per cent per annum. There were environmental concerns, too: the Atatürk Dam alone meant that 155 villages were submerged, and there were twenty-two other dams in the GAP. Archaeological sites were covered before they could be excavated and examined. There were ominous indications that, far from preserving small farmers and family holdings, the government had in mind agri-businesses on a grand scale, with the consequent dispossession of farmers and an accelerated drift to the cities to swell the unemployment pool there, as well as the obliteration of a way of life in the countryside, with its customs, crafts and traditional methods allowing large families to live from relatively small holdings. There was concern, too, about the methods of irrigation chosen, and the crops that would be grown. From the Atatürk Dam two 26 kilometre tunnels, almost 8 metres in diameter, carry water to Şanlıurfa for distribution by an open canal system throughout the arid Harran Plain. The tunnels will deliver 328 cubic metres per second, which will irrigate 327,725 hectares by gravity feed and 148,649 hectares by pumped water, and they will provide power through a hydroelectric plant at their outlet. But the open canal system is a wasteful method of distributing water, with a high evaporation loss and a tendency to breaks and spillages which will waste water on unproductive ground. Against this it is argued that the initial lower costs will be worthwhile, and that the farmers of the region are familiar with this system.

Another problem is the type of crops to be grown. Given the agricultural history of the region, the farmers seem most likely to opt for cotton, but there is no shortage of cotton in Turkey or on world markets, so that returns are likely to be poor. Wheat, the other traditional crop of the area, is also plentiful worldwide and in Turkey.

Only the Euphrates is involved in the first stage of the GAP, but when it is complete it will involve the Tigris as well, thus enlarging the area affected from Gazientep right across the south-eastern provinces to the Iranian and Iraqi borders. This is the heartland of Turkish Kurdistan, and will clearly have a huge impact on the people and the economy of the region. The government argument is that as a result of geography, not political discrimination, the Kurdish provinces have been neglected and have always been poor and backward, their bleak mountains and narrow valleys unsuitable for large-scale agriculture and their distances from urban centres making them unattractive to industrialists. The GAP, the government says, will result in improved communications, irrigated agriculture and a concentration of people into new towns where all modern facilities can be provided. The Kurds say that the new towns will be similar to the protected villages that Iraq built in the north of that country, places where the authorities can watch and control what is going on, where fields of fire will govern town planning more than pleasing vistas. The object, they say, is to deny their champions, the guerrillas of the PKK, the environment in which they can operate.

No doubt that will be the result, but the government rightly points out that is a bonus from the whole scheme, not the reason for it. It is prosperity that will defeat the guerrillas, not force of arms, say the economists. In the course of time south-east Anatolia will become as well off as the rest of the country, and when that happens the Kurds will be as Turkish as the Turks. Kurdish exiles say that that can never happen. It is a recipe for disaster, they say, and warn that unless economic growth is allied to political reforms, eastern Turkey will remain as it is now – a lawless region where the army rules the roads and towns, and the guerrillas control the mountains and the remote villages. Neither the government scenario nor the predictions of the PKK fighters seem likely to come true: the involvement of Syria and Iraq makes the South-Eastern Anatolia Project an international concern, which sooner or later will need, and get, international action.

4

The Nile: Egypt's Prime
Security Concern

When President Anwar Sadat signed the peace treaty with Israel in February 1979, he was determined that there would be no more war between Egypt and the Jewish state. At the same time, he was very conscious of Egypt's overriding strategic consideration – the safety of the Nile. All Egyptians know that their nation's vital interests go 7,000 kilometres into the heart of Africa, but the Egyptian military has a special role. There are several different levels of national security in Egypt, and only one in Category A: something that comes under the direct protection of the armed forces. Any threat to the Nile allows the Egyptian High Command to order an immediate military response, without having to wait for Parliamentary approval.

To the world, Sadat's stunning visit to Jerusalem in November 1977 was the greatest personal diplomatic coup of the century. 'Let there be no more war between Arab and Israeli,' he said, and millions of supporters around the world believed that by his actions the Egyptian leader had made that possible, ending three decades of hostility.

In the Arab world, it was not like that: many governments saw Sadat's initiative as a great betrayal. They understood immediately what Israeli Prime Minister Menachem Begin would do: detach Egypt from the rest of the Arabs and so make it impossible for them ever again to pose a credible threat of war against Israel.

In Cairo, opinion was deeply divided. The foreign minister resigned, and so did his deputy and then his successor. Senior officials and army officers held anxious consultations, but in the streets and coffee houses there was joy. The Egyptian people were tired of war, of what they saw as their sacrifices on behalf of the Arabs with whom they did not always identify. Sadat had the popular support he always craved.

Yet within the year, Sadat was very close to being toppled in a military takeover. From information we have unearthed in Cairo, Washington and Jerusalem, we have been able to piece together the details of two quite separate plots to depose the Egyptian president: and the reasons for both were not only that he wanted to make peace with Israel, but also that as an inducement to Israel to agree, he was considering diverting water from the Nile to irrigate the Negev desert of Israel. Water came close to causing the downfall of Sadat long before the bullets of fundamentalist extremists killed him in 1981.

It was at a meeting of the political committee set up during the conference between Israel and Egypt at Camp David in 1978 that Israeli delegates first mooted the possibility of cooperation on water projects between the two countries. It was not a new idea: diverting about 1 per cent of the Nile's flow through a pipeline to Israel had been discussed by hydrologists for many years, and made economic sense. Israel would not only pay for the water it received, it would also share its expertise with Egypt, while the work would be jointly financed and would employ both Egyptians and Israelis.

Sadat liked the idea, and with his international outlook saw that it could lead to cooperation with other neighbouring states: extending the pipeline would enable Lebanon and Jordan to be linked into a regional water network. What Sadat did not understand was the strength of the opposition to what he was doing, both at home and abroad.

The Egyptian intelligence service, the Mukhabarat, was well aware of Arab plans to cause trouble for Egypt by backing Mengistu Haile Mariam in Ethiopia and the rebels in southern Sudan – both of whom could affect the flow of the Nile. The security men were ready to fight these schemes and to protect Egypt, but they were not prepared to see Nile water going to Israel. One officer told us: 'It was bad enough trying to convince our people [in the service] to protect plans to make up with the enemy of thirty years, but when it came to seeing a branch of the Nile, no matter how small it was, going out of the Egyptian border, then the majority would prefer to lose their eyesight rather than see this day.'

Instead of acting alone, the intelligence men leaked details of what was going on to politicians, former ministers and army officers. The first coup plot was born: rioting and demonstrations would be organized by shop stewards and student activists supporting the opposition, then the army officers would move their units into the streets, ostensibly to restore order but actually to join forces with the protesters. Sadat was to have been arrested. The signal for action would have been any announcement of an agreement with Israel which included Nile water.

To gain added legitimacy, the plotters approached a popular and vocal member of the Egyptian parliament, Kemal Ahmed, known for his honesty as well as his outspoken anti-government views. But Ahmed was experienced in the ways of Egyptian political life: he feared he was being set up, and although he vigorously denies it now, it seems that he opted for caution. He reported the two officers who approached him to a contact in the State Security Police. The officers were arrested and this particular plot was foiled. To this day the names of the two officers involved, like the whole episode, remain top secret. According to murmured explanations from serving officers, the two were quietly dismissed without standing trial, as it was feared they would have revealed the extent of disaffection in the army if they had appeared before a tribunal.

The Americans warned Sadat of the second and more serious attempt being made to get rid of him. Stansfield Turner, then the head of the Central Intelligence Agency (CIA), personally delivered the message while Sadat was negotiating with President Jimmy Carter and Begin at Camp David. The defection of an Egyptian intelligence officer in London had alerted the Americans. A major in Egyptian Intelligence serving as an attaché at the London Embassy had secretly joined the Egyptian opposition National Front, but it was six months before he was reported to his superiors in Cairo. By that time he had seen details of the planned agreements with Israel and had learned the secrets of the coup planned by the opposition.

Well used to political intrigue, he quickly realized that if it was to have any chance of success, a coup against Sadat would have to be led by a figure known and respected by all Egyptians. The only man who fitted that bill was General Saad el Shazli, the charismatic officer who commanded the Egyptian troops when they crossed the Suez Canal in the 1973 war. General Shazli was dismissed by Sadat after the war – made a scapegoat, his supporters said, for the Israeli successes – and went into exile in Algeria. Major Noor el Dine-el-Sayyed (also known as Mahmoud Noor el-Dine), the intelligence officer in London, flew to Algiers with documents proving that Sadat was planning to divert Nile water to Israel, sure that his information would persuade General Shazli to act. Then, with his professional expertise, he realized that his activities were known; he went underground and later surfaced in Cairo. An accomplice of his – later found dead – leaked valuable information to British intelligence. The information was passed on to the CIA, and as a result of what they learned the Americans began monitoring General Shazli's telephone conversations. Details of what was being planned soon emerged.

In this second and more advanced plot units from the special forces were to have occupied the radio and television building once the news that Sadat was prepared to give Nile water to Israel was announced. To demonstrate apparent public support, exiled Army generals who served under Nasser were contacted, and in turn persuaded the powerful Nasserite movements in the universities and trade unions to give their backing by staging 'spontaneous' demonstrations of support for the new regime once it took over. General Shazli would be installed as a credible and popular alternative to Sadat – most Egyptians thought the general was the real hero of the 1973 war and was unjustly dismissed. The plotters were able to recruit influential Egyptians abroad, who provided the money needed, and also controlled newspapers read by Egyptian expatriates and three anti-Sadat radio stations, one broadcasting from Iraq, another from Libya and the third from a ship moored near Malta.

Told by the CIA chief what was going on, Sadat was incredulous. He could not believe that the Egyptian army would turn against him, the leader who had restored their credibility and their morale in the 1973 war. But Sadat was out of touch: even the carefully controlled Egyptian media were turning against the agreement with Israel as more and more details were leaked by officials who were aghast at what was being done. The army was reflecting the mood of the people.

Kemal Ahmed, though he exposed the first plot, had not changed his mind, and when the Camp David accords were brought to the Egyptian parliament for ratification, he spoke for many when he shouted: 'This is high treason, Anwar.' When a government MP sitting behind him slapped the back of his neck Kemal Ahmed kept up his chant, and the incident only ended when the Speaker expelled both.

In Washington, the Americans advised Sadat to drop all ideas of cooperating with the Israelis over water. Always inclined to think he knew best, Sadat wanted to ignore this advice, but was finally persuaded to take notice when the most senior Egyptian commander warned American officials that the Egyptian army was opposed to any further concessions to Israel. The officer was Field Marshal Abdel Halim Abu Ghazala, the defence minister, who told his president that he would not be able to guarantee the loyalty of the army if officers told their men that a coup was 'to stop Israel stealing the Nile'. That was the end of the talks on water, a decision that allowed Sadat to remain in power. It has since emerged that the offer of Nile water might not even have achieved what Sadat set out to get. When the Israelis were told of the end of the planned water diversion project, Begin sent a message to Sadat, according to Mohamed Heikal, the former Egyptian minister and editor of *Al Ahram*: 'Our principles are not for sale for Nile water,' Begin wrote. 'Israel's security and the sacredness of Jerusalem are not for sale for Nile water.'

When he was considering diverting a small part of the Nile's flow to Israel, Sadat was deliberately abandoning an Egyptian policy of aligning itself with the northern group of Arab states in favour of returning to the country's traditional concern with events in Africa and along the Nile. Sadat, whose mother was black, saw himself as an African as well as an Egyptian, and shared the Egyptian idea that the country was not really part of the Arab world at all. 'We survived as a great nation for over 5,000 years without the Arabs,' Sadat said to the Egyptian journalist Mousa Sabry in Aswan, where he held talks with Menachem Begin in 1978. 'But look over there, Mousa,' pointing south as the morning sun sparkled on the Nile. 'We cannot survive without Africa.'

After reaching his preliminary agreement with Israel, Sadat saw events in Africa as the greatest potential danger to Egypt, and was particularly worried at developments in Ethiopia, a country he believed Israel was using to put pressure on Cairo. 'The only matter that could take Egypt to war again is water,' Sadat told a close group of his aides, among them Dr Boutros Boutros-Ghali, now the UN Secretary General. His warning was directed to both Israel and Ethiopia, the upstream state that controls 80 per cent of the annual flow of the Nile.

In December 1979, when Sadat's warning was repeated in much tougher language to the Ethiopian ambassador in Cairo, Israel was known to be directly involved. This time, to back up its verbal warning, Egypt despatched a naval flotilla to the southern waters of the Red Sea. The reason for this was that Egyptian agents had reported that Israeli engineers were helping the Ethiopians plan new dams on the Nile.

One of the oddities of the situation was that Ethiopia was just as concerned at Egypt's actions as Egypt was worried by what was going on in Ethiopia. The KGB, which in 1979 still had a good intelligence network inside Egypt, had warned Ethiopia and Arab countries opposed to Egypt that Sadat was considering diverting up to 800 million cubic metres of Nile water annually to the Negev desert in Israel. While the news was considered politically outrageous by the Arab countries, in Ethiopia it was seen as a dangerous precedent. If carried through, it would involve a disposal of Nile water outside the Nile basin, something that had never occurred before. Ethiopia was opposed to any such transfer in principle, and was determined that at the least, if such an idea was considered, it would have to be a matter for all the states concerned.

As the Nile is almost the only source of water for Egypt, the country's main security concern is not to let any other country or group of countries of the eight other states on the Nile dictate policy to her. The Egyptian High Command has contingency plans for armed intervention in each of the countries around the Nile basin in case of a direct threat to the flow of the Nile. Some of those plans date back to the early nineteenth century, to the days when Mohammed Ali was rebuilding the Egyptian army. All have been updated several times since then, several by the British around the turn of the century. Today, a full-time staff at the Nasser Military Academy in East Cairo reviews and adapts the plans to changing circumstances. Naturally, Egyptian officials emphasize that they would always prefer diplomatic solutions, and say they want comprehensive agreements among all states concerned. Nevertheless, the military planners work on.

One of the problems is that conflicting interests make it difficult for the very different countries of the Nile basin to cooperate, so that diplomats find it very hard to bring order into a chaotic situation: there are hardly any treaties or agreements among the nine states on which to build, or to use to control exploitation of the river. The only treaty that is still respected is the Egyptian–Sudanese Agreement of 1929. Other African states which have in the past signed agreements with Egypt or with other states hold that they are either out of date or null and void, since they were signed under colonial rule. Since achieving independence, most African states have either refused to abide by the old agreements or announced that they want to cancel or renegotiate them. Immediately after they became independent, Tanzania and Kenya, for example, argued that Britain, which was an ally of Egypt and shared the same strategic and security interests in Sudan, had signed agreements with Egypt on behalf of the two countries but could not have represented their real interests. The problems facing the governments involved now reflect the need for swift development to meet growing needs, against a background of inherited mistrust and a lack of organizations for regional cooperation or laws regulating the use of shared water resources.

The situation is complicated by the geography. The complete river is made up of the two sub-basins of the White and Blue Niles, which form nearly separate systems before they merge. The equatorial sub-basin is also known as the White Nile basin or sub-system, and is itself geologically and geographically divided into two sub-systems of tributaries.

The first group of tributaries, also known as the lakes terrain, contributes 30 billion cubic metres of water annually. The sub-basin of this group also embraces Lakes Victoria, Albert, Edward and Keoga. The second group of the Equatorial sub-basin is known as the Semliki River tributaries, most of which flow through Zaire and Uganda. They contribute 8.5 billion cubic metres annually as they join the other group north of Lake Albert to form the Bahr el-Jabal, the mountain river, in which the White Nile begins its long journey: at this point the river holds some 50 billion cubic metres.

The White Nile contributes only about 15 per cent of the flow when it joins the Blue Nile 2,500 kilometres to the north. An estimated 36 billion cubic metres are lost to evaporation and natural seepage as the White Nile flows through Bahr el-Jabal, the bottle neck at the Sudd, the great expanse of swamp and marsh in southern Sudan. The high temperatures of the region combined with the shallow swamps and dense vegetation mean that millions of cubic metres are lost through evaporation. The White Nile is left with only about 14 billion cubic metres to flow north. The second sub-basin, known as the Abyssinian Highland tributaries, is divided into three sub-systems. The main river is the Blue Nile, which flows from Lake Tana. The Blue Nile and its smaller tributaries lose hardly any water by evaporation in these uplands, where the rivers foam through narrow gorges gouged out of the hills. Its flow is measured at the Roseires Dam in Sudan at 54 billion cubic metres a year. Four hundred kilometres further north it merges with the White Nile just south of Khartoum, where the two rivers can be seen flowing side by side, quite distinct in the same bed. Khartoum, founded only in 1825 as the administrative capital of the Egyptian empire in Sudan, means elephant trunk, an allusion to the long spit of land formed by the confluence of the two rivers. From Khartoum the river is known simply as the Nile.

The second tributary in this group is the Sobat River, which contributes 13.5 billion cubic metres a year as it joins the White Nile south of Malakal. The third is the Atbara, which adds 12 billion cubic metres as it joins the main river at Atbara some 250 miles north of Khartoum. Thus the two main sub-systems pass through eight of the nine Nile states before joining each other at Khartoum to flow majestically on through Egypt to the Mediterranean: Rwanda, Burundi, Tanzania, Zaire, Kenya, Uganda, Ethiopia and Sudan.

Although the Blue Nile floods only after the monsoon rains, it contributes over 80 per cent of the water that reaches Egypt. The White Nile, fed by the equatorial tributaries, flows all year round, but only provides about 15 per cent of the Nile water because of the massive loss by evaporation. The 1929 Egyptian–Sudanese agreement reflected that position by ignoring other countries, and also by allocating 48 billion cubic metres of water annually for Egypt, while giving Sudan only 4 billion. The Aswan High Dam resulted in an additional 22 billion cubic metres, with Egypt taking 7 billion and Sudan taking the remainder, according to the 1959 agreement. Since the completion of the High Dam, Egypt's total water allocation has reached 55 billion cubic metres while Sudan's annual figure has increased to 18.5 billion cubic metres.

It took eight years of drought in the 1980s to force the Nile basin countries to recognize the crisis they were facing, and to begin to try to do something about it. But just as Uganda, Ethiopia and Sudan were coming up with ideas for new dams, for diversions and canals, Egypt was dusting off plans for military intervention in all those countries. During the first eight years of the 1980s, rainfall on the Ethiopian hills and the central African mountains reached an all-time low. The drought which first hit the Ethiopian hills in 1979–80 lasted until late 1987, and at its worst in 1983–4 the Nile flow measured at Aswan was only 42 billion cubic metres, half its normal flow. In chaos because of civil war and the maladministration of the Mengistu regime for many years, Ethiopia is still struggling to cope with its problems, many of which affect Egypt. Specialists at an international seminar on desertification estimated that deforestation was costing Ethiopia between 6 and 9 per cent of its GDP a year through loss of farming land. Cost-free water for irrigation had led to salination and waterlogging. All the Egyptians note is that Ethiopia's planned new dams might result in a 20 per cent loss of Nile flow for them.

In July 1988 Egypt was forced to release 10 billion cubic metres of the total 17 billion stored in Lake Nasser, the vast reservoir formed by the Aswan Dam, into the main river. The total amount of water stored behind the High Dam went down from 125 billion cubic metres in 1980–1 to 46 billion in 1986–7, while the level of Lake Nasser dropped to 148 metres in summer 1987, the lowest in its thirty-year history, and a level which threatened to stop the electricity generated from the High Dam power station. So bad was the drought that the Egyptians were forced to update, redefine or change many irrigation and domestic water consumption laws and regulations, and to modify some old practices and irrigation methods.

Those years of drought changed the national mood in Egypt, shaking people out of their comfortable assumptions about the Nile and forcing them to think about the dangers to that vital asset. For the first time people worried about the water crisis. The records of water flows and lake depths made them realize, perhaps for the first time, that the Nile was not inviolable. Speeches by politicians, newspaper articles and lectures brought the severity of the crisis home to the Egyptian intelligentsia. A national atmosphere of concern, almost of crisis, was induced, and with it a feeling that 'Egyptian water security' should be at the top of national priorities. At worst, the new mood induced nationalist feelings and even xenophobia among the many Egyptians who saw conspiracies all round them and feared that enemies were seeking to use the Nile to weaken their country.

The Egyptian parliament was given an up-to-date assessment of threats facing the country's water resources in a hitherto unpublished report by Dr Hamdi el-Taheri in 1992. Dr el-Taheri, an internationally known expert on water, concentrated on the external dangers because, he said, the internal difficulties were well known: the rise in water consumption owing to the expected increase in population, misuse in agriculture, urban waste, poor distribution networks and so on. Studies were under way to see how those matters could be rectified, but for the external dangers Dr el-Taheri had no ready solutions. He merely identified them in his report to the Parliamentary Select Committee on the Nile, implicitly accepting that these were political problems which would require political solutions, not the answers which hydrologists might be able to suggest.

The most immediate danger, the Committee heard, was that either Uganda or Ethiopia, or both, would implement plans to build new dams on the White or Blue Nile. Egypt was also extremely nervous about the problems in South Sudan, as it was feared that the southern part of the country might split off; that would have a direct effect on the future of the Jonglei Canal project, already halted because of civil war. Later, when Dr el-Taheri outlined his fears to a special session of the Egyptian parliament, there were shouts of 'When are we going to invade Sudan?' and 'Why doesn't the air force bomb the Ethiopian dams?' from the angry Deputies.

The war in southern Sudan also had a serious effect on Egypt, as continued delay on the Jonglei Canal made Egypt more susceptible to natural drought, with the loss by evaporation at times greater than the amount flowing into the area of the swamps. During the 1980s low rainfall in central Africa meant that hydroelectric generation, irrigation and even tourism were all affected by the lack of rainfall and the resulting low level of the Nile.

The other threat, considered even more dangerous by Arab nationalists, is what they see as Israeli intentions and Israel's desire to have a share of the Nile water. In both his paper to the Egyptian parliament and his book *Water Future in the Arab World*, Dr el-Taheri directs attention to Israel's declared wish to use 1 per cent of the Nile water flowing to Egypt, an idea lately put forward by Professor Ben Shahar. Dr el-Taheri also described Israel's old Zionist rallying cry (the land of Israel from the Nile to the Euphrates) as 'a hydraulic slogan'. Dr el-Taheri, who represents a large constituency of politicians and Egyptian officials, argued that Egypt's repeated refusal of Israeli requests to use the Nile water would lead Israel to try to exert indirect pressure on Egypt by getting involved in Ethiopia's plans to build dams on the Blue Nile.

The school of thought represented by Dr el-Taheri sees 'Israel's hand behind the problems and tensions in Sudan and Ethiopia'. Whether the allegations are true or not is irrelevant since they have already persuaded powerful figures in Egyptian political life; there is now a faction in the Egyptian decision-making establishment which takes potential Israeli actions into account when considering water projects. This powerful group also influences decisions made by Egypt's friends and allies throughout the Arab world. Ministers and officials who subscribe to the theory of Israeli involvement see Egyptian water policy as inseparable from the broader issue of Arab relations with outside powers. They believe Egyptian strategic security over the Nile is linked to the Arab–Israeli conflict, and to the Syrian–Iraqi quarrel with Turkey as well as to the Gulf state's dispute with Iran.

The shock of the 1980s made many Egyptians fear a water crisis was on the way. Their reaction was that they would not object to the country going to war if there was any threat to the flow of the Nile – an idea seized on by the nationalist parties. Many influential writers of Nasser's era and those who still favoured the idea of pan-Arabism found in the Nile water crisis an excuse to go back to their old ideas: they argued that Egypt should join with like-minded Arab countries to confront what they saw as Israeli intrusion into Africa, especially in Ethiopia.

These new pan-Arabists were opposed by the traditional Egyptian nationalists, who saw Africa, not the Arab countries, as the natural geographical sphere of influence where Egyptian diplomacy and strategy planning should be concentrating. They believed that just as the incipient water shortage in Africa could threaten to propel countries towards war, it could just as well force them into negotiations.

It was not until June 1990 that the moderates of the Egyptian nationalist school, led by Dr Boutros-Ghali, managed to convene an African water summit in Cairo. It was attended by government delegates from forty-three African nations, and in the end it was a political success for Egypt, enabling it to regain its former leading role in Africa. The conference also gave prominence at last to what hydrologists in many countries had been arguing: the need for regional cooperation. This was particularly important in Egypt, where there was a real national debate about the policies to be followed, with the government apparently favouring closer links with the Arab Gulf states at the expense of relations with Egypt's African neighbours. 'Cooperation between African countries is essential in order to make the best use of the Nile River,' said Dr Boutros-Ghali, then Egyptian Foreign Affairs Minister. 'Through solidarity we will be able to achieve a common policy.'

It was at this Cairo conference that the current idea of 'interdependence' was first formulated. Practical politics means that no country wants to be totally dependent on another for any of its vital strategic supplies. Whether it is a question of procuring oil or grain or water, a state wants to have an alternative in case relations deteriorate with one supplier, who would then be able to take advantage of a monopoly position. In the case of water, countries have little choice of where their supplies come from. So to ensure that downstream states are not at the mercy of those upstream, the idea is to make the upstream countries dependent on those lower down for some vital need. Given the potential of water, then electricity and food are the obvious commodities that a downstream country could exchange with its upstream neighbour. Egypt, with its wealth of hydroelectric generating capacity, could export cheap electricity to the less populated upstream African countries in exchange for water.

Another popular theme that emerged from the conference was the idea of sharing information. This would be particularly useful if floods threatened densely populated areas, or if there was a potential water shortage that might affect industries that relied on certain water levels to operate machinery. 'The floods that hit Sudan in 1988 might not have been as disastrous if Khartoum had known how much rain had fallen in Ethiopia,' according to Tagelsir Ahmed, under-secretary in Sudan's Ministry of Irrigation.

The trouble was that while downstream countries like Egypt and Sudan, with a possible water deficit of 10,000 million cubic metres by the year 2000, might be desperate for a regional agreement, nations like Ethiopia were not nearly as keen. In 1990 Ethiopia was using only 600 million cubic metres of the Nile water each year, but it feared that new policies might limit its sovereignty over the Nile and delay planned development. The end of its civil war, the fall of the Marxist government of Mengistu Haile Mariam and its better relations with its neighbours mean that Ethiopia is now on the road to development and will need more.

As African populations increase at a rate of about 3 per cent a year and water levels fall, the need to negotiate comprehensive water-sharing agreements between countries becomes more critical. But the ideas that seemed to offer hope at the time of the Cairo conference have remained mere ideas. Instead, there has been a noticeable increase in tension and concern over the situation in Ethiopia. The consensus is that it is that country which will be the next flashpoint, and that Egypt will precipitate a crisis by intervening militarily. The danger has been aggravated by those in the Egyptian establishment who are alarmed – with some reason – by Israel's presence in the Horn of Africa and its ready acceptance of Ethiopia's invitations to supply Israeli agricultural and irrigation expertise. The fear among these Egyptian strategists is that Israel will push Ethiopia into developing projects on the Nile which would affect the flow of the river down to Egypt. Pan-Arabists among Egyptians, as well as those in Libya and other countries which espouse Arab nationalism, argue that Israel is once again trying to keep Egypt tied up in Africa and too busy to come to the aid of members of the Arab League Defence pact.

Unfortunately, the actions and policies of successive governments in Addis Ababa over the past twenty years, and the presence of Israeli military advisers as well as agriculture and irrigation experts, have strengthened the hands of those in Egypt calling for military action in Africa to secure the flow of the Nile.

One outcome of current Egyptian policy towards the Nile basin states has been the establishment of the working party known as 'the *undogo* group' – *undogo* is the Swahili word for brotherhood – which is a practical forum for discussion of problems affecting all Nile states and an expression of the new Egyptian policy of cooperation rather than confrontation. This policy was not seriously pursued in Egypt until the death of President Sadat in October 1981, when his successor Hosni Mubarak allowed Egyptian diplomats and foreign relations advisers to demonstrate the new conciliatory attitude. The aim was to reduce tension with Egypt's African neighbours and to concentrate on improving relations with the Arab League countries who froze Egypt's membership when it signed the peace treaty with Israel. 'Cooperation between African countries is essential in order to make the best use of the Nile River,' Dr Boutros-Ghali told the 1989 conference in Cairo. 'Through solidarity we will be able to achieve a common policy.' But as Dr Boutros-Ghali told us on another, more private occasion: 'Just to agree on a single joint project, one needs two years of discussions and study.' Raising funds for each project would take up to three years, he said, since none of the countries in the Nile basin can currently afford projects of any significance. 'Even if we were to start today, it would take us ten years, and by that time Egypt would have had another fifteen million added to its population.'

By summer 1990 there were at least two groups trying to forge a water-sharing agreement between Nile basin states. First and most important is the *undogo* group, which groups all the Nile states except Ethiopia and Kenya; it meets once a year to discuss politics and technical cooperation. The *undogo* group is Egypt's most ambitious diplomatic initiative, and could have far-reaching consequences. The annual meetings discuss cooperation not only on the questions of water, but also on policies related to energy saving, the environment, education and cultural cooperation. The Egyptians pushed hard to put electricity generation and cooperation in joint hydroelectric projects at the top of the agenda. The proposed *undogo* power-grid is one of the world's most ambitious projects: to join the national electricity grids of the nine Nile states. It would link the hydroelectric power station at Inyanga Falls – the world's largest waterfall – with the Aswan High Dam power station. The project when completed would supply all the needs for industrial and domestic use of the nine states, and at very low cost. The second phase would be to export electricity to North Africa and Europe.

The other group is favoured by the UN Economic Commission for Africa and the UN Development Programme, the two UN agencies trying to get the Nile countries together by having them implement specific water development projects identified by the UN groups. Ethiopia has now agreed to participate in these meetings.

Unlike in the Jordan Valley, water allocation in the Nile Basin need not be a zero-sum game. Cooperative water development efforts could lead to increased usable water supplies for everyone, as well as other benefits like hydro-power generation and cooperation on projects that would lead to creating jobs and prosperity in areas which are unlikely to have any other chance of development.

Since the flurry over Ethiopia, greater concern has been growing in Egypt about the intentions of Sudan, which in 1991–2 moved into the Islamic fundamentalist camp, and at the same time fell under the influence of Iran. Particularly disquieting to the West – and Egypt – was the high-profile presence of Iranian revolutionary guards. Egyptian officials were reluctant to detail what action they might take to ensure that Sudan was not going to pose a threat to Egypt's Nile security. Instead they emphasized that Egypt and Sudan were very close, Nilotic peoples who share the same interests irrespective of what type of government each has. At the same time, Egypt carried on a discreet propaganda campaign designed to persuade the Sudanese people that it would be in their interests to cooperate with Egypt – and if necessary to go over the head of their government. 'Egypt and Sudan were the first two countries in the Nile basin to sign an agreement on the shared use of the river water,' Ambassador Mahmoud Ibrahim told Cairo TV in April 1992. 'In the last agreement between the two countries we raised Sudan's quota from 4 billion to 18.5 billion cubic metres per year while Egypt's quota was only raised by 14.5 per cent, from 48 billion to 55 billion cubic metres per year. This was part of the Aswan High Dam agreement. We compensated the Sudanese and we agreed to build the Roseires Dam for them.'

For all the soft words and the efforts to appear sweetly reasonable, Egypt is the Oliver Twist of the Nile basin: it always wants more. Thus its policy is not only to maintain its own current supplies, but also to prevent, if possible, other countries from increasing their take, and to induce those upstream states to go in for projects that will benefit Egypt as well as themselves – the Jonglei Canal in southern Sudan is the prime example of this.

One senior Egyptian planner told us:

Although Egyptian officials always talk of cooperation, and appear to favour cooperation among the nine states on the use of the Nile water, they always add a footnote in the way of 'yes, but as soon as civil wars, political troubles and other conflicts end', or 'when the African countries are politically stable . . . etc.' It would be naive to think that the Egyptians don't have plans to exploit the politically unstable situation in some African countries – those which have unfriendly governments or are considering plans that would affect the flow of the Nile. Egypt always wants those plans postponed – indefinitely.

Another diplomatic method used by Egypt is shown by its representatives in international gatherings. Their opening argument is always that many riparian countries can rely on rainwater for irrigation, while Egypt is totally dependent on the Nile and Sudan relies on the river for half its needs. These diplomats, hydrologists and other experts also argue that downstream countries – by which they mean Egypt – are more advanced and more densely populated than those upstream, which are economically backward. The Egyptians also try to show that the demographic situation is such that upstream countries have no need for additional water, while Egypt and Sudan are under constant pressure.

Rising population, industrialization and inefficient use of available supplies meant that in 1975 Egypt needed 46.3 billion cubic metres; by 1992 it needed 49.7 billion; and by the year 2000, when the country's population is expected to reach 70 million, Egypt will need 55 billion at least, 63 billion if the worst case is taken. Experts talk of the need to reclaim 42,000 hectares annually, and of adopting a new plan for irrigation and the use of water. If something is not done to improve efficiency, they say, then turn of the century needs will rise to 73 billion cubic metres.

These grim figures do not seem to have made an impact on most people, or even on legislators who should know better. The same perception of constant abundance that led an Egyptian MP some years ago to advocate selling Egypt's 'surplus' Nile water to Saudi Arabia seemed to be held more recently by Hasballah Kaftawi, minister for housing and the development of new lands. He announced to the Congress of the National Democratic Party that 'the Ministry had prepared its major plan for the reclamation of 2.8 million feddans (1.8 million hectares) . . . after it had been confirmed that there was sufficient water for such projects until the year 2000.'

It is difficult to see how such ignorance can remain, as throughout Egypt the alarm is being sounded by former ambassadors and senior army officers, many with pan-Arabist beliefs from the Nasser era. One of their spokesmen is Dr Hamdi el-Taheri, whose 1991 book on water prospects was financed by Sheikh Kemal Adham, former head of the Saudi Arabian intelligence service. The 'water activists' in Egypt advocate a two-tier strategy to ensure adequate supplies. The first tier is Egypt's diplomacy in Africa, which includes public policy and secret diplomacy, clandestine action and military contingency plans in the event of an emergency threatening the Nile. The second layer of action consists of new plans for international water use, and improved technology to reduce consumption and minimize wastage.

In Egypt, where rain-fed agriculture is virtually non-existent, water is distributed through an inefficient 30,000 kilometre network of public canals, some of them as old as Egypt itself, though the majority were built in the early nineteenth century. Now used mainly to irrigate croplands bordering the Nile, they are currently being upgraded. Some canals are being lined to minimize seepage, while 120,000 hectares of new lands east and west of the Nile Delta are supplied with more efficient drip irrigation.

It is obvious that Egypt has some hard choices that it must make soon. While water conservation projects on the Upper Nile will become a reality some time in the next century, over the next few decades Egypt must make its first priority the establishment of the most efficient domestic patterns of water use and allocation possible. This will entail a reduction in land reclamation targets, careful selection of crops based on their water needs, substantial reduction in conveyance losses and on-field waste and efforts to recuperate domestic and industrial waste water. Dr Ewan Anderson of Durham University says that plants are available which, if planted in sufficient quantity on land irrigated even with saline water, could feed all the donkeys in Egypt and produce enough oil to keep all the lamps burning too.

What is already in hand is the vast Cairo waste water scheme, which will replace all the capital's crumbling, old and decrepit sewers, installed by British engineers in 1906, will add another 80 kilometres of tunnelling under the capital and will also recycle large amounts of water. Of the E£800 million (US$1.2 billion) cost of this scheme, E£245 million (US$358 million) was made available to Egypt from Western governments that saw the dangers if the work was not done. President Mubarak, a favourite of the West, warned that the situation was so bad that there could be widespread outbreaks of typhoid, cholera and other water-borne diseases. If that happened, he said, there might also be civil unrest so serious that Egypt would be a liability to the West, rather than the asset it now is in the Middle East. Western governments accepted the analysis and put up the money. In 1985, during her visit to Cairo, Prime Minister Margaret Thatcher duly inaugurated the work and promised a further £4 million sterling (US$6 million) grant.

In the meantime, Egypt continues its arguments with its fellow Nile states, and still seeks basin-wide cooperation. Its demands – for that is what they usually are – are always advanced apologetically and as part of a plea for cooperation. But they demonstrate a somewhat unhealthy Egyptian arrogance and are part of Cairo's constant pressure for additional water quotas. The other hidden, but well understood, message is that Egypt is quite able and willing to resort to force if necessary – and any interference with the Nile without prior consultation would certainly be a *casus belli*.

5

The Nile: Egypt and Ethiopia

While Egypt and Sudan, the two countries which have always given a lead in cooperation in management of the Nile, continue to show that technical cooperation can continue even if political relations are strained, Ethiopia does not yet appear to have learnt that lesson. Obsessed with its own huge difficulties of rebellion, civil war, disintegration and famine for the past two decades, Ethiopia is only now slowly emerging once more on the international stage like some suddenly awakened and still bemused giant. Locked away in its mountainous heartland, Ethiopia has always had a grandiose self-image, and has not hesitated to see its plentiful water supply as a gift to be exploited. It was as long ago as the seventeenth century that an Ethiopian ruler first threatened Egypt with 'the water weapon': in 1680 Abyssinia's Christian King, Takla Haymanot, warned the Egyptian ruler: 'The Nile would be sufficient to punish you, since God hath put into our power His fountain, His outlet and increase, and that we can dispose of the same to do you harm.'

Ethiopia has been called the water tower of Africa, and has its hands on the taps that supply Sudan and Egypt. Until comparatively recently this did not matter, as Ethiopia, or Abyssinia, had neither the means nor the will to interfere with the flow of the waters to the Nile. For centuries it was aloof, remote, inward-looking. Then in the late twentieth century it was the unhappy victim of great power experiments, until it went its own way to internal strife, fragmentation and near dissolution. Only now is it coming together again as a nation, to the fear of the countries downstream, particularly as Israel, which first made contact with Mengistu Haile Mariam's Marxist regime, has remained well poised to take advantage of any opportunities – in other words, to damage Sudan and Egypt if that should prove to be in its interests.

Ethiopia's power over the Nile is the effect of eleven rivers that rise in the Ethiopian highlands and flow across its borders to Somalia and the Sudan. By far the largest river is the Blue Nile, known as the Abay in Ethiopia, which on average delivers about 50 billion cubic metres to Sudan each year, or about 60 per cent of the total discharge of the main Nile. In addition, in the south-west the Baro and Pibor rivers, which form the Sobat river, and in the north-west the tributaries of the Atbara supply respectively 14 and 13 per cent of the main Nile's discharge.

Although Ethiopia itself is mainly semi-arid, there are soaking downpours over its mountains during the rainy season. This means that Ethiopia exports not only water but also the rich soils that once made Sudanese and Egyptian agriculture so productive. The result has been the irremediable erosion of the Ethiopian highlands, with something like 2,000 tons of solid matter per square kilometre washed away from the highlands each year.

The erosion of the Ethiopian highlands has been caused not only by the steep slope of the westward flowing rivers but also by centuries of deforestation as Ethiopians have chopped down their trees for firewood, a process that has accelerated greatly in the past fifty years. With 80 per cent of its population living in rural communities, Ethiopia's need over the centuries has been for fuel for cooking and heating, a need made worse by the ravages of the civil war that divided the country for nearly twenty years, making distribution and central control impossible.

Today, technology allows Ethiopia to harness the swift drop in its rivers to provide huge amounts of hydroelectric power, which will make up for the loss of the trees. All that is needed is money and expertise; so far, only Israel has offered both, and at a price. The most obvious payment extracted was permission for the Falashas, the Jews of Ethiopia, to emigrate to Israel. The second was that Ethiopia should take Israeli advice on where, when and how dams should be built. What the Israelis did not spell out to the Ethiopians was that while helping to develop the country, Israel would also take the opportunity to exert pressure on Egypt in particular, on the Arabs in general and on Sudan. The Ethiopians, their officials have since told us, understood that as well as anyone else, but carefully ignored the issue. They did not want to see proffered aid withdrawn, nor were they particularly upset if the downriver countries suffered a little; Ethiopia has lately taken to complaining about the amount of water appropriated for themselves by Sudan and Egypt without any consultation with Addis Ababa.

So Ethiopia is pressing ahead with dams and power stations to exploit its western watershed, something of vital concern to its downstream neighbours. Egypt is well aware that its threats of military intervention are little more than bluster, and that some other means must be found of keeping Ethiopia from exploiting its position. The Egyptian Foreign Office has always believed that Churchill's idea of the whole of the Nile basin as one hydrological–political unit to be ruled from Cairo should remain the cornerstone of their policy, and so is pursuing the idea of basin-wide agreements. In his study *Water Battles to Come*, Dr Mahmoud Samir Ahmad, former Egyptian ambassador to Ethiopia and the adviser to the parliamentary all-party committee on water, bases his argument on that theory, then develops it to make the whole of the Nile valley a hydroeconomic–political unit. He cites any rules he can find in international law to argue that old treaties and agreements must be upheld. So the diplomatic answer from Cairo to Ethiopian or Sudanese plans has been renewed insistence on the need for a Nile authority to regulate things, something which would obviously be of benefit to Egypt and Sudan but would do little for the other states. Ethiopia realized very well that any new agreements forced on it by Egypt and Sudan might limit its sovereignty over the Nile waters and delay planned development. But the end of its civil war, the fall of the Marxist government of Mengistu Haile Mariam and its better relations with its neighbours mean that Ethiopia is now on the road to development, and will need more water.

Ethiopia could over the years have benefited from various projects, but as long ago as the 1930s suffered from the rivalry of what were then the great powers. There was a plan to use Lake Tana for storage, and a New York company was given a contract to construct a dam at the outlet of the lake. But when the project was formally proposed to the UK, Egypt and Sudan in May 1935, the UK opposed it to avoid antagonizing Italy, which was then bent on conquering the country.

In the mid-1950s the Lake Tana dam scheme was revived, this time by the USA, which had become the dominant foreign power in Ethiopia, with the vast Kagnew airbase near Asmara being used as a watching and listening post over the whole Red Sea and Indian Ocean zone. By 1959 Britain was against the idea, ostensibly for the benefit of its East African dependencies. In a statement on behalf of Kenya, Uganda and Tanganyika, Britain said:

> The territories of British East Africa will need for their development more water than they at present use and will wish their claims for more water to be recognized by the other states concerned. Moreover, they will find it difficult to press ahead with their own development until they know what new works the downstream States will require on the headwaters within British African territory. For these reasons the United Kingdom Government would welcome an early settlement of the whole Nile Waters question. A conference of all riparian states has been suggested. In principle the United Kingdom Government favours this idea but thinks that a conference is unlikely to be successful until the Sudan and the United Arab Republic have settled the difference between them.

Egypt and Sudan did settle their differences in November 1959 by amending the old Nile Agreement to give Sudan more water from the new storage provided by the Aswan High Dam, but the British suggestion was not taken up. The Egyptians were suspicious: it looked to them like a trap in which Nasser would be bogged down in complicated negotiations that Britain could manipulate, and which would be used to take revenge on Nasser for the ignominy of the Suez Canal débâcle three years earlier. It was also plain that London had no mandate to speak for the East African territories.

It has also been noted that it was after work began on the Aswan

Dam, with Soviet backing, that the United States suddenly became interested in development of the Blue Nile among other projects in Ethiopia. The beginnings were apparently innocent enough. In 1957 the US Bureau of Reclamation agreed to carry out a detailed survey for the Ethiopian government, which was completed in 1963, with the results published in seventeen heavy volumes. American researchers such as John Waterbury, currently a professor at Princeton University, have suggested that it was no coincidence that the five years of the study coincided with a period of growing tension between Washington and Cairo. Colonel Nasser had entered into close economic and military relations with the Soviet Union, and had embroiled the Egyptian armed forces in the civil war in North Yemen on the opposite side to Saudi Arabia, then rapidly becoming America's client state in that region. The Bureau of Reclamation study was taken as a thinly veiled warning and a reminder to Egypt of its geopolitical vulnerability. The High Dam could do little to protect Egypt against any determined policy on the part of Ethiopia to divert significant amounts of water from the Blue Nile. Egyptians who knew of the existence of the American survey certainly took it as a reminder of their country's vulnerability and as new evidence of the 'imperialist' West's conspiracy against Egypt's anti-colonial role in Africa and the Middle East.

The Bureau of Reclamation recommended that twenty-six dams and reservoirs should be constructed to provide water for both irrigation and hydroelectric power. The survey estimated that if all twenty-six projects were implemented the annual water requirements for irrigation and storage losses would reduce the discharge of the Blue Nile at the Sudanese border by 5.4 billion cubic metres. In the early 1960s that would have meant a major reduction in the supply available to Egypt and the Sudan. Today such a reduction would be near to catastrophic.

Fortunately for Egypt – and perhaps for international peace – Ethiopia did little to implement the ideas of the US survey before the 1990s. If it had done so, it might have involved the Soviet Union at a time when Moscow and Washington were vying for power in the Horn of Africa and in the Levant. Only the internal conflict in

Ethiopia prevented work being considered, and so perhaps stopped an international conflict taking place in that remote country.

Development cannot be delayed indefinitely, however. Ethiopia's population is expected to grow from 54 million in 1992 to 94 million in 2010. Industrialization, urbanization and improved agriculture will all mean that more water will be needed once the country achieves stability and settles down to catch up on the rest of the world, as it has begun to do. Ethiopia will no longer be content to remain as the water tower of Africa, using little of its own abundant supplies. A crisis of one sort or another seems certain as time goes on.

As the Ethiopians declared at the UN Water Conference at Mar del Plata, they would welcome an accord on the utilization of the Nile with their downstream neighbours, but in the absence of such an accord they reserve the right to carry out their plans on their own. That did nothing to reassure Egypt and Sudan; on the contrary, it reinforced the growing distrust of Ethiopian intentions being felt in Cairo. There is a section in the 1991 report of the Arab Affairs Committee presented to Majlis El-Shaab, the Egyptian parliament, entitled 'Water crisis in the Arab region'. The general tone of the report is pessimistic, and it concludes that the Middle East is likely to witness the first water war. The committee was concerned not only with Egypt: it noted that 85 per cent of water coming into rivers of member states of the Arab States League Treaty (ASLT) comes from non-ASLT member countries, some of whom have a history of hostility towards Arab countries. The report emphasized Israel's involvement in Ethiopia and Israeli plans to help Ethiopia construct six dams, which would have a direct effect on the water flow into Egypt. It suggested that Israel was 'trying to breach Egypt's southern defences and lay siege to the strategic sources of the Nile'.

The report recommended that the Egyptian Foreign Ministry should acknowledge that Israel's assistance to Ethiopia was an attempt by the Jewish state to put Egypt under pressure and exert greater control over the Blue Nile. The committee said this was a grave security matter that would justify the use of military force and it would recommend that the parliament should back the government whenever such option became necessary. In chaos because of civil war and the maladministration of the Mengistu regime for many years, Ethiopia is still struggling to cope with its problems, many of which affect Egypt. Specialists at an international seminar on desertification estimated that deforestation was costing Ethiopia between 6 and 9 per cent of its GDP a year through loss of farming land. Cost-free water for irrigation had led to salination and water-logging.

The modern problem began when Ethiopia announced it would no longer abide by accords and protocols already signed early in the century by Emperor Melenik II. This announcement in the official newspaper *Ethiopian Herald* in February 1956 added that 'Ethiopia had the right to exploit Nile water running within its borders.' That declaration was followed by Ethiopian statements stressing its right to carry out any plans or projects that were considered essential for the Ethiopian economy, and to meet the agricultural, water and energy needs of its 55 million people. To emphasize the seriousness of its attitude, Ethiopia chose to set out these objectives in a letter to all diplomatic missions in Cairo.

For all the apparent reasonableness of the statements from Addis Ababa, it always seemed that the urgency or otherwise of projects that might affect the Nile flow was governed to a large extent by the state of relations between Ethiopia and Egypt. And the state of play between Cairo and Addis Ababa was in turn governed by the situation in all the other countries that had a stake in the Ethiopian civil wars: Libya, Sudan, Saudi Arabia, the two Yemens, the super-powers (up to 1991) and lately Iran.

The first major incident occurred in 1958, at a time when Egypt and Ethiopia were on opposing sides in the East–West conflict. Under Colonel Nasser, the Egyptians were in an anti-American, anti-Western mood. The World Bank had in 1955 turned down an Egyptian request to finance the building of the Aswan High Dam. Nasser retaliated in July 1956 by nationalizing the Suez Canal, which led to the armed confrontation with British, French and Israeli forces. Then came American help to Ethiopia as a means of embarrassing Cairo.

This game of nations with Ethiopia as the pawn was carried a step further when in 1983 Ethiopia took advantage of a UN conference for underdeveloped countries to present a list of forty irrigation projects, some on the Blue Nile and some on the Sobat river. The Ethiopian delegation repeated their country's policy: that Ethiopia reserved the right to implement the proposals unilaterally if there was no agreement. But by this time Egypt and Ethiopia had swapped seats in the cold war game. The Soviet Union saw a chance of reasserting its position with Cairo, as President Sadat had by now been eliminated. Moscow was hoping that Cairo would mend fences, so it persuaded its client regime in Ethiopia to put a temporary freeze on Nile projects. Discussion of new Ethiopian schemes quietly died away.

According to Ethiopian and Sudanese representatives talking unofficially during water conferences, one cause of the constant friction is the Egyptian obsession with history. Cairo, these officials say, tries to carry out the policy that Britain applied to the Nile basin but, unlike the Britain of the nineteenth and early twentieth centuries, is not in control of most of the countries concerned. As early as 1891, Britain signed a protocol with Italy, which was then acting for Ethiopia, forbidding the construction of anything that would affect the flow of water into the Atbara river, which feeds into the Nile. Another accord signed in Addis Ababa in 1902 gave Britain and Egypt a veto over the construction of any projects on the Blue Nile, Lake Tana or Sobat river that would affect the discharge of water to the Nile. Then in 1929 the final brick was put in place: an agreement was signed allowing Egypt a right of veto over any work in Sudan, Kenya, Tanzania or Uganda which Cairo might interpret as interfering with its right to Nile water. According to this treaty, Egypt has the right – and it still makes full use of it – to inspect any part of the River Nile, from its distant beginnings before the streams discharge into central African and Ethiopian mountain lakes all the way to the Mediterranean.

This agreement gave Britain and Egypt a greater say in the construction of the Owen Falls Dam in the early 1950s than Uganda itself. Egypt put up some of the money for the dam and sent engineers to help, and today an Egyptian engineer is still resident there, with the daily duty of giving permission for the amounts of water to be retained or discharged.

Egypt is now more concerned than ever at what is going on in Uganda, Ethiopia and Sudan because of the potential effects on the High Dam at Aswan. Completed in 1971 with Soviet help, the High Dam was supposed to solve Egypt's perennial problems of flooding and drought but, given the huge population increase since that time, it has done no more than enable the country to stand still instead of sliding backwards. Egypt naturally wants to see more water delivered into its system at Lake Nasser, the artificial lake on the border with Sudan created by the dam, and so opposes greater water retention upstream. There has in fact been a small increase in the amount of water flowing into Lake Nasser in recent years in comparison to the 1905–55 average, which is the basis of the 1959 Sudan–Egypt Nile Water Agreement, one of the more successful examples of regional cooperation. But recent events in Khartoum have made the Egyptians wary of relying on that treaty always being observed, or of the flow of water being maintained from Uganda or Ethiopia.

The water shortage of the 1980s focused attention on the High Dam again, though it had always had its critics. Neither when it was built nor later did they object to the project itself, but they were concerned at the lack of proper studies and the disregard of possible negative effects. They pointed out that two dams near the Delta, with a canal diverting water to the Qattara Depression south-west of Cairo, would have minimized evaporation, avoided the loss of silt and left untouched the Nubian areas, where many villages had to be flooded and large numbers of people displaced.

It was recognized from the start that the silt brought down from the African highlands would no longer be spread into Egypt, but would be stopped at the dam, where special silt traps were built. The problem was seen as one of restoring fertility artificially, putting up costs to farmers and leading to pollution. Statistics show that Egypt now uses 300 kilograms of fertilizer per hectare, one of the highest levels in the world. The 90–140 million cubic metres of silt the Nile flood used to deposit each year is still carried by the river, but only as far as the dams will allow. What was not forecast was the major trouble occurring now: the build-up of silt, which not only hurts those downstream but also shortens the dam's life. A study commissioned by the World Bank estimates that the world's dams are losing 1 per cent of their storage capacity to silt each year. The Roseires Dam in Sudan is badly affected and needs work, but Aswan seems worst off of all.

In July 1992, Hamdi el-Taher, chairman of the General Authority of the Aswan High Dam, warned that the silt deposits, which have been building up behind the dam for twenty years, could eventually stop the flow into Lake Nasser and divert it west into the desert. 'The accumulating silt could form a delta in the south or, even worse, the river could change its course, running west into the desert or even Libya. The problem spells disaster,' Mr Taher warns today, four years after he first sounded the alarm. The Ministry of Irrigation dismissed Mr Taher's claim, and said there was no danger because the High Dam had been designed with areas for silt deposits. Later, however, hydrologists from the ministry quietly joined a team of experts who travelled to the southern end of Lake Nasser, beyond the Egyptian border and deep into Sudan, to study the rate of sedimentation and silt movement and to install equipment to monitor water levels.

The silting at the High Dam increases Egyptian concern over events in Sudan, as the hydrologists believe they must always be free to study the Nile above the dam and fear Sudan might restrict that access. The leader of the Egyptian Green Party, Dr Ibrahim Kamel, reports that silt built up during the autumn flood turns into a solid wall when it is exposed to the sun during the dry season, and so creates a new natural dam. This effect is repeated annually, with new dams emerging every few miles. Dr Kamel argues that in a year of unusual flood, which occurs periodically, the first natural earth dam would disintegrate under the weight and pressure of water. This, he argued, would create a massive wall of water that would knock down all the other dams, and would gather momentum until it reached the High Dam, which would be swept away. 'A massive wall of water 40 metres high would reach Cairo in no time,' he concluded, 'and if that happened you would be able to collect bodies of dead

Egyptians on the shores of Greece.' When the Egyptian parliament heard that prediction, MPs warned the government it had to ensure that work could be carried out in northern Sudan if necessary.

6

The Nile: Egypt and Sudan

It stands alone and forlorn, like some futuristic sculpture, a twentieth-century reminder that man, after all, is stronger than metal, that technology and development are the playthings of politics. The Bucketwheel, a triumph of German engineering, was one of the mechanical wonders of the late twentieth century, a machine that could do the work of 1,000 men, and do it better. Behind it now lies the evidence of that proud boast, a ditch 267 kilometres long, stretching off into the distance of the Nilotic plain like the trail of some gigantic beast, the useless remnant of the dream the Bucketwheel was supposed to make come true.

The invention of the Bucketwheel made the Jonglei Canal possible. For years the idea of a canal across the Sudd, the vast area of marshes and swamps which separates black southern Sudan from the Arab north, had been discussed by hydrologists and the swarm of Egyptian, Sudanese and international officials concerned with the Nile. To many, the need seemed pressing and self-evident, the benefits immense and the increase in water availability a conclusive argument in favour of going ahead. To others, the consequences seemed likely to be disastrous, the ecological damage unjustifiable and irreparable, the human cost even higher and the benefits dubious. On only one point were the two sides united: the difficulty of cutting a navigable canal through almost 300 kilometres of marshland in one of the most remote parts of the world, in a country with poor communications, few resources and no pool of trained labour. The lobby that wanted nothing to be done won by default, as even in the 1960s the most conservative estimate was that it would take twenty years to build the Jonglei using the most sophisticated machinery then available, draglines and dredgers.

Egypt was the country most anxious for the canal to be built, for Egypt would benefit most – and would suffer none of the adverse consequences, which would all be confined to southern Sudan. Egypt, after all, has no significant agriculture other than that which is irrigated. Sudan, by contrast, has about 4 million feddans (1.7 million hectares) under irrigation and another 14 million cultivated under rain-fed conditions. It is the long-term objective of Sudan to raise the irrigated surface to about 10 million feddans and the rain-fed to about 60 million, according to a study by A. Ibrahim. The irrigated acreage would be developed mainly in the rich plains between the Blue and White Niles, though according to the experts nowhere near all the Sudan's land suitable for irrigation will ever be developed. Water is the limiting factor.

Egypt was driven by political considerations as well as the practical. Egypt has always regarded Sudan as within its sphere of influence, its own backyard, and as Sudan became independent of Britain, Egypt wanted to demonstrate that was still the case. No matter what the international situation, Egyptian leaders always found an excuse to emphasize Cairo's commitment to Khartoum, no matter how untrue that may have been at times. Just before his assassination Sadat spelt it out again – this time in a warning to Colonel Gaddafi, who in 1980 was meddling in Chad and encouraging raiders to move into southern Sudan: 'I say to him so that he hears it well, any operation against the Sudan and we will be there in the next instant at the Sudan's side.'

It was the practical considerations that were paramount in the arguments over the Jonglei Canal: only 22 per cent of the Nile water that reaches Egypt comes from the Central African mountains, but this amount could increase dramatically if the estimated 25–50 billion cubic metres of water lost due to evaporation in the swamps of southern Sudan were available. At its simplest, building a canal there, perhaps by deepening and enlarging existing channels, would speed the current and thus reduce the loss of evaporation. But the sheer scale of the job and the time it would take seemed to rule out this apparently simple way of increasing the amount of water available to northern Sudan and Egypt.

Like most Nile projects, the Jonglei Canal had a long period of gestation. From the time the first explorers penetrated into the Sudd, or those heading north from Central Africa found their way barred, it was realized that a canal would be the obvious way to carry the water safely through to the north of Sudan and Egypt – and the old dream of a Cape to Cairo road played its part too, as the waste from excavation could obviously be used. The first formal suggestion of a Jonglei Canal was put forward in 1936 as part of the 'Century Water Scheme', the plan to use the central African lakes as huge reservoirs which would regulate the flow of the water between seasons. The outbreak of the Second World War stopped any chance of work in the 1940s, though feasibility studies were begun as soon as the fighting stopped, with the World Bank playing a leading role. Britain, still the colonial power, was the moving spirit, but that came to an end with independence in 1956, when neither the new government in Khartoum nor Nasser's Egypt was anxious to espouse controversial ideas, that had first been proposed by London. So serious study did not begin until September 1969, when a subcommittee of the Permanent Joint Technical Commission established by Egypt and Sudan under the terms of the 1959 Agreement set out the broad outlines of a revised Jonglei project. In December 1971 a draft proposal was submitted to both governments, and in February 1974 President Sadat and President Jaafar Numeiri of Sudan signed their integration agreement to launch a new era of Egypto-Sudanese cooperation. As part of a number of joint projects, Jonglei I was given formal approval by both governments in April 1974.

The basic problem remained: the canal would take decades to complete and would cost an immense amount of money. The two governments concerned could not provide the funds, and international agencies were not inclined to do so given the dubious environmental situation and the political uncertainties of the area.

The Bucketwheel changed all that. Originally developed for open-cast mining, it was in effect a huge revolving wheel carrying buckets which could scoop up earth and deposit it to one side, all done while it was moving forward on a careful line and digging to a specified depth. This masterpiece of engineering by the German firm of Orenstein and Koppel was specially adapted for canal digging, and first used, with great success, on the Chasma–Jhelum canal in Pakistan in 1968. It was there that it was seen by Yahia Abdel Magid, the Sudanese hydrologist who became minister of irrigation, and he suggested its use in digging the Jonglei. As it rusts away now at kilometre 267, it has proved that the Jonglei can be dug by modern methods, and one day it probably will be; but it has also shown that the wishes and desires of a people have to be taken into account, not just the ideas of their governments.

The Jonglei Canal did not cause the civil war in the Sudan – that began in 1955, while the canal was not agreed until 1959 – but over the years the canal certainly played its part in it. Nor was support for Jonglei the monopoly of one side or the other in that continuing tragedy. What happened was that for the people of the region the Jonglei Canal came to symbolize all that they were fighting against. The Bucketwheel, the air-conditioned camps for the technicians, the Egyptian interest and the support of the government in Khartoum seemed to the people of southern Sudan to be the visible expression of northern domination, of Egyptian imperialism, of Islamic arrogance and of the broken promises that had originally persuaded them of the benefits the canal would bring. In 1984 the Sudan People's Liberation Army decided that work on the canal had to be stopped. They attacked the base camp at Sobat – after giving a warning which, owing to the inefficiencies of Sudan, was never delivered – abducted some of the expatriate workers and warned the French contractors not to try to resume work: nothing has been done from that moment to this day. The US$400 million spent so far by Egypt and Sudan has caused more harm than good. If the canal is ever completed, it may cost as much again; and the benefits are still not at all clear.

The technicalities of it all have been known since the sources of the Nile were found in the nineteenth century, though long before that explorers, traders and soldiers had reported how their way upriver was barred by impenetrable masses of floating vegetation, and attempts to abandon the river and march south overland were made impossible by swamps and marshes. This was the Sudd, where the Nile that emerges from the central African lakes is converted from a rushing torrent through mountain gorges, or a placid but determined waterway along valley floors, into a dispersed series of basins and lagoons, where the flow sometimes seems to go from east to west rather than south to north, where channels that are clear on one visit are blocked on the next, where the shallows mean vast losses of water through evaporation, where cattle breeding depends on the spread of the flood outwards to the plains on either side and where the high waters mean better fishing. The local people have no wish to see the basis of their life sweep on northwards. Yet from the beginning of this century, the people of southern Sudan have realized that the only way they can get the benefits of modern life is via the great waterway. From early in this century successive Sudanese governments have spent many millions in trying to keep the rivers open, so that administrators and troops, doctors and traders can penetrate into the southernmost regions of the biggest country in Africa.

The heart of the Sudd is a permanent swamp some 9,500 square kilometres in extent, though the area varies from year to year depending on the rainfall over the lakes to the south. Because it is so shallow, the amount of evaporation is very high; estimates are that only half the water which flows into the Sudd at its southern end at Mongalla is available for the White Nile at Malakal. It is because of this huge loss of water, which far outweighs the value of the swamps as a reservoir regulating water flows in seasons of high and low rainfall, that the idea of a canal to carry the water swiftly and efficiently through the marshes was first evolved. Different routes were suggested and different methods examined, but in the end the project always foundered on the impossibility of carrying through the work in a reasonable time and at a fixed cost.

Politically, the 1959 Nile Waters Agreement between Egypt and the Sudan cleared the way for the Jonglei Canal. The agreement was pushed through by General Ibrahim Abboud, who seized control in Khartoum in November 1958 after bickering politicians in the first two years of the country's independence had ruined the economy and deepened the rift between north and south. General Abboud quickly restored financial stability by removing unnecessary taxes on cotton, and curbed rival movements within the army. Abroad, he saw his most important task as establishing good relations with Egypt, and the key to that was an agreement over the Nile waters. So on November 1959 a treaty was signed in Cairo providing for the High Dam at Aswan and a more modest one at Roseires in the Sudan, and in Article Three agreeing that a canal across the Sudd should be dug, and that Egypt and Sudan should share the costs.

At last the way was clear, except for the old problem of how to do the work. Ten years later the Bucketwheel solved that, but could not settle the other hazard – the war in southern Sudan. The product of centuries of separation and discrimination, the civil war began in 1955 when a company of Southern Sudanese troops mutinied as they were being transferred to Khartoum. The mutineers from No. 2 Company of the Equatorial Corps went on a rampage around their headquarters at Torit, hunting down northerners and killing more than 260 before taking to the bush to avoid northern troops sent to restore order. The mutiny was a warning signal that went unheeded: independence went ahead on 1 January 1956, with the northerners in control making little attempt to integrate the south into the new country. As usual, southern needs and aspirations were ignored.

As resentment mounted, so too did lawlessness and attacks on the institutions of government, until in 1963 a united and violent opposition emerged with the formation of the Anyanya, made up not only of the original mutineers from Torit and those who sympathized with them, but also attracting professional men and intellectuals. If the mutiny was the first action of the civil war, the emergence of the Anyanya turned it from a guerrilla conflict into a pitched battle between two peoples, the black south and the Arab north. General Abboud could not cope, and handed power back to the civilians; they did no better, while the Anyanya prospered, helped by arms captured from the demoralized army, smuggled across from Uganda or donated by Israel, always anxious to see trouble on the borders of Egypt.

General Jaafar Numeiri, who was chief of staff in the Sudanese

army, was sickened, like General Abboud before him, by the inepti-
tude of the politicians and took over in May 1969. Facing opposition
from the communists and from the Ansar, the followers of the Mahdi,
he sought an accommodation with the south, offering regional self-
government, development schemes and more posts for southerners
in the administration in Khartoum.

General Joseph Lagu, who had taken over the Anyanya, agreed to
talks, which were held in Addis Ababa in February 1972 and in which
Dr Boutros-Ghali played a crucial role. Two weeks of negotiations
produced an agreement giving autonomy to southern Sudan, with
an elected assembly responsible for public order and the day-to-day
running of the region. The central government retained control of
defence, foreign affairs, customs and planning – including the Nile
projects, which suddenly looked possible as peace broke out, with
the Anyanya integrated into the Sudanese Army, refugees allowed
to return home and hundreds of southerners given important posts
in Khartoum. Abel Alier, a southerner who was also a Dinka and a
Christian, and who had done most to push through the Addis Ababa
agreement, was appointed regional president and gained the support
of a majority of the assembly when it met later in 1974. Economic
development was the most urgent consideration, and was seized on
by the advocates of Jonglei, who revived the scheme as soon as
Numeiri reached a new accord with Egypt. On 6 July 1974 Egypt
and Sudan entered into a formal agreement to construct the canal
and to share the costs. On 28 July 1976 the contract with Compagnie
de Constructions Internationales (CCI) was signed, though there
were serious misgivings even then among the more far-sighted
members of the Southern administration. To the people of the upper
Nile, establishment of the regional administration was seen as no
more than a step towards implementing the canal scheme. The most
far-fetched rumours persisted, not least the idea that hundreds of
thousands of Egyptian *fellahin* were to be brought in to farm land
recovered from the swamps. Nor was the idea of the canal helped
by a comment from Abel Alier, one of its most committed supporters:
'If we have to drive our people to paradise with sticks, we will do so
for their own good and the good of those who come after us.'

Suddenly, Sudan became the hope of Africa, the one country where everything was going right. Not only was the neglected south going to be developed and brought a prosperity which would enable it to join the north on equal terms, the whole country was to benefit from an infusion of Gulf oil money to turn it into the greatest beef-producing region outside the Americas. It was recognized that political instability and a poor infrastructure were handicaps, but the theory was that if enough capital was forthcoming those problems would take care of themselves.

While it might have been advantageous for the Sudanese government to side with the Arabs against Egypt, its history and geography gave it little choice but to follow Cairo. Sudan backed Egypt when that country signed the two Camp David accords and the peace treaty with Israel, something seen by most of the Arab governments as an act of betrayal by which President Sadat recovered Sinai for Egypt by abandoning the Palestinians and the greater Arab cause, making it impossible for the Arabs ever again to pose a credible military threat. Given the Sudanese government's dependence on Egypt for funds as well as for military support to enable it to remain in power, President Numeiri had little choice. President Numeiri's political adviser at the time told us that Numeiri was also better informed of President Sadat's long-term plans and designs in Africa at the expense of his commitment to the Arabs than were other Arab rulers with little vision into the future, like Colonel Gaddafi in Libya or the Arab Baath regimes in Iraq and Syria. President Numeiri therefore saw his country's future in siding with Egypt; but his action meant that the projected inflow of funds from the Gulf was substantially reduced, although it did not completely stop. Not surprisingly, with Arab money staying away, Western investors were scared off. Then, to cap it all, the Iraq–Iran war drove petrol prices up further, absorbed the interest and the finances of the Gulf states, and finally put the lid on the grandiose schemes for the development of Sudan, which only a few years earlier was being projected as the 'bread basket of Arab nations' by Arab governments. The country began its steady slide into the chaos which still persists today.

In October 1974 those opposed to Jonglei took to the streets of the regional capital, Juba. The ordinary protesters who smashed shops and burnt cars were opposing not only the idea of settling Egyptian peasants in their region – something never even considered – but other rumours just as wild: that the canal would drain the swamps and the surrounding pastures, and make cattle herding impossible, ruining the lives of the Nilotic people; that in place of the swamps there would be desert; or that the whole climate of the region would change. None of it was true but much of it was believed, so those politically opposed to Alier and what was called 'the southern Dinkacracy' – the domination of small tribes by the Dinka – were able to use Jonglei as a means of getting rid of those in power. Demonstrations quickly turned into riots until an alarmed central government joined forces with the southern assembly to head off trouble; but they just stored it up for the future. Numeiri and his ministers promised that Jonglei would not be merely a canal, but the engine of the development of the whole region, bringing improved communications, the great north to south road – a revival of the old imperial Cape to Cairo dream – and an end to underdevelopment, backwardness and poverty. They argued that if excess water were drained off there would be increased land for cattle and flood protection for the future. Abel Alier gave an assurance that the people of the upper Nile would not be removed for the benefit of Egypt 'as the Nubians had been when the Aswan Dam was built', and there would not be a single Egyptian settler or soldier in the whole area. The Juba administration issued a statement saying it would not be associated with politics aimed at perpetuating the economic status quo in the region. 'We will not remain as a sort of human zoo for anthropologists, tourists, environmentalists and adventurers from the developed economies of Europe to study us, our origins, our plight, the size of our skulls and the shape and length of customary scars on our foreheads.'

President Numeiri promised that schools would be built, that there would be mechanized farming, veterinary and medical services, clean drinking water and jobs for all. The Jonglei Canal would herald a new era of prosperity for the south, and especially for the 250,000 people living in the canal zone. Soon, criticism of the project was quietened, though it did not disappear; instead, the canal became the symbol of all the promises the president had made. The canal and the prosperity of the region had become linked. Alas, the government could not deliver – at least, not in the time allowed by the sceptical southerners. The people of the upper Nile wanted instant action, not surveys and studies and visiting experts, which is what they got. Deprived for so long, they saw all the preparations as no more than a way of putting off doing anything. Words were not enough for them, so when the things they wanted could not be delivered immediately, the old disillusion returned. Its first expression came in the elections to the regional assembly in 1978, when Abel Alier and his colleagues were defeated to be replaced by General Joseph Lagu. He took over just as Idi Amin's terrible regime in Uganda was in its death throes, forcing thousands of refugees across the border into Sudan – many of them bringing with them stores of weapons which were quickly distributed. The south became a more lawless place than ever, its convoluted politics matched by banditry and factional fighting. Abel Alier was brought back by Numeiri, only to be replaced again, this time by General Gasmallah Abdullah Rassas, who, although a southerner, was a Muslim. Then Khartoum's decision to build the refinery for the oil from the south in the northern city of Kosti made things worse, with President Numeiri trying to divide the opposition by setting up new provinces and regional institutions, a move which would have put paid to the Addis Ababa agreement by removing a southern centre of opposition. With the economy declining again, Numeiri turned to Egypt for help, signing yet another integration treaty with Cairo. This time the agreement gave formal permission for the Egyptians to send military advisers to Sudan; that rang more alarm bells in the south.

In Cairo a quiet debate was going on. Should Egypt help General Numeiri's government put down the revolt in the south, perhaps sending troops and armour or just air units? Or should it back the other side, and support the rebels on the grounds that they were likely to win in the long run anyway, or that they would be in control if Sudan split into the two sections of which it was obviously composed, the black south and Arab north? The Egyptian military, like the military everywhere, were basically in favour of the devil they knew, and so wanted to support Numeiri – they had a core force at the Sudanese Military Academy outside Khartoum, where special Egyptian army units had been quietly insinuated with the instructors and other staff needed to train the Sudanese cadets. Although they did not say so, the Egyptian commanders may also have had in mind the need to keep their large standing army in shape; and all commanders know there is no better way of doing that than by sending their men into action.

Against these considerations, the Egyptian foreign ministry was concerned at the dangers that intervention would pose. They believed an Egyptian presence would certainly lead to increased Israeli clandestine activity in Sudan, and perhaps open Libyan intervention. It might also alienate African countries whose goodwill Egypt always wanted, to ensure the safety of the Nile waters. So with very little emerging in public, the debate continued in Cairo; and nothing was done.

Through all this turmoil, the political in-fighting, the agonizing over policy in Cairo and the desperate attempts by Numeiri to hang on to power, the Bucketwheel kept turning, ploughing its huge furrow across the flood plain. It was the one thing that did go ahead: none of the promised benefits materialized as more and more experts conducted new studies and UN and international agencies competed for the limited materials available in the area and for the small number of skilled people.

Just as an army unit refusing to obey orders had sparked the civil war back in 1955, so now it was the 105th Battalion of the Sudan Army in its garrison at Bor that provoked the new outburst. And again, the cause was an order that they should be moved to the north. These soldiers, most of them former Anyanya fighters, had their families near them, and many of them supplemented their army pittance by working farms around the town. They refused to move. Numeiri ordered an investigation, which found that many of the northern officers had behaved stupidly and paid no heed to the soldiers' complaints. Then Numeiri made his biggest mistake: he sent Colonel John Garang, director of research at army HQ in Khartoum, to sort things out. Colonel Garang was himself a southerner, a former member of Anyanya and a highly qualified agricultural economist, with a PhD from Iowa gained with a dissertation on the Jonglei Canal. On 16 May 1983 Garang abandoned the Khartoum government and accepted the soldiers' request that he should lead them. He took to the bush with the men of the 105th, and was soon joined by thousands of other disaffected troops. Garang named his organization the Sudan People's Liberation Movement, and quite soon had 4,000 experienced troops in the Sudan People's Liberation Army (SPLA), which quickly defeated a rival grouping known as Anyanya II. Garang then turned his attention to government targets, taking over police and army posts which had not defected and finally striking at the government's two foreign prestige projects, Chevron's oil rigs and CCI, the French canal builders. In November 1983 the SPLA ordered work on Jonglei to halt; it did so, it explained, because promises made to the southerners had not been kept. Chief of these, it said, was the provision of clean drinking water and an irrigation network. It was also clear, the SPLA said, that no moves were being made to provide schools or medical centres. Another complaint was that not enough bridges over the canal were being built, or crossing places for cattle. In a letter to the French company, the SPLA said: 'Agricultural projects, hospitals, towns and model villages that were to be carried out in the canal zone will remain only in the text of your agreement never to be executed after you have completed your work on the canal. You can therefore see our determination to see to it that the work on the canal stops.'

The French company shut down the Bucketwheel and began evacuating personnel from the camp at Sobat. On 10 February 1984 the camp was taken over by the SPLA. The French finally left, announcing that all work on the canal had ended. Jonglei would have been completed ahead of schedule in March 1985.

Sudan is, perhaps, the perfect example of man proposing and other forces disposing. On paper, the engineers and hydrologists of the international agencies, of Britain, Egypt and Sudan, all had wonderful schemes to maximize Nile flow to the benefit of both countries. After Jonglei, there were to be three other projects involving the

Upper Nile and Equatorial lakes that together should have yielded an extra 14 billion cubic metres annually below Malakal. Draining the Machar Marshes would have been next after Jonglei, then the Egyptians and Sudanese would have turned to the vast area west and south-west of the Jonglei Canal to work on the Bahr al-Ghazal project. This would involve building two more canals, one of them almost twice the length of Jonglei. Finally, the paper plans call for the original Jonglei Canal, if ever completed, to have its capacity doubled by the digging of a second canal parallel to it. In the end, in the extremely unlikely event that all those projects were implemented, Sudan would have a little less than 30 billion cubic metres a year to meet a projected demand of upwards of 32 billion cubic metres. This is hardly a significant figure if the estimates of future demands made by hydrologists are no more accurate than their projections of the costs of their schemes or the time needed to carry them out.

Today, an Islamic government has taken power in Sudan and is attempting to prosecute the war in the south, where the people are more determined than before not to be subject to the will of the extremists now in control in Khartoum. Egypt is more worried than ever. It has its own fundamentalists and is deeply concerned that those extremists now have a source of men and arms on the border, and a refuge when they need it. While maintaining the outward courtesies essential between neighbouring states, Egypt has been doing what it can to make life difficult for General Omar Bashir and his government. Egypt has been giving covert military assistance to the SPLA, and willingly gives sanctuary to opponents of the Khartoum government. The former commander of Sudanese forces, General Fathi Ahmad Ali, defected when the Islamic extremists took over and was warmly welcomed in Cairo, where the opposition to the present Sudanese government, the National Democratic Alliance, has its headquarters. More than a million Sudanese live in Egypt, and careful propaganda from Cairo means that most of them are now opposed to the regime in Khartoum.

Egypt has been using an old point of contention between the two countries to mask its basic objection to the Islamic government, which it blames for supporting its own increasingly active fundamentalists. The disputed region of Halaib on the Red Sea coast has been used as an excuse for Egypt's increasingly strident opposition to the Khartoum government: according to a treaty dating from 1899 the area of Halaib lies in Egyptian territory, but it is administered by Sudan under the terms of a second agreement reached in 1902. Egypt therefore claimed to be particularly incensed when in December 1991 the Sudanese government granted an exploration concession to the International Petroleum Company of Canada, a move which Egypt denounced as illegal. In apparent retaliation for Sudan's assumption of sovereign rights, Egypt has announced plans to resettle 4,500 families from the Nile valley in Halaib.

Egyptian worries over the government in Khartoum have been made worse by the growing links between Sudan and Egypt's opponents, particularly Iran, Libya and Iraq. With its inexperienced and internationally unpopular government, Sudan has been looking for friends anywhere it can find them, and is also seeking cheap and regular supplies of oil. Libya and Iraq are equally anxious to find backers where they can, while Iran saw an opportunity to export its revolution and perhaps eventually to gain some economic advantage. Sudan has signed a number of food-for-oil agreements with Libya, and a comprehensive trade agreement with Iran under which Iran would supply 100,000 barrels of oil a month and pay for much of Sudan's military expenditure until the defeat of the southern rebels.

As a result of all this, there has been a bitter propaganda war between Cairo and Khartoum; yet throughout it all both sides were careful not even to hint at using water as a weapon between them. Instead, Egypt and Sudan emphasized the need for cooperation, and at times even pushed once again that doubtful proposition, the unity of the Nile basin. Technical discussions on water issues continued, and the Egyptian Ministry of Agriculture still offered training courses to Sudanese agronomists.

Sudan did occasionally allow itself a touch of bitterness: in a paper it presented to the conference on water in Dublin in 1992 it noted that the dry regions of the world make up about 30 per cent of the land mass, but their share of fresh water resources is only about 1 per cent of the total.

African sub-Sahara, the Sudano-Sahel belt, has been seriously affected by the severe, prolonged drought extending over three decades. Eight African states of the region have been drastically hit, and suffered from hunger, thirst and the collapse of their socio-economic structures, while humanity, morality and mortality have become real issues. It is true that human misery has been focused on by the international media, and that there was world aid, but the entire aid for this really vital human case, for eight countries within three decades, was far less than the armament support sometimes provided for one country in one year.

What was not in the report, but was discussed by delegates, was that if all the Upper Nile projects on the drawing board were carried through – something extremely unlikely given the shortage of money and the continuing turmoil in the country – Sudan would still not have enough water to exploit all its agricultural potential, or even to provide its people with a clean and adequate supply. It is one of the ironies of the region that while water-rich Sudan suffers shortages and is unable to utilize all the agricultural land available, its difficult next-door neighbour, Libya, a dry and barren country, is tapping a vast reservoir whose waters might be claimed by Sudan as well as by Egypt and Libya, and is embarking on vast reclamation and irrigation schemes which would be much easier to implement in fertile Sudan. Yet through it all, the practical cooperation between Egypt and Sudan continues. The two countries most dependent on Nile water realize that neither transitory political disagreements nor fundamental ideologies must be allowed to affect the more important issue – the regulation, management and continued availability of the waters of the river on which they both depend.

7

Great Artificial Rivers:
Libya and Iraq

In 1977, Egypt and Libya waged a four-day war in which one of the main factors was Cairo's determination to protect its water supplies. Before the end of this century, Egypt and Libya may well go to war again. If that happens, water is likely to be the sole issue.

In the 1977 conflict, the world's superpowers came close to being drawn into a confrontation in the Middle East, just as they had been four years earlier, when the Americans declared a world-wide alert – 'defcon 1' – to warn the Russians that they would not tolerate Soviet troops going to the aid of the Egyptian Third Army, cut off and surrounded by the Israelis. In 1973, the war was brought about as Sadat deliberately tried to break the stalemate in the Middle East, and in a sense prepared the way for his trip to Jerusalem in late 1977. In 1977 it was again Sadat who was deliberately going to war, and risking a superpower clash; but this time Egyptian concern about water was a prime consideration dictating Cairo's actions.

Colonel Muammar Gaddafi had been in power for seven years and, feeling secure at home, was seeking to expand his influence and settle old scores: chief of these was his quarrel with Egypt, and in particular with President Sadat. When he took over in a bloodless coup in Tripoli in 1969, the 28-year-old Captain Gaddafi hoped to emulate his hero, Gamal Abdel Nasser. In particular, Gaddafi hoped to unite his country with Egypt – he rightly saw that Libya's oil riches and Egypt's people could together be a highly successful combination. But Nasser died in 1970 and his successor, Anwar Sadat, was unenthusiastic: Sadat had a broader vision, and Libya had little place in it. To his chagrin, Gaddafi was not even consulted before Egypt and Syria went to war in 1973.

So Gaddafi turned to other adventures: he annexed a 95 kilometre wide swathe of northern Chad, the Aouzou Strip, where he tried to take over the revolt being carried on there by FROLI NAT, the Muslim movement opposed to the government in Ndjamena. Even more important to Gaddafi, the Strip gave him additional access to Sudan, where President Jaafar Numeiri was backing Sadat and receiving Egyptian help in return. So Gaddafi turned his guerrillas loose on Sudan, where they encouraged the southern breakaway movement, supplied arms to dissidents and spread anti-Egyptian propaganda. Ever sensitive to events that might affect the Nile, Egypt suddenly discovered all sorts of Libyan-inspired plots, Libyan spy rings and Libyan-backed dissidents inside Egypt itself. Sadat had decided that Gaddafi had to be curbed and taught a lesson. The excuse was the 'plight' of the million Egyptian workers in Libya, said to be hostages held by Gaddafi, though there was little evidence of that. Egypt went to war, and for four days sent its planes on bombing raids in border regions. Unfortunately for Sadat, everything did not go according to plan: the air defences supplied by the Russians to the Libyans proved more effective than expected and the Libyan army put up a stiff resistance. Sadat gratefully accepted the various mediation efforts made by Arab and Third World countries, and called the war off.

The 'lesson' Sadat had sought to teach the Libyans was not effective enough to stop them continuing their efforts to take over Chad, and the French eventually had to intervene there to prop up fumbling regimes in Ndjamena. Eventually, a strengthened government was able to send effective forces north, and after several battles Gaddafi's Libyan and Palestinian troops were defeated, and the two sides signed a ceasefire agreement – though help from France, Egypt and the USA was still needed to maintain the government in power in Ndjamena, and the Libyan threat has still not disappeared. Just like the Israelis, Gaddafi knows very well how to annoy and worry the Egyptians, so he even sent his army into Uganda, site of one of the sources of the Nile, to support the infamous regime of Idi Amin. To his dismay, the Ugandan army disintegrated and the Libyan forces were left to defend the capital, Kampala; in a six day battle the Libyans were soundly beaten and forced to withdraw.

This failed to deter Gaddafi, who went on meddling in Sudan, switched support from the Eritreans to back Mengistu Haile Mariam in Ethiopia – again to Egypt's annoyance – and attempted to divide Chad into French and Libyan spheres of influence. To the Egyptians and their allies all this was annoying, even exasperating, but it was not worth going to war again for. Today, the Egyptians are rethinking that attitude, and the reason is the near-completion of Gaddafi's most ambitious project, the 'Great Man-made River'.

'The Great Mad Man's River', as it has been dubbed by the Egyptians and the Libyan opposition, is a grandiose scheme to bring water from a vast aquifer below the sands in the south of the country to the coast. Already, 120 wells have been sunk to tap the water there, and another thirty are being drilled. The artificial river made by pipes wide enough for a car to be driven through will eventually form a 4,200 kilometre network, as long as the Rhine, to carry the water from the oases of Kufrah and Sarir to the coast, and east and west to distribute it among the country's most heavily populated regions. It is hoped to move 2.2 billion cubic metres per year from the arid and thinly populated south to the north of the country, where the majority of Libya's population live, in cities, small towns and a few farming settlements. It is estimated that 80 per cent of the country's agricultural production is found in the region between Tripoli and Benghazi.

Gaddafi first tried to persuade his citizens to move to giant desert farms that he planned close to the wells at Sarir. But after a decade of easy living in which the oil wealth allowed Gaddafi to provide the infrastructure and welfare his people needed, they were reluctant to move from the urban coast to the desert. Gaddafi's solution was to move the water to the people. The Great Man-made River could also be justified on the grounds of national food security. The greening of the desert, with its analogies to the Koranic paradise, was a popular idea, and would bring the backward desert oasis villages into the modern era. Above all, Gaddafi, like his hero Nasser, would have his monument. The viability of the scheme at first seemed a secondary consideration. Told that in many places the water must be pumped over hills more than 100 metres high on its nine-day journey to the coast, Gaddafi replied: 'With the will of Allah, His guidance and the work of our people, we can make water go higher than the Empire State Building.'

Until today the main source of water along the coast, for both domestic use and agriculture, has come from coastal aquifers, but a rising population and more intensive farming have led to over-pumping, allowing seawater to seep in. The idea of moving water from a place where there are no people to the coast where it is desperately needed, seems to make sense in a country where oil combined with a small population gives a massive per capita national income. The trouble is that the water comes originally from the Kufrah aquifer, which is believed to extend from Libya into Chad, Egypt and Sudan. Studies commissioned and paid for by the Libyans have been carried out, and in many cases have concluded that Libya will in fact only be drawing Libyan water and that the aquifer being tapped is only in Libyan territory; but the neighbouring countries are deeply suspicious of these findings, and fear they may have been carried out by those with vested interests in the continuation of the lucrative Libyan project. Egypt, most sensitive of all over water as well as the major regional military power, is particularly disturbed, anxious that Libyan pumping may worsen the damage already being done by silting behind the Aswan Dam. What is agreed by all the experts is that the 60,000 cubic kilometres of water in the Saharan aquifers can only be mined once. It is fossil water, trapped there hundreds of thousands of years ago when the now-baking Libyan desert was covered in ice.

When the Egyptians were investigating the situation caused by silt at Aswan, they sent teams deep into Sudan and into the surrounding countryside, and made no secret of the fact that their scientists were being reinforced by men from the Egyptian Army Corps of Engineers. Officially, these officers were 'putting their experience at the service of the Ministry of Irrigation and Public Works'. But the real reason was to give the army experience of the area, as the military would take over the region in certain circumstances – if, for instance, changes in the Nile meant the appearance of new streams flowing towards the Libyan border. Egyptian officers have told us that in classified contingency plans drawn up in Cairo, the Egyptian High Command envisages taking control of large areas south-west of Lake Nasser, as well as parts of south-east Libya, if the need should arise; that is, if the silting at Aswan did show signs of forcing the river into new channels flowing into Libya.

Egyptian military plans, known as *Waraa el-hidoud* (Beyond the Borders) were traditionally associated with Nile water. Plan Aida provides for intervention in Ethiopia, where the end of the civil war may allow a government in Addis Ababa to revive old irrigation schemes and build new dams. The Egyptians are already worried about the threat to the Blue Nile and the help being given to Ethiopia by the Israelis: as we have seen, during a closed session of the Egyptian parliament in January 1990 MPs called for the bombing of any new installations on the Blue Nile. That could well lead to Operation Aida being implemented.

Al-Timssah (Operation Crocodile) sets out the modalities for a campaign in Sudan, and the silting at Aswan, detected early in the 1980s, prompted the Egyptians to map out a scenario for an invasion of Libya, plans which were put into practice in 1976 when relations between the two countries reached crisis point. They remain in the inventory of contingencies studied at the Nasser Military Academy.

Two operations using commandos from the elite Egyptian special force Al Sa'iqua (Thunderbolt) – called Amaliyat al-Arba'een (Operation Arba'een) after the medieval caravan route from Egypt to what is now Chad, and Amaliyat Ashay al-Akhdar (Green Leaf Tea Operation) – were rehearsed during border battles with Libya. The operations are designed either to disable or to control the key water pumping installations that might affect the Western desert aquifer in a massive region inside Libya, Chad and North Sudan. In 1989 Operation Arba'een was modified to turn it into a massive commando assault designed to secure a bridgehead for a full-scale invasion by Egyptian troops. The aim would be to occupy hilltops overlooking the plain where Egypt meets Sudan and Libya. The Engineering Corps would then go into action to prevent any diversion of the Nile into Libya, by a massive earth-moving programme, achieved mainly by blasting sand barriers into position with explosives. The aim would be to change the whole topography so that any new branch of the river was kept within Egyptian territory. The initial estimated time for the operation in 1988 was 180 days, but after the Western intervention in Kuwait in 1990, the time scale for all such operations was cut by half: everything would have to be done before outside powers could interfere.

It was significant that just as the Egyptians very publicly involved the army in their survey of the Nile above Aswan, another Egyptian department began preparing public opinion for action by accusing Libya of underestimating the effects of pumping fossil water from areas close to the Egyptian borders for the Great Man-made River. Egyptian geologists warned that pumping water from the aquifer beneath the Egyptian desert west of the Nile valley might create a partial vacuum that would increase the speed of seepage of water from the Nile to the underground reservoir. That, they said, could lead to sudden depressions, subsidence, that might destroy Egyptian oases from the border with Libya all the way east to Fayoum. Since long before Gaddafi appeared on the scene, the Egyptians have had plans to expand the 80,000 feddans (33,600 hectares) of cultivated land in the Qattara Depression, traditionally watered from underground sources, to the full potential of 500,000 feddans. They also want to extend from 350,000 to 800,000 feddans (147,000 to 336,600 hectares) the arable land in Siuah, Frafrah and Abu Minkar oases, all situated between the Nile valley and the Libyan border.

Egyptian studies in the 1950s showed that there were two natural underground aquifers in that region, one north of Siuah, which was estimated to be able to supply 140 million cubic metres per year for 200 years, the other south of the same oasis, with fossil water in an underground reservoir 28 square kilometres in area. Since Libya began constructing its pipeline, Egyptian hydrologists have taken to claiming that these aquifers in the Western Desert are connected to the Libyan aquifer, and warning that Libyan actions could affect the situation in Egypt.

This sensitive area between the Nile and the Libyan border was the centre of the earthquake that devastated parts of Cairo in September 1992. Discussing the disaster in the Officers' Club in Cairo that evening, a very senior Egyptian officer, who was attending his retirement banquet, said: 'It's a pity the earthquake didn't wait until Gaddafi started pumping our underground water in his mad project. Then we could have done something about it.' The clear implication, from a man involved in policy-making, was that Egypt would welcome an excuse to move against Colonel Gaddafi yet again.

It was also remarkable that 'The Organization for Solidarity with the Mountains of Nubia' started its campaign in the autumn of 1992, seeking autonomy for the Nubian mountain region north of Kurdfan. This is the area in which the Egyptians have set up their water monitoring equipment, and would be involved if the Nile changed its course towards Libya, or if Egypt decided to move into the Libyan border areas. This sudden and hitherto unheard-of organization called for the withdrawal of all Sudanese troops and paramilitary organizations from the area, and the opening of the border between the two Nubias – in effect, southern Egypt and northern Sudan, an area last administered as one entity when Britain ruled both countries. In the past, efforts by the people of Nubia to gain greater local self-government have been thwarted by Cairo, so there can be little doubt that the 1992 campaign had been sanctioned and encouraged by the Egyptian government. The aim seemed to be to show that there was local support for a single authority administering the area on both sides of the Egyptian–Sudanese border, again a useful move if operations against Libya from that area were proposed.

The Great Man-made River in Libya was begun in September 1984, and for the next seven years it was the largest civil engineering operation in the world. More bulldozers and excavators were assembled in the desert than had ever been brought together in one place before. By the end of 1992, Libya had spent more than US$5 billion of the initial US$14 billion allocated to the River, and the first section had been completed. The opening was celebrated with a typically Libyan extravaganza on 1 September 1991, the country's Revolution Day. After 667 kilometres the pipeline had reached Ajda- biya, where a reservoir has been built, and the line splits into two spurs, one the 150 kilometre link to Benghazi, the other going south- west to Marsa el-Brege where another pipe manufacturing plant has been built. From there the line will extend west to Sirte – not an agricultural area but Gaddafi's family home – and finally to Tobruk. In the last stage the Sirte pipe will be continued west to Tripoli via Misurata.

At the opening ceremony hundreds of delegations from revolu- tionary movements all over the world, and the last remaining Com- munist groups, listened to the usual confused and interminable speech by Colonel Gaddafi as scores of young Libyan men in Italian- made designer swimming trunks dived into a massive pool filled by the water gushing out of a four-metre pipe, water which had made a nine-day journey from beneath the Sahara, where it had lain un- touched for hundreds of thousands of years. As the ceremony went on, officials boasted that the huge pipes which bring the water from Kufrah to the present coastal terminal of Ajdabiya, all made in Libya, will last as long as the water does – but no one is quite sure how long that will be. The Libyans themselves say at least fifty years; the Egyptians say forty years at very moderate rates of use; and the contractors say perhaps as long as hundreds of years. The short answer is that no one knows, and of course everything will depend on the rate of extraction.

Libya set up two plants to manufacture the thousands of kilometres of pipes needed when the project began, but that is about the only part of the project which is Libyan. Even the factories that make the pipes were designed by American and European engineers and built by the Dong Ah construction company of South Korea, the main contractor, which has brought in 10,000 Korean and Thai workers, with the few locals employed usually coming from across the border in Chad.

It is certain that, like oil, underground water beneath the Sahara is not going to last for ever. Hydrologists are not sure how long it would take for the aquifers to recharge naturally; certainly the three

Saharan aquifers took at least 2,000 years to fill while the area was going through a wet period. It is now accepted by environmentalists that the recharge rates in the North African zone are so slow (and will become slower) that, unlike surface water, the underground water in the aquifers extending from west of the Nile valley to Senegal can only be pumped once. However, there are no rain gauges in these remote hills, so estimates of the annual rate of recharge vary from the five million cubic metres suggested by Dr Moid Ahmad, professor of hydrology at Ohio University in the USA, to the 600,000 cubic metres suggested by Ed Wright, a British geologist who prospected in Sarir for British Petroleum in the 1960s. A study by Fred Pearce in the *New Scientist* found that at the current rate of water exploitation, and even without the Libyan project, things are not promising. The rainfall in the Saharan region is less than one centimetre a year, though the main recharge of the central and southern Saharan and north Sahelian aquifers comes from rainfall on hills in northern Chad. Most of that is lost by evaporation before it can make its long journey through the layers of sand and rocks to the underground reservoir. And as the estimated four cubic kilometres of rain which fall on the Chadian hills can find its way to at least three aquifers, less than half the total will go to recharge the Libyan aquifer.

It does seem clear that the recharge will not be anywhere near the amount pumped by the Libyans each day. Studies of parts of the Kufrah aquifer, in an area developed in the 1970s for irrigation pilot schemes, when pumping was going ahead without any limits being applied, found that the water table fell by as much as fifteen metres a year, a figure twenty times higher than the rate predicted by the planners of the Great Man-made River. According to Professor Tony Allan of London University, the water table in the Sarir area will certainly fall by as much as two metres a year once the Libyans start pumping at full capacity. This will raise the price of the water, and thus the cost of agriculture, since deeper pumping will be needed and that will require more energy – extra fuel. It is also likely that as events prove that the Libyan dream of food self-sufficiency cannot be attained, the temptation will be to pump more and more water.

That will certainly lead to trouble with Libya's already concerned neighbours, who have begun to make preparations for action. Many Libyan opposition groups are now supported by Egypt – as well as the American CIA – and operate from Chad, which cannot supply money but can provide a base, and is happy to do so to protect its water. The guerrillas of the Libyan opposition are being encouraged to cross the border into their home country, and may well see the Great Man-made River as a legitimate target. Neither Gaddafi nor his people would agree; the potential for an escalation of actions would be immediate.

The constant increase in the price of the total scheme will also have to be taken into account when figures are worked out for the cost of growing the crops to be irrigated. The whole project is being carried out under the supervision of the American company Brown and Root, which oversees the operation from a branch in Britain. The total cost was estimated in 1990 at US$27 billion, but that figure is likely to rise still further: in 1985 the total cost was expected to be US$20 billion; in 1980, US$14 billion. Angus Henley, who monitors Libyan affairs for the London-based *Middle East Economic Digest*, said: 'The whole idea of using this valuable resource for agriculture is very open to question. Libya's experience with post-revolutionary farming has not been very good. It followed the Soviet collective idea. There has been gross incompetence.' Interviewed by Reuters in September 1991, Mr Henley noted that for the same US$5 billion the Libyans spent to get the water to Ajdabiya, they could have built up to five desalination plants each producing nearly four million litres every day. He and others predict that it will cost the Libyans at least ten times as much as farmers in Western Europe to produce a bushel of wheat. Professor Tony Allan includes the Libyan project in his book *Natural Resources as National Fantasies*, a very critical study of some of the wilder schemes being considered around the world. He believes that it is madness to use water which can never be replaced to grow wheat. That message seems to have got through to the Libyan government, which is now considering replacing wheat with other high-value crops on the farms to be irrigated by the southern water, though optimists – the builders of the project among them – still claim that the Great Man-made River could eventually irrigate more than the acreage originally forecast, and produce more than the million tonnes of cereals said to have been produced each year in the time of the Roman Empire.

Even Libya had some difficulty in finding all the money needed, but given the country's oil reserves, it was not surprising that when Colonel Gaddafi sought a loan from the Arab Fund for Growth and Development in 1985, the Fund was only too happy to lend. But the Fund did lay down one condition: it asked for a study to determine the effect of the project on the environment. The Libyans agreed, and the money was forthcoming even before work on the study had begun; the results will not be known until 1994.

The idea of exploiting underground water first attracted the Libyans in 1967, a couple of years before the military coup that brought Gaddafi to power, when drilling by Western oil companies regularly produced water. Further investigation proved the presence of a massive aquifer of fossil water in the south-eastern part of the country. When Gaddafi and his 'Free Officers' did take over, the idea of food self-sufficiency appealed to them: one of their ideas was 'self-reliance', and food production seemed to be something they could manage. So as a result of that early ideology, and following a number of studies in which those consulted were given fairly clear ideas of what was expected, the Libyan government is committed to establishing more irrigated farms – hugely subsidized – in the coastal area near Sirte. The aim is to have about 180,000 hectares there, and a further 320,000 hectares in Jabal al-Akhdar and the Jefra plain. But even with the Great Man-made River – which Colonel Gaddafi calls the eighth wonder of the world – food self-sufficiency seems impossible in Libya, where food now accounts for 20 per cent of all imports, where less than 20 per cent of the people work in agriculture and where only 1.4 per cent of the land is arable.

Economists estimate that water demand for urban and industrial use will sooner or later pre-empt supplies, taking priority over the agricultural sector. Population growth as well as the difficulty of the environment mean that the dream of food self-sufficiency is never likely to be realized. And even those who are enthusiastic about Gaddafi's plans agree that they make little economic sense. 'It is clear that the cost of food raised by irrigation with the new water will be uneconomic,' according to Professor Allan.

An additional difficulty is that, just as few Libyans were willing to move south to new farms in the 1970s, even fewer Libyans want to be farmers in the 1990s. The Libyan ministry of agriculture took full-page advertisements in Cairo newspapers in 1991 to invite Egyptian peasants to Libya to cultivate the new fields to be watered by the Man-made River. But the Egyptians are reluctant, remembering the bad treatment many received in Iraq when they answered a similar call. Others suspect that Gaddafi only wanted to attract Egyptian farmers in their thousands to make any move against him by Egypt more difficult.

The Libyans may be able to get around the practical difficulties, but they will have a lot more trouble in placating their neighbours. The Egyptians, the Sudanese and the Chadians, backed by the French, all insist that the underground aquifer is shared. The Egyptians have already warned Gaddafi against over-pumping, while the Chadians fear that Gaddafi's future reliance on water from the shared aquifer might induce him once again to occupy the north of their country.

The possible effect of Libya's actions has not yet made any impact on the Egyptian public, as most of those who write about water in Egypt see Ethiopia and Israel as the dangers. But official Egypt is deeply concerned, while senior army officers have told us they regard Gaddafi as an unpredictable, hot-headed demagogue who must constantly be prevented from causing mischief.

That is a description which might also be applied to another Middle East leader for whom Cairo has no affection – Saddam Hussein of Iraq. Egypt's President Mubarak took the lead in coordinating Arab resistance to Iraq's invasion of Kuwait, sent Egyptian forces to fight beside the Americans and, just like President Bush, has seen his stature diminished by Saddam's continued presence long after the battle of Kuwait was supposed to have put an end to the Iraqi leader's pretensions.

In the same way that Egypt is worried by what might happen in Sudan or Ethiopia, Iraq is concerned at events in Syria and Turkey. Regarded as water-rich in Middle East terms, Iraq would be in difficulties if upstream states put their own concerns first. Iraq is especially worried, as Saddam Hussein has invested huge capital and his own prestige – still high internally, no matter what the world may think – in a vast project with implications for the national psyche as well as tremendous practical potential.

In December 1992, Mesopotamia, the land between two rivers, celebrated the inauguration of a third waterway, also described as a river by the Iraqi publicists. The 565 kilometre Saddam River between the Tigris and Euphrates starts near Baghdad and ends close to Basra in the south, and is ostensibly designed to reclaim polluted land by washing it with surplus irrigation water, which should remove 80 tonnes of salt a year to rehabilitate 150 million hectares over five to ten years.

'The project is a great wonder to be accomplished under the unjust blockade,' said the official Iraqi media, which blame all the country's troubles on the international embargo applied against it at the end of the war to liberate Kuwait. This time they have a point, for it was a huge scheme; what was not acknowledged was that something had to be done to occupy demobilized troops, already causing trouble in many parts of the country. Above all, there was no mention of the secondary aim of the project: it is the first step in a plan to drain the marshes between Amara and Basra, and thus remove the last haven in the country for anti-Saddam dissidents – destroying the homes and way of life of the Marsh Arabs.

The new river, as it was called, was also a useful focus for a nation in danger of fragmentation and in need of some cause for pride. Although the project was formulated as long ago as 1953, it was presented as the latest battle Iraq had to wage to make the country self-sufficient in food, and so defeat the Western-led enemy. The Baath regime always has to have an outside focus to distract people from their internal miseries.

It was also one more monument to the man who dreams of the ancient glories of Babylon, and sees himself as the reincarnation of the great leaders of ancient times, Hammurabi or Nebuchadnezzar, whose empires were based on the riches provided by the fertile land between the Tigris and Euphrates. So the new canal became 'Saddam's River' – just as the Iraqi people called the Iran–Iraq struggle of 1980–8 'Saddam's War'. As 60,000 labourers shifted 76 million cubic metres of soil and built eighty-four bridges, their work was lauded by the regime's speechwriters, songs were composed and television features broadcast. Until the newly reclaimed land yields crops to feed the population, that will be the daily diet of the Iraqi people: the Baathist regime not only needs outside enemies on which to focus, it has to have victories to celebrate. So the day on which the first phase of the scheme was completed was declared a national holiday, and the morning lesson in Iraqi schools and universities was a discussion of the project's strategic importance. 'Saddam River Day' will be celebrated every year 'as an embodiment of the greatness of this achievement through which the Iraqis have opened wider horizons, a bright future and a chapter of glory of which history and coming generations will be proud'.

The opening ceremony turned into a victory parade, with soldiers in the vanguard, carrying a giant portrait of Saddam in army uniform. They were followed by grey-suited engineers, uniformed pilots and stewardesses of the grounded Iraqi Airways, and the small fleet of earth-moving machines which was all that could be mobilized and kept working. In a message read at the ceremony and broadcast on Iraqi television and radio, Saddam emphasized the achievement of completing such a project under sanctions. 'When planning such a plot they [the allies in the Kuwait war] had in mind the present pictures of starvation and death in Somalia, and they wanted the same thing for the Iraqi people.'

There is another side to it all: the draining of the marshes where 30,000 Shia dissidents sought refuge after the abortive uprising of 1991. During the Iran–Iraq war, Iraqi engineers constructed vast water defences on the line between Amara and Basra, the site of the main Iranian push. But the canals and artificial lakes were not only obstacles to an enemy advance, they were also built in accordance with a long-standing plan to drain the marshes. Now the plan is being implemented, and these magnificent wetlands, where the Marsh Arabs have lived and evolved their own distinctive way of life for 3,000 years, are in terminal danger. The reason is that the mass of canals and waterways beside the Shatt al-Arab, and feeding into it, make it easy for Saddam's opponents to cross back and forth to Iran, which supports the Shia of Iraq in their fight for autonomy. Deserters from the Iraqi forces have made their headquarters there too, preying on surrounding towns and villages and attacking travellers. By drying out the marshes and making them easily accessible to his forces, Saddam will be able to rid himself of his most determined and persistent enemies. Saddam's River, the third waterway in the Land of Two Rivers, will eventually be linked to a fourth canal that will complete the project and end the virtual independence of the marshes. In response, the Marsh Arabs, who face the destruction of their homes and villages and the end of their traditional way of life, have declared their own hydro-jihad, as they call it. Drying up the marshes is another of Saddam's crimes, they have told the United Nations, a crime as bad as any he has committed in the past against the Kurds, the Shia or his own people. These new militants have not said what they intend to do, but they are at home on the water, understand its ways and its uses; destroying the installations so laboriously built on the new river would be an obvious method of attack. Saddam will certainly respond to any such attempts as he has in the past: with extreme violence, perhaps again using poison gas; it was in the marshes that Iraq first tried chemical warfare in 1984.

To stay in power, his most important objective, Saddam will continue to portray Iraq as a beleaguered country, and will evoke the spirit of 'the mother of all battles' to keep his people engaged. That means focusing on the latest achievement, the Saddam River, and it means, too, that any interference with the water supply to the project will provoke another crisis. If Turkey or Syria undertake works that lessen the flow of the two rivers – as they are committed to doing – Saddam will react, diplomatically or by retaliatory subversion now, by military means when he again becomes strong enough to do so. In the same way, aid to Iraqi opposition groups by Kuwait or Iran, the regional sources of support to them, would certainly provoke an Iraqi reaction.

In many Arab countries there is now a grudging admiration for what Iraq has accomplished, and Saddam himself remains something of a hero to many individual Arabs. The Iraqi experience is also engaging the attention of planners in many countries: until its 1990 invasion of Kuwait, Iraq was one of the world's leading food importers, paying either from its annual US$18 billion oil revenue or with subsidies given by Saudi Arabia and other Gulf states that supported Iraq during its eight-year war with Iran. In the 1980s farming was seriously affected by rapid urbanization, with 75 per cent of the 18 million population living in towns and cities, and by shortages of labour as a result of the general mobilization and the terrible losses of the war. By 1987 Iraq was buying 80 per cent of its food requirements, accounting for 26.7 per cent by value of imports.

Then came the terrible miscalculation of the Kuwaiti invasion, which led to huge losses in Iraq, damage to many of its basic installations and the collapse of its economy when the world applied and maintained sanctions. Suddenly, Iraq had to rely on its own food production. It responded by upgrading plans for irrigation and agricultural development that were first proposed in the 1950s, and had been on hold ever since. And despite sanctions, despite the hostility of most countries of the region and the world, Iraqi expertise and sheer hard work has worked a small miracle – though at an incalculable future cost to at least one section of the Iraqi people, the Marsh Arabs. The month-long bombing campaign by the American-led coalition formed to force Iraq out of Kuwait meant that, when hostilities ended, only one important water project on the Tigris and Euphrates, the Darbandikhan Dam, emerged in a usable state, having suffered 50 per cent damage. The Dokan and Haditha Dams were 75 per cent destroyed and the Ramadi Barrage, Saddam and Samarra Dams were put out of action altogether. The destruction of dams and pumping installations, water purification plants and power stations had a serious effect on electricity generation, and therefore on food production and the provision of potable water. Crop failures were widespread in 1991 because of shortages of fertilizers, pesticides, spare parts for tractors, pumps and other machinery, power failures, and restrictions on aerial crop spraying and harvesting in border regions. The wheat and barley harvests were down by 50 per cent, while the date crop was even worse, as it was irrigated by the Tigris, which became heavily polluted by the discharge of raw sewage into the river. Saddam Hussein, as brilliant a domestic politician as he is a disaster as an international strategist, decided to turn the misery of his people to advantage.

As soon as the UN Security Council imposed sanctions against Iraq, on 6 August 1990, the Ministry of Agriculture in Baghdad launched a campaign to increase the cultivated area and improve cereal production by 50 per cent. By the end of 1990, the cereal crop was 70 per cent greater than that in the 1987–9 period, as farmers planted 80 per cent of their land with cereals in response to generous government subsidies. Combined with strict but fair food rationing, introduced in September 1990 and still in force, this enabled Iraq to survive.

Iraq had always had a policy of trying to achieve self-sufficiency in cereal production, and the new measures at last enabled it to reach its goal and averted what might have been a serious famine. This has been noted by economic policy-makers in the region, who had been advised – usually by Western experts – to continue to rely on food imports, as they could easily afford to do so. Now, that policy is being re-examined, and Saudi Arabia, which exports wheat, has a new justification for its expensive production.

8

The Arabian Peninsula

Sultan Qabous, the Sandhurst-trained ruler of Oman, was a dis-appointed man on the day we saw him in his garish palace in Muscat. He had just been handed the results of a programme of test drilling in a promising inland area of his barren country, and it was a familiar report: traces of oil but no water. The Sultan sighed and told the minister who brought him the news that they would just have to go on trying. Oil was important to Oman, but water was vital. And as in many other places in the arid Arabian peninsula, instead of grow-ing to keep pace with the booming population, the country's water resources were reducing as over-pumping lowered the water table and allowed seawater to contaminate the coastal aquifers. There was another problem too: wherever the test rigs operated by the newly established Ministry of Water Resources went, they were closely watched by the farmers and landowners of the area, and when water was found dozens of new wells were immediately sunk, so that the new source of supply was soon as over-extended as all the others. A system of well registration was being introduced, and a ban on new drilling, but in a country as large as Oman that was difficult to enforce. More radical solutions were needed, so in 1990 Sultan Qabous, true to his military training – as a British army lieutenant he served in Germany – put a senior officer of the Sultan of Oman's armed forces in charge of water resources. Although it was never announced, the aim was to curb excessive water use by the better off members of the community, to prevent illegal well digging and to enforce Draconian preservation measures.

In Oman, on the southern rim of the Arabian peninsula, cut off from most other Arab countries by the Rub al Khali, the Empty Quarter, or by the Hajar mountains, it might be thought that while regrettable and difficult internally, lack of water could not lead to conflict. Certainly the chances are fewer, but they are there: Oman has only managed to patch up a fragile peace with Yemen, it objects to the way the sheikhdom of Fujaireh (in the United Arab Emirates) bisects its land in the north, and it is uneasy about the intentions of Iran, just across the forty kilometre wide Strait of Hormuz. Above all, it worries that any compromise over a disputed border area might deny it access to water; one of the reasons why Oman and Saudi Arabia were able to define and agree the long frontier between them was that there was very little chance of any water being found anywhere in that stretch of desert.

The events of 1990 and 1991 caused most concern to Oman and all the other countries of the Arabian peninsula. The Iraqi invasion of Kuwait not only demonstrated that the unthinkable was possible, that one brotherly Arab state could attack another without reasonable excuse or provocation, it also showed the vulnerability of the smaller Gulf countries to outside attack and to man-made disaster. The security of the Arabian peninsula is supposed to be assured by the alliance of the six countries of the region grouped in the Gulf Cooperation Council: Saudi Arabia, Kuwait, Bahrain, Qatar, the United Arab Emirates and Oman. These six countries set up a military headquarters near Riyadh, held joint military manoeuvres and committed themselves to provide forces for collective defence in time of need. Yet when Iraq invaded Kuwait it was forty-eight hours before Saudi Arabia even allowed news of the attack to be given; and though forces from many of the states eventually took part in the liberation of Kuwait, they were quite unable to do so on their own. Worse still, as the Iraqis were forced out of Kuwait they engaged in an orgy of damage and destruction that is still affecting the Gulf today, and that pointed to the greatest danger of all: damage to the desalination plants which supply the basic water needs of every state in the area. As the vast oil spill caused by Iraq's destruction of Kuwait's oilwells crept south along the Gulf shore in those desperate days in 1991, one by one Saudi Arabian desalination plants along the country's north-eastern shore had to be closed down, in case the oil reached the intake ports. By good luck and the vagaries of wind and weather, the oil slick never went far enough to cause trouble, and within days the plants could be reactivated; but there were some anxious moments in the towns and villages along the Gulf shore, right down to the big industrial port of Jubail. The incident was watched with horror by all the Gulf countries as they examined once again the security of their own plants.

Two-thirds of the world's 7,500 desalination plants are in the Middle East, 60 per cent of them in Saudi Arabia, the biggest country in the world without a river. By the end of 1991, there were 4,500 desalination plants in the Gulf – half of them in Saudi Arabia – with a total output of 1.4 billion cubic metres per year. The output is usually mixed with underground water of higher salinity when used for irrigation.

The annual requirement of Gulf countries for desalinated water is expected to grow to 5.4 billion cubic metres by the year 2030, but given their riches and the fact that 97 per cent of the world's water is salt, the potential for converting that to fresh water would seem to answer the need: unfortunately, it does not work like that. Although the principle of desalination – vaporization – is simple and has been known for centuries, the quantities required today need huge and sophisticated plants. The development of steam power in the nineteenth century enabled large plants to be built; the first land-based plant was built in Aden towards the end of that century. The basic technique is to apply energy to seawater so that it is evaporated, then to capture and condense the water vapour. The earliest methods used boiling. Then 'flashing' was developed, by which the water is heated but is prevented from boiling by high pressure. The water is then fed into a 'flash chamber' at low pressure, which gives rapid evaporation of water that can be condensed. To increase efficiency, a number of linked chambers are used.

Heavy reliance on desalination by vaporization can lead to difficulties: most plants in the Gulf do not use solar energy but are fuelled by natural gas. Western experts advised that gas could be used to generate electricity at the same time that water was evaporated.

But this means that the oil-producing country has to keep pumping a minimum supply of crude oil in order to produce enough gas to fuel the plant. This in turn means that the producer country has lost the option of reducing oil output in order to maintain prices.

Aristotle described how Greek sailors evaporated seawater 2,500 years ago, while the Romans passed water through clay or wool to reduce the brine content, a method similar to that applied today in the increasingly used reverse osmosis method. The most commonly used desalination technique now is multistage flash distillation or condensed vapour refining. But a multistage plant is economical only when it is combined with power stations or powered by a cheap energy source, limiting the scope for further development.

While research into new energy sources continues, the current high cost has caused reverse osmosis technology – a method of straining water through a permeable membrane – to be put forward as an alternative. Japanese technologists have already produced more efficient, longer-lasting membranes for the plants. All commercial desalination plants in the world still use conventional power sources, but energy research is making solar power feasible. The ability to produce and store heat at high temperatures inexpensively gives solar power advantages in seawater desalination. Solar desalination plants using reverse osmosis may soon be commercially attractive.

Israel is another country that has concentrated on desalination, though unlike Saudi Arabia it does have available water on its territory. Israel decided to turn to desalination because it wanted alternatives if, as at one time seemed likely, the enemies surrounding the country decided to try to cut off its water supplies.

Starting in 1965, Israel built thirty-five desalination facilities, which had a total annual production of about 18 million cubic metres according to Pinhas Glickstern, an engineer with Mekorot, the public company that supplies two-thirds of Israel's water. Eight plants worked by vaporization, twenty-three desalinated mineral-rich water by reverse osmosis and four were experimental. Of these only the mineral water plants are functioning today, producing 4 million cubic metres of water a year. Seawater desalination plants were gradually shut down in the 1980s because the mineral water plants were much cheaper to run. 'Water desalination technology is capable today of producing limitless amounts of water at a price that makes it available for home or industrial usage,' Dr Dan Zaslavsky, the Israeli water controller, told us. 'The problem lies in energy, not in water production.'

Energy-use improvements in the past decade have been incorporated into a Mekorot plant at Sabha, near Eilat, probably one of the most up-to-date and efficient in the region, though Saudi Arabia is planning several new plants within the next few years. The Sabha plant produces 15,000 cubic metres of water daily, is remote controlled for fourteen hours a day and uses only half the energy such installations did ten years ago.

Desalination of seawater is only cost effective in quantities over 20,000 cubic metres per day. At current prices, desalinated seawater is available for US$0.65 per cubic metre, but its estimated real cost – taking out the subsidies – is US$1 per unit. Both prices are too high for desalinated water to be used for agriculture. Mineral-rich water can be desalinated in any quantity for US$0.25 to 0.45 per cubic metre, but most hydrologists believe that, rather than either of these, agriculture will use purified sewage water for many years to come, not least because governments usually subsidize this heavily. However, during the next twenty years, inexpensive power sources may make it possible to produce desalinated seawater for something like one-third of the present cost. It would then also be economically practical to purify water which has been contaminated by man-made chemicals.

The difficulty in the Middle East is that vast quantities are needed, particularly as governments seek greater industrialization and there is then a natural inclination towards urbanization. Tens of millions of cubic metres per year will be needed, not in twenty years' time but within three years, according to predictions by Israeli engineers. 'If one wishes to make peace and bring prosperity to these countries, one must make sure that in the next decade 500 million to 600 million cubic metres of water will be desalinated. The investment needed for such a project is about $2.5 billion, less than the cost of a small war,' says Dan Zaslavsky.

This was one of the considerations that induced Israel to agree to take part in the negotiations over water as part of the Middle East peace process, though not surprisingly after so many years of conflict no real progress was made on any of the subjects on the agenda, including water. But none of the meetings broke up in disarray, and in the conference on water both sides at least agreed to set up a data bank. Israel's tactics in the negotiations were to seek the widest possible agreement on sharing of water resources, knowing it was bound to gain; the Palestinians sought to extract political concessions in return for their agreement to discuss specifics; Syria, which has the return of the occupied Golan Heights as its main political objective, refused to attend and forced its client-state Lebanon to join its boycott. Golan Heights water, which now supplies nearly a quarter of Israel's supply, is a factor adding urgency to Syria's efforts to regain its lost territory.

The meeting did give the Arabs a rare opportunity to publicize the disparity in the treatment of Palestinians and settlers in the occupied territories, but more important was the impact made by one of the few suggestions put forward by the American organizers of the whole process. They suggested to both sides in the talks that one of the most attractive confidence-building measures, with an immediate beneficial effect, would be jointly built and owned desalination plants. Coming from the Middle East to talks in Washington or Europe, Arab and Israeli representatives alike could see the sense of that proposition, and unofficially accepted that the most useful project would be an Israeli–Jordanian plant long planned for the border between Eilat and Aqaba. But this would not go far in satisfying the projected demand. More would be needed, and with unlimited seawater the real need would be money. The fact that the rich Gulf countries have joined the Middle East peace talks indicates some possibility of progress, with the Gulf financing desalination plants in the north – a reasonable insurance to prevent the much heavier cost of a new war.

But desalination plants are tremendously expensive to install and costly to run. They can produce only a limited amount of fresh water and have to depend on a constant supply of energy, and their output is also limited by the amount of mineral salts contained in the water fed in. It is no surprise that it is the oil-rich countries of the Gulf that have turned mainly to desalination, as they have the wealth to pay for the plants and the running costs, the energy supplies to keep them going and, above all, the need for these expensive investments. Yet every desalination plant built is a hostage to fortune: they are easily sabotaged; they can be attacked from the air or by shelling from off-shore; and their intake ports have to be kept clear, giving another simple way of preventing their operation.

It is an oddity of the Arabian peninsula that the countries there have until now been content to place their reliance on desalination plants, while turning their backs on the possibility of importing water from available sources nearby. The argument has always been that imported water would give the supplying country a stranglehold over the importing state, that in a literal sense the supplier would have his hand on the tap and could turn it off at any moment.

One of the earliest suggestions for exporting water was made in 1930, when Kuwait was suffering from a particular shortage that was leading to unrest among the people. The Iraqi Prime Minister Nuri Said offered to divert water from the south of Iraq through an extension of the Khor Abdullah Canal. But the shrewd Sheikh of Kuwait – Ahmad al-Jaber al-Sabah – turned down the offer as he saw that the project would give the Iraqis a stranglehold on his vulnerable state. Nuri Said, like all other Iraqi leaders, upheld Baghdad's claim to Kuwait. So Kuwait continued to rely, as it had for decades, on importing drinking water from Basra and the surrounding areas in tankers driven across the border or dhows sailing down the Shatt al-Arab. Efforts to revive the project were made in 1953, when the idea was that a waterway should be constructed from the Shatt al-Arab to Kuwait. This time, the Kuwaitis were worried that a canal could be used for military purposes. They commissioned an expert study, which suggested a pipeline instead.

The old objections applied to the pipeline as well, so it was never built, but in the 1970s the Iraqis and Kuwaitis did sign an agreement to pipe 700 million gallons a day from the Euphrates. This time the Kuwaitis felt more secure, because in return for Iraqi water they would supply electricity; then any break in water supply could result in the whole of southern Iraq being blacked out. But even this apparently sensible idea was never carried through. Border clashes between the two countries made relations so bad that no joint projects were possible, and then when things improved, the Iran–Iraq war stopped everything. After Iraq invaded Kuwait in 1990, and declared it the country's nineteenth province, one of Saddam Hussein's first announcements was that the plan to pipe water to Kuwait would go ahead. Not surprisingly, once Kuwait was liberated in 1991 the ruling al-Sabah family decided there should be a ban on all talks about projects linking their country with Iraq.

There are a few other water exporting ideas, some of which have been studied. One is to divert water in a pipeline from Pakistan through Baluchistan to a pumping station on the Iranian coast. At first, tankers would carry the water across the Strait of Hormuz to Ras al-Khaimeh, the rest of the UAE and Oman; later, pipes would be laid on the sea bed. But with the example of what happened between Iraq and Kuwait, Sheikh Zeid of the UAE, which was financing the project, decided against it.

Today, five countries of the Middle East, Turkey, Syria, Jordan, Iraq and Egypt, have given approval in principle to a plan to integrate their national electricity grids, though without any agreement on water. The initial cost of US$185 million will be financed by the Kuwait-based Arab Fund for Economic Development. If it goes through, the proposed network will serve 150 million people, and it is seen as the first stage in joining up with the Gulf countries, which have a surplus, and linking them with Europe through Turkey, while the Maghreb countries could join the network via Egypt. The grid should give a huge boost to the economies of the participating countries; more importantly, it could inspire the confidence in each other so lacking today.

Turkey sees itself as a regional superpower now, and is busy trying to extend its influence into the Asian republics of the former Soviet Union. It also has ambitions to the south, and for years has been seeking influence in the Arab world to balance its aim of membership of the European Community – perhaps to make its application more acceptable. In 1986 it proposed an ambitious plan to take water to Arab countries. The brainchild of Turgut Özal, the project would take water from southern Turkey to the six countries of the Gulf Cooperation Council, as well as to Syria, Jordan and Israel. The Turkish argument was that the US$20 billion project would be a means of increasing security in the region. Mr Özal claimed to believe that such a pipeline would create a new interdependency among Middle East states, though Arabs immediately saw it as a ripe provider of new disputes.

Arab governments are just as wary as the cynical Arab-in-the-souk. Far from promoting harmony, they said, the plan would greatly benefit Turkey while making the Arab countries dependent on Ankara, and might also lead to quarrels between the recipient countries – those at the end of the line might well worry about the possibility of damage in states traversed by the pipelines. Turkey would certainly gain economically if the plan went ahead; the aim would be to pump 6 million cubic metres per day to the south. Customers would pay about half the cost of water from a desalination plant. The Turkish water pipeline would be the largest water carrying project in the world, according to Texas-based Brown and Root, its proposed contractors. The north–south pipeline would extend over 6,000 kilometres from its source in southern Turkey to the southern tip of the Arabian peninsula, with branches to Kuwait, Qatar and the United Arab Emirates. Western branches would take the water into Lebanon and Israel.

When the project was first proposed, most Arab states rejected the idea of such a Middle East water complex, as the potential participants saw it as a means of extending Turkish hegemony over the whole area once again. Yet the growing need for water meant they could not reject it outright, and could not afford to offend Turkey. Both Syria and Jordan viewed it with intense suspicion, but they merely said diplomatically that they would have no need for imported water as they have enough from local resources. Their shortages, they argued, were caused by excessive use by Israel, and that country's diversion of Jordan water, something which might be rectified in a general Middle East peace agreement.

Despite the growing needs, opinion among Arab governments has been hardening against the water pipeline project, and the pace of work on the South-East Anatolia Project and tough statements by Turkish politicians have not made the Arabs any more understanding. Turkey's closure of the overland oil pipeline from Iraq during the Gulf war reinforced Arab prejudices against relying on the Turks for water. Syrian spokesmen have said flatly that the pipeline 'is not in a serious stage of discussion', though even they have been careful to keep the possibility alive.

In Amman, the deputy minister of Water Resources, Mutazz Belbeisi, who acknowledges that the proposed pipeline holds major political ramifications, says cautiously that Jordan has not rejected the scheme outright. The word from Turkish officials in Ankara is things are going rather better with Israel, and that an agreement has already been signed to deliver water to that country in huge rubber bags towed across the Mediterranean; however, the pipeline project has still not been accepted there either, though Shimon Peres, the Israeli foreign minister, called the Middle East 'a dry bomb', because of the lack of water, and seemed to be one of the few non-Turkish politicians to agree with the Turks that a pipeline would increase security and opportunity for all the people in the Middle East. That has made the Arabs even more suspicious. They believe that Turkey has ambitions to revive the Ottoman Empire, and there is no desire by any Arab state to relive that era of history. Growing Turkish–Israeli friendship forces them to be careful. But like Syria and Jordan, the other Arab countries try to be diplomatic in their rejection of Turkish offers: they argue on practical grounds that the initial costs of the pipelines would be more than it would take to build several new desalination plants, and that the price of the water from Turkey would not be so much cheaper than desalinated water as to recover the costs in a reasonable time. Suggestions that water deliveries should be linked to reciprocal oil contracts have failed to persuade any of the Arabs to reconsider their opposition.

What is being seriously considered is the possibility of water from Iran, something that makes more practical sense because the distances involved are much less, and better political sense because the

Arab Gulf states recognize they have to coexist with Iran. Both sides seem anxious to put in place confidence building measures. The main project being considered is to pipe Iranian water 1,800 kilometres overland to the Gulf coast, and then 200 kilometres through an underwater pipe to Qatar. The two countries have already signed agreements to take water from the source of the Karun river in western Iran. The pipeline would cost some US$13 billion, which Qatar will pay.

A feature of the Arabian peninsula is that few in government, or the ordinary inhabitants, yet seem to appreciate the importance of conserving water. Instead, it is the Arab's view of water as an ingredient of paradise that guides the planners. Although few Arabs would take literally the idea of paradise as an oasis full of running streams, water does have a strong hold on the collective imagination and plays an important part in Islamic ritual – a worshipper is enjoined to wash before praying and fountains are provided outside many mosques. So oil wealth is used to transform the dusty towns of the Gulf and Saudi Arabia into green oases, expensively maintained parks and even more expensive golf courses, to give a physical reminder of the rewards Islam offers in the hereafter. Yet this apparently agreeable and environmentally friendly plan carries the seeds of conflict. The greening of the cities takes not only money and water, but labour as well. All the countries of the Gulf are short of labour – in all but Saudi Arabia the native-born are in the minority, and even in Saudi Arabia the proportion of 'guest workers', mainly Yemenis, has at times reached 15 per cent of the total population. In Abu Dhabi, where Sheikh Zeid was the first to go in for greenery, it takes 5,000 Pakistani gardeners just to water, trim, plant and clear the roadside verges, the acres of bougainvillaea, the palm trees and all the rest that makes the capital of the United Arab Emirates such a surprise to the traveller expecting a desert city. Abu Dhabi relies partly on desalination for its water supplies (and has successfully combined this with electricity generation), as the underground water supplies are now totally unable to keep pace with the demand of the coastal cities, for irrigation and for what is known as 'urban beautification'. Up to the late 1960s, underground water was piped from the wells of Al-Ain oasis to the coast; now, that flow has been reversed. The same pipeline which used to bring water to Abu Dhabi town today supplies Al-Ain, twenty-five years ago a peaceful cluster of oases on the Oman–UAE border, but today an ugly, sprawling city bigger than the capital. And in a town where aqueducts carried sparkling water among the palm trees only a couple of decades ago, the pipeline now delivers nasty-tasting desalinated water from plants on the coast.

Of the total output of desalinated seawater in Abu Dhabi, 18 per cent now goes to Al-Ain while 35 per cent goes to Abu Dhabi city; 47 per cent is mixed with treated sewage and waste water and used to make the city green. The problem of watering the greenery appears to have been solved, but not the difficulties caused by those who do the work. Every extra mile of verdant roadside planting needs more workers, and those workers sprinkle more water on the plants and use more water themselves. It all adds to the burden on already over-stretched water resources, as well as putting additional strain on the social make-up of the city-states of the Gulf. The local people find themselves foreigners in their own land, and many are beginning to dislike the way things are going. In Dubai, one Arab travel agent told us he has had to learn Urdu to be able to talk to the bulk of his customers. In Qatar, officials have begun to question whether continued development is necessarily a good thing: more development means more workers, who in turn require more services, which means more plant has to be developed, and yet more workers are brought in, and so on. It is a cycle that many say should be broken: at some stage government should say enough is enough, and put an end both to development and to the import of more labour.

One hopeful idea has come from the Philippines, a major provider of labour to Gulf states for many years, and far enough away not to pose any threat. A Philippine–US consortium has suggested exporting water to the Gulf states, using oil tankers sailing back empty from Japan. Describing the idea as 'the flip side of the oil trade between Asia and the Middle East', a Philippine official said his country could offer water from a deep aquifer for sale in the Gulf at an extremely competitive price because the tankers to be used would be the same large crude carriers that transport oil to the Philippines and Japan. These tankers already stop periodically in the Philippines for dry-docking and repairs. The first contract would be for the supply of 225,000 cubic metres of irrigation water a day.

The argument for calling an end to the cycle of more development, more labour and more resources has been heard more frequently since the invasion of Kuwait. An unhappy consequence of that episode has been that Palestinians, never the most popular people among their fellow Arabs, have become the object of fear and suspicion in many countries. During the Iraqi occupation of Kuwait, the PLO under Yasser Arafat appeared to be supporting Saddam Hussein, so Kuwaitis suspected the large Palestinian community in their country of helping the invaders. After Iraq was forced out, the Kuwaitis took a savage and usually unmerited revenge on many Palestinians, most of whom had acted as perfectly loyal citizens and had done nothing to earn the punishment they received. There were some collaborators, of course, and unfortunately it was those the Kuwaitis chose to remember, not the many more who had nothing to do with the Iraqis. That attitude has rubbed off on to the other Gulf states, and Kuwait's policy of restricting its expatriate community to 40 per cent of total population is being studied in the other countries. It was certainly no accident that Saudi Arabia claimed to have become so incensed at Yemen's support for Iraq during the war that it took steps to induce many hundreds of thousands of Yemenis to leave the Kingdom for home. But instead of punishing Yemen, Saudi Arabia may have saved it from its own past excesses by providing it with the labour it needs at home to preserve its ancient irrigation system.

Yemen was the site of the worst dam disaster of ancient times when the Marib Dam collapsed in the sixth century AD, ruining a carefully cultivated area which had been developed over the previous 1,000 years, watered by laboriously dug channels and regulated by sluice gates. According to legend, the collapse came when a rat dislodged a vital boulder in the dam wall, leading to the inundation of a vast area, sweeping away the mountain terraces below the dam, breaking the water conduits and destroying the primitive sluice gates.

The water network was swept away in a night, and with it a highly developed agriculture that supported thousands of farmers and their families.

According to Tony Milroy, a British agricultural engineer now working in Yemen, a similar disaster is facing Yemen today. The only difference is that instead of the terraces and intricate system of water channels being swept away in hours, they have been gradually deteriorating over the past couple of decades. Yemenis have always been great travellers, well used to spending many years working overseas before returning to their own country to live comfortably from their accumulated earnings, so as the great oil boom began to transform the Gulf in the 1960s, young Yemeni men were easily persuaded to leave their villages to work in the oilfields or on the construction sites in surrounding countries. Then the transformation of Saudi Arabia began, and there were plenty of jobs there, even more easily accessible; whole Yemeni villages became denuded of young men, and often women too, leaving the care and upkeep of the terraces, fields and waterworks to the old and infirm. They could not cope, so the terraces crumbled, the highest, narrowest and least productive first, then those further down the mountain. Trees which prevented erosion were used for firewood as wars and revolutions led to a breakdown of the old regulations prohibiting deforestation, and without shade the grass would not grow. A quiet disaster was creeping up on the mountain villages, for all their regular heavy rainfall. With 400 to 700 millimetres a year, this is one of the few parts of Arabia where it was always quite possible to grow crops without irrigation, but the rain comes in sudden savage bursts, not the steady soaking of the northern hemisphere; if it is not controlled, it merely sweeps away topsoil, runs off into the valleys or dissipates through the rock and shale. The water has to be stored, controlled and guided, and the intricate system of terraces and channels did this; but if one went the others were affected, and if the trees at the highest levels were cut down the sparse soil of the upper terraces was swept away by the next spate.

Photographs taken twenty years apart show that mountains which were covered in vegetation are now bare rock, with terraces swept away and drifts of shale where water channels criss-crossed the mountainside. While the boom years lasted it mattered very little: the young men still went off to other countries to work, and there was always a need for more men to do the dirty jobs in Saudi Arabia that the locals would not touch. Now, the recession has hit the Arabian peninsula as well as the rest of the world, so Saudi Arabia used the excuse of the Gulf war to get rid of what it saw as an excess of immigrant labour. The Yemenis had to go, and though they went at first to the big towns and cities of their homeland, they found no work there either, so those who came from villages went back home. There, they were enlisted in the local schemes that may yet restore Yemen to the prosperity it once enjoyed through the marvel of the Marib Dam. With help and encouragement from the UN Development Programme – and from the British Arid Lands Initiative – the villagers are being encouraged to rebuild the terraces that catch the water and direct it gently down the mountainside network, to replant trees and to devise better ways of constructing and controlling water channels. With the spread of education, which according to the old men in the villages fits people only for town life, not for agriculture, the young men still speak wistfully of the golden years abroad, and a new generation dreams of travelling in search of fortune. But the worldwide recession and the blunt Saudi pressure to force the Yemenis to go home mean there is nothing to do but go back to the old ways. That may yet be the salvation of an ancient and effective system of land management, and by rehabilitating traditional agriculture may avoid unrest in a rapidly growing population.

Internal dissension combined with external aggression might stir trouble in Saudi Arabia and the other Gulf states, and the lack of water might indirectly contribute to it. The emphasis on oil production and oil-related industries in all these countries has led to a huge growth in the towns and cities, a rapid urbanization which has accelerated the natural tendency for rural people to leave their homes in search of better-paid work. In Asir province in the fertile south-western corner of Saudi Arabia, there are already abandoned farms, and villages with dozens of empty houses. The Saudi agricultural labour force is declining by 0.9 per cent a year according to government figures. At the same time, the high general per capita income means there is a growing demand for 'luxury' food – good quality meat, chicken and so on. But with the rising population and large immigrant labour force, the Kingdom's own food production is falling. In 1971, 55 per cent of Saudi Arabia's food was produced locally: today the figure is much lower, probably only about 30 per cent.

In one area Saudi Arabia makes a huge effort to grow what it wants, and in the process uses water that future generations will sorely miss. In 1970, Saudi wheat production, mainly in the Asir province, which in a good year gets as much as 500 millimetres of rain, was 26,000 tonnes. Today, production throughout the country is about 3.5 million tonnes. It may be the world's most expensive wheat; it is certainly the most water-costly of all.

This remarkable increase in output has been achieved at a high monetary and environmental cost – like Egypt, Saudi Arabia now expends 90 per cent of its water on agriculture. In the mid-1980s Saudi Arabia was the world's third largest food importer but in 1991 it became the world's sixth largest exporter of wheat; wheat production is heavily subsidized, with guaranteed producer prices several times the world price and estimated annual water consumption of eight billion cubic metres. The figures tell the story: in 1972 the Saudi government allocated US$190 million for agriculture; now, the figure is US$1.83 billion. In reality it is even higher, as farmers pay nothing for the water with which they irrigate their land. Only the Kingdom's vast oil income could have made possible the annual average growth of 14.6 per cent in agriculture between 1980 and 1990, most of it accounted for by cereal production rising ten-fold in that decade. Saudi Arabia today exports a surplus of about two million tonnes of wheat a year, after supplying all its own needs; it is also self-sufficient in dates and eggs, and soon will be in chicken meat, dairy products and vegetables. But everything depends on water, and recent events showed how fragile a resource that is. During Operation Desert Storm, when an extra half a million troops had to be supplied at a time when Saudi Arabia was forced to close down several of its desalination plants, the Kingdom could not cope. Bottled water was flown in from countries all round the area, often from as far away as the Mediterranean. The cost was huge, but was never quantified. It was perhaps offset by an even worse logistic failure by Iraq, which could not provide enough drinking water for its frontline troops in Kuwait. Many of the Iraqi soldiers who surrendered did so at least partly because they were thirsty.

The cost of the Saudi wheat growing programme has been US$1 billion a year in subsidies, but much worse has been the tragic depletion of the Kingdom's water resources, even though the most modern methods are being used and the efficiency of the system is about as good as can be obtained. Saudi Arabian hydrologists acknowledge that in some places they are using fossil water 30,000 years old, and that there is no chance of it being replaced.

To achieve the dramatic increase in wheat production, Saudi Arabia has relied mainly on the aquifer on the Jordan–Saudi border, and the profligate use it has made of this ancient, unrenewable reservoir means it will be exhausted in little more than another twenty years. One consequence has been increasingly strained relations between Jordan and the Kingdom, and a sense of bitterness towards Saudis by the people of Amman (where water is rationed), who believe the water should have gone into their domestic system and not been squandered on what they see as prestige projects in Saudi Arabia.

Saudi Arabian insistence on pushing up wheat production stems from 1973, when King Feisal led the move to use 'the oil weapon' in protest against what was seen as US support for Israel. The price went up from US$2 a barrel to US$12 within a few months in a demonstration of the power of the producers, led by the Arabs and warmly encouraged by Iran. Henry Kissinger, the world's super-diplomat, made sure that the Saudis and all the rest heard what he had to say: 'If they want to hit us with the oil weapon, we'll hit them with the food weapon.' For 'food', the Arabs correctly read 'wheat'. The USA remains the world's greatest grain grower and exporter, while all the Arab countries then had to import wheat. Fresh daily bread is the staff of life to all Arabs, and a government that failed to assure its supply would swiftly fall. King Feisal, wisest of all the Saudi monarchs, quietly ordered a new agricultural policy, redirecting some of the national investment away from industry, and adopting measures not only to try to keep people on the land but also to increase the 2.5 per cent of the land mass which was all that could be cultivated out of Saudi Arabia's 2.25 million square kilometres. Water cannot have seemed a problem to King Feisal: with oil revenues soaring, there was always money to buy what was needed. Another desalination plant? Fine. And another, and another ... In many ways, King Feisal was right. In 1970, the Kingdom's desalination plants were producing 23,000 cubic metres a day. Now, they produce 2.5 million cubic metres of potable water each day, and US$2 billion has been budgeted for new plants at Jeddah, Jubail and Yanbu. In the years since 1970, 200 dams have been built to collect water run-off, the number of wells has doubled to 4,717 and there are 1,300 reservoirs. It might seem that King Feisal's understandable belief that money could buy everything needed is correct: alas, it is not. Despite all the money spent, all the efforts made, all the building, well-boring and new desalination plants, the Kingdom is still short of water, and is having to tap into its deep fossil supplies to grow its wheat and provide its people with drinking water – though only 94 per cent of the population get it from a tap.

Despite the ill-feeling that Saudi use of the aquifer on the Jordan border has caused, the disparity in relative strengths as well as the fundamentally friendly relations between the two countries mean this is unlikely ever to lead to conflict. But it has caused a great deal of ill-feeling in Jordan. Amman, the capital, is desperately short of water, so that as well as general rationing, at times the different districts receive supplies on only one day a week. The Jordanians' sense of seeing 'their' water squandered, added to Saudi Arabian displeasure at Jordan's role during the invasion of Kuwait, has led to coldness between these two neighbours.

As in all countries heavily dependent on irrigated land for food production, Saudi Arabia is beginning to suffer the consequences of heavy use of fertilizers and the build-up of alkalinity owing to the concentration of salts in much of the water used. The problems caused by irrigation and over-pumping are now being realized, and a national water policy is being drawn up with an emphasis on conser-

vation. But until now there has been very little control in the Kingdom, with the result that there has been a fall in the quality of
available water, with seawater seeping in along the coast.

In neighbouring Yemen, some of the regulations have contributed
to the problem: a decree that wells should be 500 metres apart, for
instance, was taken by farmers as an encouragement to drill more
wells, rather than a restriction; they promptly put down wells every
500 metres, leading to serious depletion. Another regulation providing that well drilling in the Sanaa basin should be restricted to 5 per
cent of the area was generally ignored, with the result that between
20,000 and 25,000 wells were sunk, and the water level has fallen
dramatically. In neighbouring Oman, which has far greater reserves,
legislation has been introduced providing for fines for people illegally
digging wells. But in both these countries, as in the rest of the
Arabian peninsula, regulations cannot alter the main problem they
face: populations increasing more quickly than the resources available to them.

9

Ancient Desert Rules and International Law

A lone figure dressed all in black, tall and proud-stepping, materializes out of the mirage formed by the intense heat where the dry sky glare meets the hostile desert. As he slowly moves forward, his attitude becomes tense, and his eyes blaze with hatred as he reaches the well. There, a stranger plunges his head into the water to slake his thirst then looks up in sudden terror. With a single stroke of his sword, the man in black strikes off the wet head of a man taking more than his due. 'He was sullying my well,' the executioner explains.

This scene is taken from the film *Lawrence of Arabia*, based on a passing reference in *The Seven Pillars of Wisdom*, and though it is a mythic event it still gives a graphic illustration of the harsh reality of the desert and a clear warning that water in the arid environment of the Middle East is a matter of life and death. The tableau shows, too, the uncompromising rigidity of the laws and rules that grew out of the customs of the desert. A thirsty man can drink from another man's well, but only in the manner prescribed: he should lower a container, and the water in the container will become his property; but he must not dive into the water or immerse himself, which would pollute the well.

For centuries the history of the desert lands of the Middle East centred on the wells and watercourses as tribes followed the vegetation with their herds and traders staged from well to well as they opened up the great caravan routes. In this century, Arabs and Turks, with the occasional involvement of the British, Germans, Egyptians and Jews, fought for control of the wells along the desert routes to determine the outcome of the First World War in the dry and hostile wastes of Arabia.

Eighty years on these old adversaries are still fighting over scarce and quickly diminishing water resources, though they are now provided with more destructive weapons thanks to the riches provided by oil – the resource to which the water is a key. Whoever controls water or its distribution can dominate the Middle East and all its riches.

The cinematic scene at the well demonstrates another truth: water cannot be owned. What can be controlled is the means by which it is transported or distributed. Only when there is a dispute does water itself become a strategic commodity, to be denied to an enemy or even contaminated in a way no desert-dweller would normally consider. At times a whole civilization can be wiped out by the destruction of an irrigation system, as the Moguls did with the Persians, or the Iraqis are now trying to do to the Marsh Arabs. In times of peace – or non-war, for that is the reality in the Middle East today – there are other rules, and today there is a slowly evolving set of basic criteria to complement the customs that for decades succeeded, in general, in organizing the sharing of water resources. When the system failed, as it often did, it led to bloody conflict, but on a small scale among tribes or between villages. But the map of the Middle East has changed, the tribes have acquired flags and national boundaries, and the customs and rules that were once effective in governing water sharing between cousins and tribes related by blood no longer work when the cousins have become sovereign nations.

The increase in demand for water for agriculture, industry, river navigation and municipal and domestic use in recent years has not been matched by a corresponding increase in attention from experts and academics in the field of international relations. The few who have concerned themselves with the new problems soon realized that it is only a matter of time before water becomes a valuable commodity for many societies and nations in a number of regions in the world – the Middle East is not the only place where water crises and disputes exist, but it is the region in which the potential for conflict over water is at its most extreme, and where a long history of war, as well as of border disputes, plus the presence of oil make the need for binding international agreements most pressing, even though history gives little confidence that international laws can avert wars in the area. To complicate matters, though the region is generally treated as a whole, it is full of contradictory values, ranging from those of the desert, shaped by the needs of nomads, to the ideas of the shepherds of the plains and the farmers and urbanized people of the few areas rich in water. And the regional and local rules, no matter how contemporary they might seem, were founded on values that grew out of religious and social customs, and as a result were often more rigid than the harshest of state-made laws.

Often, one set of customary laws is in conflict with newer codes of laws and regulations forced on a state by colonial rulers, then modified again by the new entities recently born. One example is in the West Bank, where the Israeli military occupation is selective in applying Ottoman or Jordanian law, or the new military orders, something that adds to the burden of occupation and deepens the sense of oppression of the Palestinians. They believe – on apparently good evidence – that the Israeli occupiers manipulate the mass of regulations available to them to deprive the Palestinians of their fair share of water. 'One rule allocates each Palestinian in the West Bank less than fifteen bathtubs full of his legally owned water every year,' says law consultant Dr Anis al-Qasem. 'Another set of rules allows the neighbouring illegal settlers to fill their swimming pools from the same water resources.'

Inter-state disagreements reflect the same state of affairs, with the powerful seeking to impose their will on the weaker. Without water-sharing agreements one state can limit water flow to others, as Turkey did to Syria and Iraq in January 1990 when it stopped the flow of the Euphrates to fill the Atatürk Dam. At the same time, Cairo received reports that Israel was helping Ethiopia to erect dams on the Blue Nile, threatening to lower Egypt's water levels. In both those cases, diplomacy took over and the situation was resolved peacefully – at the time. But the potential for conflict was there and has not disappeared.

At the end of 1992 an Egyptian Supreme Court Judge, Dr Awad el Moor, set out his country's position: 'No rigid international rule . . . can be equally applied to all riparians.' The same judge, from the highest legal circle in Egypt, was asked about outside help – that is, Israeli help – being given to Ethiopia to build dams on the Blue Nile. His reply left little doubt about the way Egypt would interpret international law when the Nile was involved. 'Egypt will never tolerate or accept the construction of any projects that affect the flow of the Nile or the amount of water reaching the Egyptian part of the Nile,' the Judge said.

In the same way, the Turks impose their own legal interpretation of the situation when they claim that the Euphrates is a Turkish river within the national boundaries. 'We don't tell Arabs what to do with oil in their land, so they mustn't tell us what to do with water in our land,' say Turkish officials, adopting the line set by Süleyman Demirel.

In addition to minimizing the danger of conflict, there is another reason today for trying to codify the use of water resources. Environmental issues demonstrate an urgent need to balance optimum use of water resources with concern for the environment, as well as a need to husband resources for the future. International laws are needed to protect natural water from the excesses of man and to safeguard contiguous areas; projects in the upper reaches of international rivers can clearly affect those downstream. Turkish and Syrian projects on the Euphrates and the Tigris, for example, would affect the quantity, quality and type of water draining into the Persian Gulf, thereby affecting the environment of countries geographically outside the basin of the two rivers.

Today, water use is increasingly attracting the attention of international lawyers, a tribe quick to spot the lucrative potential of new concerns. There is much to do: there are no international guidelines on inter-state water share, for example, which is left to the international courts to decide on the strength of legal arguments, if the case gets that far. More often, it is left to the military on the ground to take the decision in the Middle East.

The attempts by the International Law Association and its UN-appointed commission to address the issue of inter-state water share are fairly recent, as the earliest efforts go back only to the Helsinki conference of 1966. In the Middle East the first serious attempt at regulation was the Johnston plan, which called for permanent international supervision of the Jordan basin, including water sharing, approval of new projects and settlement of disputes. The credit for addressing the issue most forcefully must be given to the World Bank, established after the Second World War to develop a rational and effective way of exploiting natural resources. By the end of 1991, the Bank had lent US$19 billion for irrigation and drainage, US$12 billion for water supplies and sewerage, and about US$3 billion for hydro-power projects, an apparently impressive total of 13 per cent of Bank lending. World Bank officials say that they believe such water-related activity will increase, since their studies – recognized as the most comprehensive and accurate – indicate that twenty-two countries have renewable water resources providing less than 1,000 cubic metres per capita, the accepted level to indicate water shortage. It is claimed that the World Bank has through its practices laid the groundwork for rules and principles governing treaties and accords between states sharing a watercourse, and its work should become an important base for developing international law.

The World Bank rules were developed as a result of economic necessity: the Bank had to make sure there was a proper return on its investment, and to do so, had to ensure that there were water resources to carry out a project. 'The political will to cooperate in the international integration of river basin development makes it easier for the World Bank,' according to Guy LeMoinge, one of the Bank's senior advisers on agriculture and water resources. 'We cannot supply funding unless there's agreement between the various countries,' he told the *Christian Science Monitor* in 1990.

The first procedural guideline for the World Bank staff was formulated in 1956, about the time Johnston was in the Middle East drawing up his ambitious plans and the Americans – at the insistence of the

British – were pressuring the Bank to turn down Egypt's application to finance the Aswan High Dam. In 1949 the Bank's policy was to avoid making loans for projects involving disputed waters, but it found that did not stop the applications coming in. One test was the Indus system, where India wanted to build the Bhakra Dam and the Nangal project while Pakistan wanted the lower Sind Barrage. So in making loans the Bank moved on to require agreement among the riparian countries on the use of waters of international rivers before it would consider financing a project. The same criterion was applied to Egypt and Sudan in 1956, and to Syria and Turkey in 1950.

As history has shown, this policy could only work if the state embarking on a project had no means of financing the work except the World Bank. In practice, Egypt went to the Soviet Union and paid no attention to the World Bank when it was confronted with the need to reach agreement with its neighbours, while Israel relied on finance from Western Jewish sources to build its controversial national water carrier. In the 1980s, Turkey severely damaged its own economy by financing the development of the Euphrates rather than agreeing to try to negotiate with Syria and Iraq – and also helped to bring a bloody Kurdish war on its head.

The World Bank also faced a dilemma when development projects could not be held up until international law agencies settled a dispute. One example was the Ghab project in Syria in 1950, involving the drainage of a swampy area of about 32,000 hectares and its conversion into irrigated land, and the change of another 13,000 hectares from rain-fed to irrigated agriculture. The Bank considered four different approaches:

1 To treat the river and its basin as one unit and consider projects only if they were part of a comprehensive scheme.
2 To require the assent of all riparian states.
3 To follow the doctrine of established use and recognize only vested rights.
4 To follow the flexible approach and treat each project on its own apparent merits and effects.

In the event the bank opted for the flexible approach, thus setting an interesting precedent that not only helped the Bank to establish its own guidelines, but could also be used as a model for future agreements. In reaching the decision to finance the project the Bank had three considerations in mind: there were no threats to the project from an upstream riparian; a downstream riparian could not lodge a substantive protest with the Bank claiming that the project was causing harm to its existing uses; and neither the upstream nor the downstream riparian could lodge a substantive protest on account of damage to potential uses. The Bank was determined not to permit any other watercourse country to veto the project, and to make sure of that undertook a comprehensive study of the legal and technical aspects in order to be able to offer informed advice that unsubstantiated protests would be disregarded. The conclusion reached by the Bank was that there was no real risk to the project from an upstream riparian, the project benefited the river valley downstream by controlling winter floods and there would be a sufficient summer flow of water below the area to be drained under the project.

There was then a long delay of three decades before the next positive contribution, this time from the United Nations General Assembly. On 15 December 1980 it voted to accept Resolution 35/163, which paved the way for the International Law Commission (ILC) to draft a statute organizing the non-navigational uses of international watercourses. The committee presented the General Assembly with a draft of seventeen articles, which are still the subject of discussion and amendment. This is not surprising, as they were intended to regulate the use of water from shared resources, ensure equitable use, organize sharing and exchange of data, protect the environment and minimize pollution, control water projects, provide basic legal criteria for controlling the flow of rivers, ensure the security of water and hydraulic installations, settle existing water disputes and reduce the possibilities of new ones.

Like the World Bank, ILC experts are faced with legal, technical and political difficulties. There is, for example, the problem of definitions. Finding a term that would accurately define a water resource that crosses borders between states is a typical exercise. It has been called: 'contiguous waters', 'non-national', 'boundary', 'successive' or 'transboundary'. Add to all that some concepts and words used to describe rivers that could, in the same or related legal or political documents, refer to the same watercourse: 'the river basin', 'drainage basin', 'international river', 'river system', 'international watercourse' and 'international watercourse system'. All these terms are still in use, especially in situations where one or more parties to a dispute are deliberately trying to sow confusion. However, the International Law Association at its fifty-first conference in Helsinki in 1966 did manage to adopt the term 'drainage basin', and laid down that 'An international drainage basin is a geographical area extending over two or more states determined by the watershed limits of the system of waters, including surface and underground waters, flowing into a common terminus.' This is progress. When it came to the question of underground aquifers whose limits cannot easily be defined, the story was even more complicated. Because many borders in the Middle East are disputed, even if a convention could be drawn up it is difficult to see how it could be applied or who would enforce it.

The seventeen-article draft convention, also known as the Helsinki Principles for the Use of International Rivers (HPUIR), was a major step forward, seen by many as a useful starting point from which to develop an international law for cross-boundary rivers and waterways, since the articles summarized already existing legal principles accepted by many nations. Yet there was also criticism of what it did not contain, particularly in regard to the Middle East. Of overriding concern was the question of the legality of diverting water outside the river basin, as in the case of Israel with the Jordan, Litani or Yarmouk, Egypt's offer to give Nile water to Israel, Turkey's planned sale of Euphrates water to Israel, Jordan and the Gulf States, or Pakistan's suggestion of shipping water to the UAE. The proposed convention also failed to provide guidelines on sharing the cost of collecting international water data, on sharing the data or on organizing cooperation in controlling the river flow.

The HPUIR were based in turn on four basic principles of international law accepted during the forty-eighth session of the International Law Association in September 1958 in New York. These laid down that: each river or lake system draining into a single basin must be treated as one integrated unit, not separate systems; unless agreed in separate treaties or accords, every state on the system has the right to a reasonably equitable use of the water within the system draining into the basin; the states sharing the basin must respect the legal rights of other states in the basin; and there has to be a commitment to respect the rights of other riparians, which in turn means a duty to bar others from violating the rights of the riparian states.

These guidelines have not become a legally binding law that might deter a potential aggressor from usurping a water resource, nor could they be used to defuse a possible conflict over water. The Helsinki Principles have become a useful basis for settling some disputes in cases being legally tested, and have perhaps influenced some parties who were already interested in formulating bilateral or multilateral accords on the use of shared water resource. The legal problems are huge, and do not relate merely to the pedantic use of legal terminology; there are political, economic and social considerations and, in addition, the tremendous added difficulty of the religious interpretation of water laws, particularly in Islamic countries.

By the forty-third session of the ILC in June 1991, the draft of the proposed convention on the Non-navigational Uses of International Watercourses had grown from seventeen articles in 1980 to thirty-two. International lawyers, including many from the Middle East, saw this as marking a successful conclusion of the task given to them by the UN back in 1970. As usual, the articles were transmitted through the UN Secretary General to member states for their comments and observations. At the time of writing fewer than a handful of nations had responded – none from the Middle East.

One significant phenomenon was the change in emphasis of the draft as it went along, with those responsible usually reflecting the concerns of their own countries. Two competing principles were involved: the first refers to the right of a riparian state to 'equitable and reasonable utilization' as set out in articles 5 and 6. The second was the obligation of all riparian states 'not to cause appreciable harm' in the course of its use of water, as stated in article 7. Not surprisingly, the first principle is held to be most important by upstream riparians, as it benefits them most, while downstream states or the ones that were the first to be developed put the emphasis on the latter principle, since, historically, downstream riparians – especially those near the sea – have been technologically, demographically and economically more advanced than the upstream states; Egypt and Iraq are obvious examples.

Another feature noted is a third principle that can bridge the huge gap created by the contradictions of the two opposing principles: 'The general obligation to cooperate in the attainment of optimal utilization and adequate protection of international watercourses', as referred to in article 8. Since cooperation in the Middle East is still a hope rather than a reality, it is only natural to conclude that the relationship between the first and second obligations, i.e. the equitable utilization and the prevention of appreciable harm, is not free from controversy.

A country like Jordan, as an upstream riparian from Israel, would obviously benefit more from the draft giving priority to the equitable utilization of a watercourse, the Jordan River. Yet the country's international lawyers and hydrologists rejoice at the current emphasis on prevention of appreciable harm. 'We are pleased for Egypt, as the big sister will be the first to benefit from the rule,' said a Jordanian lawyer who is one of King Hussein's advisers. Thus does Western logic, which puts one's own benefit first, seem to come to grief in the Middle East. There is little doubt that Israel would use the doctrine to prevent Jordan from developing projects that would affect Israel's share of water. But this would equally give the Jordanians the right to invoke such principles against Syria. What the Jordanians really have in mind is much more complicated. They believe that 'prevention of appreciable harm' would enable Egypt to stop Ethiopia from interfering with the Blue Nile. That, plus, perhaps, completion of the Jonglei Canal, would enable Egypt to revive the idea of diverting about 1 per cent of the annual flow of the Nile to Palestine and Israel. And that, according to the Jordanians, would finally solve the problems of the Jordan Valley and its inhabitants, Palestinians, Israelis and Jordanians alike.

The main concern in the Middle East, however, is the realization that regulations and recommendations by the UN International Law Commission are not binding, and that there is a great deal of confusion over the interpretation and meaning of water rights, especially if there is an inter-state use of one water resource, either a river or underground, extending across national borders. The members of the International Law Commission admit that conflict between obligations makes it inevitable that rules must enjoy some kind of elasticity, giving an impetus towards negotiations between interested parties – a conclusion very similar to that reached much earlier by the World Bank. In the Middle East, so far, negotiation in general has been seen by the stronger as a means to perpetuate the status quo or indefinitely to postpone the inevitable; and by the weaker as a means of keeping the world's attention on its plight, with the hope of changing the status quo in its favour one day.

Napoleon once noted that treaties usually omit more than they contain. In the latest draft of the ILC's thirty-two articles, there are certainly some omissions. One is diversion of the watercourse outside its natural basin, such as Israel's piping of the water from the upper Jordan via the national carrier to the Negev desert. Another criticism levelled against the latest draft is that it does not allocate some active role for the existing organizations to persuade riparians to implement the recommendations on exchange of data, vital to help preparations for flood or drought. The third criticism is the lack of provision for dealing with disputes related to confined underground water. While article 2 defines a watercourse as 'a system of surface and underground waters constituting by virtue of this physical relationship a unity and flowing into a common terminus', the draft did not refer to confined water sources at all. Yet these could well lead to conflict in the arid conditions of the Middle East. The Egyptians, for example, are far from happy about Colonel Gaddafi's plan for his Great Man-made River, as they fear a lack of proper studies by the Libyans might lead to a harmful effect on their western aquifer. Equally, in November 1992 the Jordanian minister of agriculture accused the Saudis of over-using their share of the common aquifer that crosses the border beneath the two nations.

The lack of clear interpretation of international law in the water flashpoints of the Middle East will only help to aggravate the already tense situation and perpetuate the existing imbalances in the exploitation of water – often based on certain states being the militarily and politically dominant powers. Thus countries downstream cannot challenge the military superiority of those upstream, as in the case of Iraq and Syria versus Turkey. Strong downstream countries use their military might to take more than their fair share of available waters, and regularly imply that they might take action that would threaten the stability of upstream countries if they attempted to develop hydrological projects on the shared watercourse: Israel against Jordan, Lebanon, Syria and the West Bank Palestinians; Egypt against Ethiopia and Sudan.

Militarily or politically weaker countries who might feel that the world has turned a deaf ear to their grievances would see their water resource diminished owing to unfair use by a powerful neighbour. At the same time, their populations would grow, ultimately facing them with a crisis from which they could only escape by linking the water issue with something else that might induce international intervention. Thus the world superpowers and the international organizations might eventually be forced to intervene to implement a comprehensive settlement in the Middle East, involving all issues, including water.

In a simpler argument, countries not in a position to force powerful neighbours to reach a fair settlement on use of water might start a war that would put Western interests at risk, again forcing an intervention. Since they could not win a war single-handedly against the neighbour who threatens their water supplies, they would create an unstable situation leading to a general regional conflict. In this weaker states would hope to achieve two aims: first, to secure allies against a powerful neighbour; second, to force a war on the international community, which would lead to water issues being on the agenda for general settlement.

One example of this came when Ethiopia called on Israel to help what appeared to be a project to build dams on the Blue Nile. Israeli involvement would minimize the danger of an Egyptian attack on the project because of Egyptian fears of upsetting fifteen years of peace with Israel. Another example is the policy of the current fundamentalist regime in Sudan of harbouring and aiding Islamic terrorists active in southern Egypt. Sudan believes that if it foments a small civil war in the south of Egypt it will be easier to persuade a weakened Cairo to settle water disputes before an international tribunal, rather than by force of Egyptian arms.

The niceties – and the idiocies – of international law can obviously hold up progress as well as facilitate it in the hands of experienced lawyers. In the Middle East, there is a further layer of difficulty and potential obfuscation in addition to the potential for error and delay already provided by the well-meaning international agencies: religion. Born in the deserts of the Arabian peninsula, Islam is deeply concerned with water, and makes it central to its rituals. In the Koran and the *hadith*, the traditional accounts of the Prophet's words and actions, water is used as a metaphor time and again. An Islamic image of life might be of an increasingly weary desert traveller striving to reach the oasis, the Muslim paradise of a garden laced with streams of running water. Yet Islam is not a monolithic religion, nor is it the only belief throughout the region; the result is a mosaic of different customs and practices, and separate criteria governing the use of shared watercourses. Most of the area is either administered in accordance with Islamic law – the *sharia* – or is influenced by it; the influence of Islam, for example, has its effect on the conduct of negotiations by the Palestinian delegation in their meetings with Israeli officials.

The word *sharia* is derived from an Arabic word for water. According to the fourteenth-century Arab lexicographer Ibn Mandhur, the *sharia* is the source from which one descends to water. In pre-Islamic times, the *sharia* was accepted by Arabs as the body of rules governing the use of water – *shuraat al-maa* – permits allowing people to drink. Scholars believe the word was later 'stretched' to encompass the wider meaning of laws and regulations that were a gift from God, and to take in the Muslim belief that water is the most pure and sacred of all those gifts.

The centrality of water to the Arabs has continued from pre-

Islamic times right down to the present day. The legend of Hagar was known before the revelations of the Prophet, but is included in the Koran: it tells how Hagar was left with her baby Ismael in the desert at the foot of Mount Arafat. As she was about to lose consciousness because of thirst and heat, she put down Ismael, who was in equal distress. In his fit, the baby kicked the sand with his feet repeatedly, eventually revealing a damp patch where Hagar was able to find water. Today, it is the desire of every devout Muslim to visit Mecca and to drink from the well of Zamzam which Ismael revealed.

The *sharia* rules on water are in general linked to those concerning the use and ownership of land. Most Muslim jurists divide land into two categories: the inhabited, used, owned or legally exploited; and that which is dead, arid, deserted, has never been owned, claimed or used by anyone and is not connected or annexed to the first category. Dealing with unowned land, the Muslim jurists take as their starting point the injunction of the Prophet: 'Three resources are common and people should share them equally: fire, grazing grass and water.'

As Islam developed – very rapidly – from a revolution into a state and then into an empire, so its laws had to be extended and interpreted, and applied to alien lands as Islam spread through conquest. Common use of water was not enough: the jurists noted that the Koran encouraged the revival of dead land, for which the use of water was essential. This in turn led to an interpretation giving a value added to water by labour, when moving water for distribution or using it to develop land.

In the fourteenth century, experts at Al Azhar university in Cairo, then as now one of the great seats of Islamic scholarship, suggested the use of the profit motive, by which developers of dead land could become the legal owners. This principle is still applied today, and has encouraged people to develop land and use scarce water to establish ownership. This phenomenon has been seen particularly in Saudi Arabia, where entrepreneurs tried to claim ownership of large plots of land in the hope of finding oil, and in the process of claiming ownership used water in a half-hearted effort at cultivation at enormous environmental and economic expense.

The *sharia* holds that water is a gift of God that should not be owned or controlled to the point of excluding others from using it, though the traditional shared use was limited to drinking and watering animals and the symbolic purifying of the body for prayer. The general legal view, traditional and modern, is that it is impossible to own water unless it is stored. The *sharia*, like law everywhere, is burdened with interpretation, often contradictory, and also relies heavily on precedents, so that there is no escape from history, another recipe for conflict in the Middle East.

There are three categories of water under the *sharia*: rivers, springs and wells. Rivers then have sub-categories: great rivers, from beyond the borders; lesser rivers within national borders; and artificially created rivers, canals, irrigation channels or aqueducts. In the first category, the flow is so great that there is no need to quarrel over it, and the Islamic rule is clear: that nobody should deny the use of that water to any human or animal. In the second category, the *sharia* lays down that if one of the lesser rivers has enough water flow for those who dwell in its vicinity (the river basin) then they must share its use generally, with no one person or group having the right to exclude any other from its use. But if the water is not sufficient, then there are recommendations about constructing barrages and other means of storing water, so that the water is then shared by those who live in the vicinity (the basin) in accordance with an order of priority starting with those who built the means of storage. In the third category, water held or flowing in artificial canals, there is common use for those who constructed the project or dug the canal, and distribution is determined according to available volume. If there is enough, then the rule of common sharing applies, but if that is not the case, then priority is given to those who dug the canal. If they are too many for the water available, then shares are apportioned according to how much each has contributed to the project and to its maintenance.

There is very little literature by contemporary Islamic groups or governments setting out a policy on water, but their thinking seems to be based on the lines of the second and third categories detailed in the *sharia*. Unusually, Islamic lawyers recognize the need for a change of definition that is being forced on them by the economic necessity of modern times – unusually, since they do not often accept the need to modify the teachings of Islam in other areas.

Dealing with wells, the *sharia* again classifies them into three groups based on the intention of the person or the group who first dug the well. The first is a well on a public highway dug for the benefit of travellers and their animals. No one, including the person who dug it, has any right to claim ownership or to control the way people use it. The second is the water of a well dug for a specific purpose, with a period of use, which then becomes the private property, for a set time, of the people who dug it. Once the period announced or the purpose of digging it has been completed, then it becomes public and those who dug it have to join the queue like everyone else. The third category is the private well, either on private land or on land claimed as owned while its cultivation depends on the use of this well.

Last comes the issue of spring waters, which are accepted as a natural resource. Muslim scholars divide them into three categories along lines similar to those of river waters. The water of a spring 'which God caused to come to the surface' is free for the use of all mankind, as long as it is available in sufficient quantity. If the amount of water is limited, then its use is restricted to those who dwell in its immediate vicinity. The second category is the water of springs 'which human beings uncovered and caused to flow'. This is held in common by those who uncovered the spring and caused the water to flow. If the amount of water is large enough, then use should be extended to give those in the vicinity of the spring the right to take what they need from it. On the question of ownership, the *sharia* regards those who uncovered the spring as its joint owners. The third category is the water of a spring uncovered by someone on his own land, where ownership is not disputed. Yet this right is not absolute. The *sharia* obliges the owner to offer, free of charge, any surplus water to others who may wish to take advantage of it.

Throughout history these rules were regarded more as guidelines than as statutory law, and interpretation varied, though the basic principle remained – that water was a gift from God, to which a value could be added by labour. Over the centuries, the *sharia* recommendations about water sharing, and the injunctions against withholding, misusing or polluting water, became the cornerstone of legislation passed by Islamic governments. The Ottoman Empire used the *sharia* as the basis for its water law in the civil code known as *Al majalla othmaniyah*, in which eighty-two articles deal with water. Those articles became an important source for the codification of Islamic law in the Levant, and remain the residual legislation for Iraq, Syria, Lebanon, Jordan and Palestine-Israel.

In the late seventeenth and eighteenth centuries there was a transformation in the Levant under Ottoman rule, with the rules of the *sharia* and the body of precedents being codified into legislation that was also affected by the influence of the French colonists. This helped to establish a more comprehensive approach to water sharing in the Levant and other countries under both Ottoman and French influence.

The Ottoman *majalla* redrafted the original laws after incorporating the French legislation known as *Code des eaux*, and these were still the rules governing water use in places like Mauritania (1921), Lebanon (1926) and Tunisia and Algeria (as late as the 1970s). Countries that came under British influence had a different approach based on customary usage, *sharia* and other rules, like Turkey, Saudi Arabia and most Gulf countries, Jordan, Libya, Sudan and Yemen. Egypt, however, was an interesting case: it was in the heart of the Ottoman Empire, came under strong French influence, and was occupied by the British in 1882. From that time it was the British who influenced the irrigation and educational systems and the army, right up to 1956; yet Egypt never implemented the *sharia*, any of the Ottoman laws or the *Code des eaux*, but kept the ancient traditional ways related to the Nile, showing once again how the state and the river together make Egypt.

While Islamic law was used by the Ottomans to promote unity and stability, today it is being used by Muslim groups as a disruptive force in their attempt to destroy what they consider an infidel society (*takfir almujtama*) in order to build the Islamic *umma* from the ruins. Water is a major weapon in their armoury.

Water is one of the basic components of Islam. 'From water we have created every organism in the universe,' God says in the Koran. Not only is water at the centre of the promised paradise, in this life it is essential for the purifying of body, mind, heart and soul before prayer. It is a ritual, a form of baptism, carried out five times a day to cleanse the organs that not only distinguish man from beast but also help him to recognize and worship God and perform the functions of everyday life. They are the means of thinking, seeing, hearing, eating, speaking, travelling and doing. Before each prayer a Muslim is required to wash the head, the eyes, the ears, the mouth and lips, the feet, the hands and the forearms with fresh water. Without this act the worshipper's prayer is not heard. Therefore, the right of a mortal to control water flow, even if it is on his or her own property, is disputed on the basis that barring people from using water to purify themselves, or charging them to do so, is committing a grave sin by interfering with the duty to worship God.

Basing their reasoning on this interpretation, Islamic fundamentalists issued a number of *fatwas* laying down that water laws issued by a non-Muslim authority such as the Jewish state or the Israeli military administrators in the West Bank were unlawful; another *fatwa* was directed against the Lebanese Christian government. Fundamentalists argue that barring Muslims of the West Bank from the free use of water found, sprung or running in their vicinity is not only an act of aggression against them but also an affront to God, so that it becomes the duty of every Muslim to launch a sacred crusade to free the water from the control of Jews, infidels and anti-Mohammedans.

A number of related *fatwas* issued by the Gammaat Islamiyah group in Egypt and Sudan, which is supported by Iranian extremists, worries the Egyptian authorities. An Islamic government in Khartoum could be forced to accept the arguments of the Islamic groups that some key articles in water agreements with Egypt contradict the *sharia*, violate Muslim rights to worship God, and are therefore null and void. The fundamentalists point out that such accords were concluded under infidel British dominion. Egyptian officials have responded by warning that any attempt in Sudan to interfere with the flow of the Nile would be a *casus belli*.

Egypt is one of the places that, although conquered by the Arabs in the seventh century, has water regulations based not on the *sharia* but on customary laws derived from ancient Egyptian and Coptic tradition that developed for thousands of years before the emergence of Mohammed in Arabia in the seventh century AD. This is anathema to Islamic fundamentalists. Sheikh Omar Abd el-Rahman, the emir – the prince or leader – of the largest Egyptian Islamic group, al-Gamaat Islamiyah, was the man who issued the *fatwa* to the fundamentalist army officer Lieutenant Islamboli and his three partners to murder President Anwar Sadat. One of the reasons for the authorization to murder was the president's proposal to cement peace between Israel and the Palestinians by offering Nile water to be shared by both. The sheikh was charged in 1982 with conspiracy to murder, but during the trial his followers made sure their testimony and admissions would not implicate their emir, so that he was released. Sheikh Abd el-Rahman, who at the time of writing this book was thought to be connected with suspects in the February 1993 bombing of the World Trade Centre in New York, now lives in New Jersey, from where he has issued another *fatwa*, copied by other principals of Muslim groups, ruling that the policy of the Cairo government in applying universal man-made laws to govern the use of water by Muslims is contradictory to the *sharia*.

Members of these groups admit that water is a useful means to achieve their ends. Interviewed in Cairo, they cited a *fatwa* of a medieval scholar Imam Safhie, forbidding any individual or group from turning water on their land into a monopoly: 'If a person takes over a piece of land which includes running water on its surface, notwithstanding that at the time of possession no one was benefiting from the water, he is still obliged by *sharia* to allow others to share it equally with him.'

The well-armed fighters of Gamaat Islamiyah, who have spread terror in Upper Egypt and created no-go areas for the Egyptian police, have now started harassing Copts, either by extorting tax from them or by applying *sharia* principles to the use of water that runs in plots of land inhabited and exclusively owned or cultivated by Copts. Given the central role of water to the ancient Egyptians, and what Copts consider their national rights predating the introduction of the *sharia*, then they can be expected to resist any interference with irrigation and their right to use water. The deliberate provocation by Gamaat Islamiyah must inevitably lead to Copts carrying arms to protect those rights. While, in the past, clashes over water were limited to quarrels between villages or between the owners of one *houdh* (a strip of irrigated land alongside the Nile bank) and their neighbours to the south, regardless of their ethnic origins or religious affiliation, new clashes could take place at any time along sectarian lines.

Muslim law states clearly that it is the duty of the imam, the emir or the ruler to force the public to obey *sharia* commands, including those related to water. This worries non-Muslims who fear that an Islamic authority might force the *sharia* on a non-Muslim population in a river basin, or even on a neighbouring state downstream.

The contrast between the complexities of modern life and the simplicities of Islamic fundamentalist efforts to apply the old simple black-and-white *sharia* rules has become an increasing cause of worry as far as water is concerned. The fundamentalists are using water as a way of involving themselves in other disputes, and hope to cause such dissension that they will be able to install local or national Islamic regimes. And they are active in many trouble spots: stirring Muslim–Copt rivalry in Upper Egypt; using Sudan as a base to attack Egypt; fomenting trouble between Senegal and Mauritania over the Senegal river; using the cover of Hizbollah in Southern Lebanon to fight Israel and the Christian Maronites, partly to prevent 'theft' of the Litani waters; with Hamas in the West Bank and Gaza Strip, rallying the faithful with the idea that the Israeli occupiers have no right to regulate water supplies; using the Muslim Brotherhood movement in Northern Syria near the borders with Turkey; and stirring up Shia groups in eastern Saudi Arabia who believe they still do not have the same rights as the Sunni inhabitants of the Kingdom.

Another way in which the *sharia* could become a disruptive influence is in the tendency by some lawyers, often acting for such rich Islamic states as Saudi Arabia, to argue that international law guidelines for water utilization in the Middle East should embrace the *sharia.* Dr Chibli Mallat, an Islamic lawyer, has argued that there are precedents in the use of domestic law by the International Court of Justice. He also saw the *sharia* as a source of international law, recalling that in 1945 at a meeting of the UN Committee of Jurists the delegations of the Muslim states of the Near East argued for the necessity to include the *sharia* as one of the principal legal systems on which international law was based.

10

The Dangerous Future

The main question at the heart of this book is whether states could use water to impose their will, and whether countries affected would decide that military means were an effective way of restoring the balance. Can an upstream state 'turn off the taps'? The message delivered by the Turks when they filled the Atatürk Dam seemed to be: yes, it is possible to deprive a neighbour of a flow of water usually received. Can a downstream state that is militarily more powerful impose its will on a neighbour that controls its water resources? The lesson from Israel seems to show that this, too, is possible. But there is an alternative way of looking at it, as such politicians as King Hussein of Jordan, President Özal of Turkey, President Sadat of Egypt and UN Secretary General Boutros-Ghali have all recognized: they all noted that while water could be a cause of war it could also be an excellent focus for inter-state cooperation. Equally, political rhetoric often does not affect technical cooperation, which may well continue quietly while the politicians rant, although water management has necessarily been politicized. Apart from local tensions, one reason for this, which could be overcome, is that the consultative process is inadequate and there is no satisfactory body of international law to deal with the issue of shared water courses. This absence of multilateral or comprehensive bilateral agreements between Middle Eastern states and their neighbours is again linked to political mistrust.

What no one knows is the degree of provocation that a state would consider insupportable, and that might force it to resort to military action. In the modern world, economics come into it: when would a war be the most cost-effective means of safeguarding the vital interests of a state? Given the huge sums involved, and the likely losses, the answer must be that warfare would very rarely be economically practical. Low-intensity operations seem to be a likelier option: installations such as dams, diversion tunnels, pipelines and desalination plants are usually vulnerable to sabotage (though Turkish engineers say it would take an atom bomb to affect their biggest dams). The international action against Iraq showed how vulnerable such installations are to air attack, while Iraqi actions in Kuwait demonstrated how easily water installations and desalination plants can be sabotaged on the ground.

There are lessons from the past to show when interference with a natural resource becomes intolerable and action has to be taken. The Arab–Israeli dispute over the Jordan, which was one of the main causes of the 1967 war, is the prime example, while President Assad's support for the PKK guerrillas was his way of inducing Turkey to negotiate over its plans to diminish the flow of the Euphrates into Syria.

There is a worrying tendency, too, for the water problems of the Middle East to spread out, to involve countries apparently far from the affected region. Ethiopia, geographically removed, is linked to Sudan and Egypt by the Nile, and is also caught up, whether it likes it or not, in the Arab–Israeli dispute. But in other cases, the connection is less clear, depending only on religion, or language, or membership of the Arab League – regarded as a club for rich countries in the 1970s, and thus attractive to poorer Arab-speaking states on the periphery of the Middle East. One such is Mauritania, where a little-publicized quarrel with its neighbour Senegal relates directly to shared water resources, and is identified by Dr Gamal Mazhloum, a strategist who advises several research institutes, as one of five flashpoints where military action is likely to escalate (the others are Turkey–Syria, the Israeli Occupied Territories, Ethiopia and Egypt–Libya). Professor Malin Falkenmark, who studies international hydrology at Sweden's Natural Science Research Council, agrees that the Mauritania–Senegal dispute is one of the most dangerous water-related quarrels, though it has made little impact in the West.

Fighting has already occurred on the banks of the Senegal river, where drought and changes in the flow of the river have over the past few years forced the tribespeople to alter their pattern of migration. They moved away from their traditional homes into areas held by others, making the struggle for access to water resources in this arid land inseparable from the ethnic and sectarian rivalries between Arab and African or Muslim and 'infidel'. Because of the involvement of other countries, the dispute did not remain one where small tribes or villagers fought each other with primitive weapons, but rapidly escalated into artillery exchanges across the disputed river.

One factor was that Saudi Arabia had been financing irrigation projects and agricultural programmes designed to improve things on the southern borders of Mauritania, and in the process to 'Arabize' the African districts affected and extend the spread of Islam. The Arab Beyadines tribes were quietly encouraged to move south, take over the land and drive out local black Senegalese.

The clashes occurred following heavy rain, which caused the river to flood. The Mauritanian explanation was that some of their farmers had been forced to abandon their holdings on the river plain by drought, and when the floods came and they returned to cultivate their holdings, they found that Senegalese tribesmen had got there before them. The now-fertile plain is inside Mauritanian territory, as the river itself is the border. But Senegal claims sovereignty over both banks of the river and argues that it needs to carry out irrigation and navigation work to develop the river, regarded as crucial for the economy of the country.

There have been claims and counter-claims on the causes of it all, but Organization of African Unity (OAU) and Islamic Conference (ICO) officials who tried to mediate recognize that the dispute over the watercourse itself is at the root of the conflict. What was most worrying was the speed with which the dispute became 'internationalized' as a result of the Arab element, largely because Iraq had used aid it was giving to Mauritania to obtain land for a missile testing range in the country. The involvement of the Iraqis alarmed not only neighbouring Senegal, but also Mali, which has a large Muslim population, and moderate Morocco.

The quarrel drew in Arab nationalists and Islamic activists, especially states that claimed a right to military intervention under the Joint Defence Pact of the Arab League. The League believes firmly – officially – that Israeli meddling in Central Africa and around the periphery of the Arab world, as well as in the Jordan basin, is part of a thought-out plan to divide and weaken its twenty-three members, and eventually to gain control of their water resources in Africa; the League sees the Mauritania–Senegal conflict as just another particularly blatant example of this Israeli 'plot', on a par with Israeli involvement in Ethiopia. Arab officials said they believed Israel's aim was to sever the southern parts of Mauritania from the rest of the country, and so to separate a member state of the Arab League from its main water resource.

Another issue deeply troubling Sudan and Egypt now, as they fear its effects on the Nile, is a wild-sounding but apparently feasible plan to build a 2,400 kilometre-long navigable canal across the heart of Africa. The modern technology demonstrated in the construction of the Jonglei Canal proves that this could be done, its proponents say, and certainly the idea is being taken seriously in Cairo – so seriously, army officers told us, that the dusty plans for military intervention in Africa are being updated and extended to include West Africa as well, while in Khartoum the fundamentalist government has asked for help with the potential problem from its new mentor, Iran. The cause of the flurry is a grandiose scheme advanced by a Nigerian, J. Umolu of Nigeria's National Electric Power Authority. He suggests constructing a pipeline similar to Gaddafi's Great Man-made River, linking the River Fafa, one of the tributaries of the Chari, with the River Oubangui. This would mean pumping water that currently discharges down the Zaire river into the ocean in the opposite direction, into the Central African Republic and Chad to increase the recharge of Lake Chad, and so to benefit Nigerian projects. Mr Umolu believes that in prehistoric times the River Zaire discharged into an ancient sea in the Chad region.

If it was ever carried out, this scheme would create a precedent that would deeply worry Egypt and Sudan, who have been concerned about any action affecting the Nile by Central African states. Today, the new pipeline is only an idea, not yet even on the drawing board, but as one Egyptian official told us: 'Egypt will collaborate with all those who will be affected to make sure this crazy project never sees the light.'

The Central African pipeline may seem too expensive for the poor countries that would have to pay for it, but other sources might be found for the finance: the UN could be persuaded that spending on such a project would be better than having to put up the same amount later to rescue countries in the grip of famine or civil chaos. Certainly some respected international companies are taking it seriously, among them Bonifica of Italy, which has produced a feasibility study of the project, named Transaqua. The Bonifica report starts with the words 'We must not be afraid of thinking big' and goes on to compare the scheme with the building of the Suez Canal or the Channel Tunnel.

Other studies for the project are believed to have been paid for by Colonel Gaddafi, who was enthusiastic about the idea when Libyan forces were fighting in Chad. Libyan businessmen living abroad, but in touch with Gaddafi, arranged for various outside firms to carry out additional surveys, and Libyan experts have been included in discussions already held between representatives of the Nigerian agricultural ministry and officials of the Lake Chad Basin Commission, which includes Cameroon and Niger as well as Chad. The idea also has the dubious backing of President Mobuto of Zaire.

As well as the Nigerian idea of a vast pipeline, there is an even more ambitious concept envisaged by Bonifica. This is to construct a navigable canal running around the rim of the Zaire basin, starting near Burundi. This worries the Egyptians even more, as it is very close to the East African headwaters of the Nile near Lake Victoria, and would drive north and north-west only a few miles from tributaries of the White Nile south-west of the Sudd in southern Sudan. The Transaqua canal would also intercept a number of lesser tributaries of the Zaire, then make a long journey across sparsely populated bushland into the River Chari, carrying a proposed 100 billion cubic metres of water each year, generating more than 30 billion kilowatt-hours of electricity, and irrigating up to 70,000 square kilometres. This is exactly the danger the Egyptians had in mind when Dr Boutros-Ghali told delegates to an African water summit in Cairo in June 1990 that 'The national security of Egypt, which is based on the waters of the Nile, is in the hands of other African countries.'

The question is how far Egypt would go to stop any of those projects being translated into fact, and to that there is no clear answer. The foreign ministry naturally says that Egypt would use peaceful, diplomatic means to try to prevent anything happening to affect the flow of the Nile. Egyptian military men say they have no faith in diplomacy or international pressure, and believe an early show of force, at least, would be needed to back up the representations of their government.

Egypt is taking developments in Africa most seriously, and making it plain that it considers it has a duty to take action if the threats become real. This is, in effect, a modern demonstration that Egypt still considers itself the dominant power in the Nile Valley. One state has emerged as the most powerful in each of the principal river basin areas of the Middle East: the Jordan (with the Litani), the Tigris–Euphrates and the Nile. Israel and Turkey operate on the assumption that their water needs and their control over water resources give them precedence over downstream countries; while Egypt, as we have seen, puts its confidence in what it sees as its military superiority over the African states that could in theory control the flow of the Nile.

At the other extreme are areas that suffer desperate shortages, have very little control over their own water supplies and lack the means to improve them: Jordan and the Gaza Strip are the prime examples. Syria and Iraq, though not in the parlous condition of Jordan or Gaza, are in the same way dependent on a neighbour pursuing its own agenda. Syria and Iraq fear the GAP is going to have a serious effect on their economies and water availability, and cannot individually hope to take on Turkey militarily. But they have a great deal of leverage, as President Assad has already demonstrated, while Saddam Hussein has shown the lengths to which he will go in pursuit of an objective. Turkey knows very well, for all its rather bombastic talk, that it has to tread warily when dealing with both those countries.

Sudan, another state that has both an adequate supply of water for itself and the theoretical ability to control the flow to its neighbour Egypt, is in no condition to exert its will. The civil war continues in the south, preventing any work on the Sudd, while Cairo makes it plain that it believes it has a right of veto over anything affecting the Nile that Sudan might propose. The new factor in the equation is Iranian backing of Sudan, which has already contributed to serious civil disorder in Egypt.

In other parts of the Middle East oil and water are interlinked: continuation of present policies or the introduction of new ideas requiring large investments depends on the oil flowing, revenues piling up and the extravagant national way of life thus being continued. In Libya and Saudi Arabia, in particular, the question is how long oil revenues can be allowed to finance agricultural schemes that are depleting irreplaceable groundwater resources. In those cases, it is not only a question of the actions being taken depleting reserves that might be claimed by other countries, but also the effect internally; opposition groups might well seize on local concerns ignored by governments to further their own ends.

It is not only Libya and Saudi Arabia that have been trying to increase agricultural production. Arab leaders, like politicians elsewhere, do not like having to rely on other countries for their food supplies, any more than they would want to be dependent on other states for their water. Experts hold that instead of embarking on new schemes, planners should ask if they need all the water they use. Geographers sometimes argue that the logical course would be to improve world trade with the Middle East so that the area of irrigated agriculture can be reduced – it is this land that accounts for the biggest loss of natural water in the arid regions. But geographers cannot ignore politics: prestige projects help to give a sense of national identity in newly independent countries and grandiose schemes often provide work, with the trickle-down effect helping to distribute wealth. Social considerations, as well as national strategy, are involved: reviving and extending agricultural land helps to stem the drift to the cities, and provides the unquantifiable benefit of maintaining rural crafts and traditions, particularly valuable in places where tourism is, or might be, a revenue earner.

The security considerations are just as important a part of reclamation, irrigation or land improvement schemes: in the GAP the integration of the Kurdish areas into the rest of Turkey is a prime concern, with the aim of making it impossible for the PKK to operate in the future. By offering greater prosperity to all, Turkey hopes to remove the water in which the revolutionary fish can swim. In Saudi Arabia, rural prosperity is seen as a means of countering a rise in tribalism, and of ensuring that dissidents among the Shia of the central and eastern provinces do not find willing followers. In Egypt, veterans of the 1973 Arab–Israeli war were given plots of reclaimed land designated for increased food crop cultivation despite their lack of farming expertise; it was more important to remove potential dissidents than to ensure high production. In Syria, priority has been given to irrigation in the Euphrates valley, though it might be better used elsewhere; but the valley is a major recruiting ground for the armed forces.

Agriculture is still a significant activity in most Middle Eastern countries, employing a high, though declining, proportion of the working population. In Morocco, Egypt, Sudan, Yemen and Turkey more than 30 per cent of the workforce is employed in the agricultural sector, which produces some 15 per cent of GDP. In the smaller Gulf states fewer than 5 per cent of the workers are in agriculture, and the contribution to GDP is much lower. In Oman, the current five-year plan aims to distribute wealth by developing rural areas, but has had to be curtailed due to the shortage of water in Dhofar province and the high population increase (3.8 per cent). The emphasis on trying to achieve food sufficiency was at its height in the 1980s, when the UAE and Kuwait, like Saudi Arabia, invested heavily in food production despite the aridity of their lands. They went in for fruit, vegetable and poultry production, even though oil revenues were large enough easily to cover the cost of food imports.

Despite all these programmes, the urban population in the region has now reached about 52 per cent of the total and the proportion is rising rapidly. One unexpected result has been increased desertification and reduction of land available for cultivation, as farmers abandon traditional areas, leaving the loss to be offset at high cost by land reclamation projects.

The drive for food self-sufficiency in Kuwait and the UAE, as in most countries which have invested heavily in schemes to increase arable land, is the single biggest drain on their water resources, a cost higher than the economic subsidies usually needed. In Oman, Yemen and Jordan water resources are being used at a rate faster than their renewal, while in the Gulf finite underground reserves are being steadily depleted. In Egypt, where 90 per cent of water consumption goes on agriculture, Nile water will have reached capacity use by 2000. Algeria, Egypt, Iraq, Jordan, Morocco, Oman, Saudi Arabia, Sudan, Syria, Tunisia and Yemen face absolute water scarcity by the turn of the century, according to one or more criteria: inadequate rainfall, number of people in relation to water resources, or proportion of water resources already utilized. Unless the shortages can be met, the likelihood of civil unrest seems bound to increase, while any attempts to improve supplies at the expense of neighbours will have international repercussions. The situation is made worse by the fact that the most acute shortages are in the poorest countries, and it is in these places that populations are growing fastest.

Studies show that 83 per cent of all available water in the Middle East now goes to agriculture, but by 2030 that amount must drop to 65 per cent as domestic use increases. The total regional population is expected to reach 348 million by that time, with an annual requirement of 470 billion cubic metres of water. That would be 132 billion more than the total available then even if the efficiency of water usage improved dramatically.

Iraq is the Arab state that is richest in water, with 5,192 cubic metres per head; Syria has 2,362, Lebanon 2,271, Oman 2,002, Sudan 2,798 and Egypt, where agriculture is most intensive, with three crops per year in some parts of the Nile Valley, just 1,050. It is worth noting, incidentally, that in Egypt, as in the rest of the developing world, women produce 50 per cent of the food supply but own only 1 per cent of the land. In Israel the figure for available water is 1,000 cubic metres per head per year if sources held to be illegal by the country's opponents are included. By the year 2000 Israel will need 1 billion cubic metres a year, without taking into account the immigration of Soviet Jews to the country; 60 per cent of that will be for direct use in the domestic network, and for industry. That would mean a shortfall of over 555 million cubic metres per year.

Looking at all the figures for the region, an Egyptian study predicts acute problems by 2000 and direct conflicts by 1994–5, which might lead within two years to armed action, raids, occupation of water resources or destruction of dams and water projects.

As a result of all that has happened, governments, institutions and prominent individuals have suddenly begun to realize just how important water is, and the way in which shortages – added to population growth – affect their economies, development and security. Yet rather than mobilizing their own people, the alarms of ministers have served more to attract the attention of outside experts and authorities, leading to a plethora of discussions, conferences and seminars, many with their own unstated objectives. At a two-day conference held in London in late 1992, for instance, there was a great deal of argument designed to show that pricing water properly was the key to conservation, and that the private sector should manage water resources, as it would undoubtedly increase them. No doubt many of those present would have expected to be invited to put their theories into practice.

Despite all the attention being paid to the situation, the Arab countries in general still blame outside forces more than they condemn their own policies, bad planning or lack of forethought. In 1991 the Abu Dhabi-based Arab Monetary Fund (AMF) formally set out the Arab belief that there was a conspiracy among the rich countries of the North to prevent Arabs exploiting their own available lands, and so approaching food sufficiency. 'The arable areas in the Arab world are more than enough to meet Arab demand if investments and proper labour were provided,' its report said. 'The Arab food gap has become a problem with political and social proportions.' Most of the arable areas are in Iraq, Sudan, Somalia, Lebanon and Egypt. The AMF estimated arable Arab land at 200 million hectares, though only 47 million hectares were being exploited. About 80 per cent of the cultivated area depends on rain, according to this report.

Annual surface water resources in Arab lands total 296 billion cubic metres. Underground water resources are 43 billion cubic metres, while the known aquifer reserves in the area are estimated at 7,723 billion cubic metres. The annual share per head in 1991 was 1,550 cubic metres, considered just enough at optimum use. By the year 2000, the figure would drop to 1,200 cubic metres, which would be on the verge of crisis even if irrigation and consumption methods were to improve. When the crisis does come, as it seems bound to do, it may be sudden and violent: there are 214 international river and lake basins in the world, of which 155 are shared by two countries, 36 by three and 23 by up to a dozen. That means that any conflict will be bound to involve national rivalries, some in the best-armed and most volatile regions of the world, particularly the Middle East.

The most dangerous places will be the cities. More than 90 per cent of global population growth is expected in urban areas of developing countries, which already suffer from lack of water, absence of sanitation and pollution of the supplies of drinking water available. Comparisons show the danger: Canada, with a population density of four people per square kilometre, has 12,000 cubic metres of water per person per year; Egypt, with ninety people per square kilometre, has 1,200. As it is, twenty-five countries are already experiencing chronic water shortages. That number will steadily rise to ninety as we move into the twenty-first century, according to the UN. By then, half the world's population will be affected, with the consequence that up to five billion people will be threatened by malnutrition, famine and disease. Already, the United Nations Children's Emergency Fund (UNICEF) believes that 35,000 children worldwide die daily from hunger or disease caused by lack or contamination of water.

In the Middle East, an additional problem is that about 20 per cent of the land is irrigated, from either rivers or underground water. In Libya, Morocco, Sudan, the UAE, Jordan, Syria and Yemen it is a little less than 20 per cent, while in Algeria, Tunisia and Turkey it is less than 5 per cent. In many countries, and especially those where farming is primitive, half of all irrigation water evaporates or seeps away through unlined ditches.

One reason for this waste, many hydro-economists argue, is that irrigation water is always hugely subsidized. Whether on the banks of the Nile or in California's Napa Valley, farmers rarely pay more than a fifth of the operating costs of public irrigation schemes, let alone their capital costs. World Bank economists and those of the IMF, who are opposed in general to subsidies, argue that other layers of support further promote the wasteful use of water. There are support payments for the crops, for instance, as well as subsidies for the electricity to drive the irrigation pumps. Raising the price of water is increasingly seen as a vital way of controlling its use. UN studies have shown that eliminating wastage through leaks, bad joints and faulty pumps can lead to 15 per cent more water being available in urban conditions, while realistic pricing policies can be used to induce large water users – factories, power plants and so on – to be sited in areas of abundant water and where they will do least environmental damage.

There is another aspect to water pricing that has not yet been quantified or, indeed, much understood. The provision of cheap, subsidized water is an important means of keeping people on the land or engaged in traditional activities. If that is not done, then hand-made artifacts will be replaced by the ubiquitous plastic, with the loss of appealing products added to the disappearance of the livelihood of many people. The dilemma can be seen in Cyprus, where the balance has almost been tipped: the island is chronically short of water, but its main industry is tourism, necessitating the construction of hundreds of hotels for visitors, who use far more water than the locals. At the same time, irrigation for such traditional crops as cherries, apples and pears is being restricted, forcing small farmers to give up and to drift to jobs in the towns. The result is deterioration of the countryside and of the towns as they become over-populated, and a loss of attractions that would make tourists visit the mountain areas as well as the seaside. That in turn means a drop in the quality of tourism to Cyprus, resulting in less expenditure by visitors and so a smaller return on investment, added to the damage done to the environment.

In Egypt, World Bank studies suggest, total annual subsidies for water are between US$5 billion and US$10 billion, the wide gap reflecting the difference between direct and indirect subsidies. In 1977 the Bank forced the government in Cairo to cut direct subsidies and to put up the price of bread; the result was riots in the streets and the swift reintroduction of price support. Any attempt to cut payments to farmers would be likely to have the same results. Although many hydrologists and environmentalists have been urging some form of water pricing in the Middle East in order to encourage farmers to use water wisely, the governments concerned recognize that such a step would not only be unpopular, it would also be unenforceable.

For all the huge expenditures on irrigation, and all the efforts made, the Middle East remains one of the world's largest food deficit areas, with only Turkey and Sudan having positive food balances. Egypt, a traditional agricultural economy, now imports 65 per cent of its food requirements at an annual cost of US$4 billion. Saudi Arabia has trebled food production since 1980, but still imports food to the value of US$5 billion annually for its population of fourteen million, a quarter that of Egypt.

One of the main troubles, according to experts of the Food and Agriculture Organization (FAO) in Rome, and those who have had practical experience of the area, is that the vast oil revenues of the Gulf countries, which by a deliberate policy were spread to other countries as well, accelerated the drift to the towns and made those who remained on the land put their faith in modern technology rather than in the old, labour-intensive methods of irrigation.

In Iran and the Arabian peninsula underground aqueduct systems have been developed over the centuries, and besides proving highly effective were so constructed that they could not extract too much water. The *qanat* system, as it is known in Iran, is made by digging and lining vertical shafts which connect with horizontal tunnels. Some extend for miles, often sloping to intersect with the underground water table. This was an inexpensive system as it was constructed with simple technology using material locally available, but most were built hundreds, or even thousands, of years ago. The best examples are five or six centuries old, and are found in Iran, where horizontal shafts recently excavated extend for as much as 25 kilometres. These long systems need constant attention. When the Mongols invaded Persia in the thirteenth century, for example, they destroyed only part of the *qanat* system, leaving the rest intact; yet a few years later, agriculture in Persia collapsed. The reason was that large numbers of peasants with the skills needed to maintain the system were either killed or displaced. The new Mongol rulers did not know how to repair the *qanats*, and without irrigation farming quickly became impossible. Today these underground channels are rarely built, and for the same reason: Iran and the Arab states lack the skilled manpower needed for their construction and maintenance.

Fortunately, there are a few exceptions. In Yemen and Oman, the *aflaj* system, as it is called in Arabic, is still the main network upon which local farmers rely for irrigation. In Oman the existing *aflaj* system supplies and irrigates 71 per cent of the cropped area. The great advantage of the system, according to Terry Evans of the water engineers Mott Macdonald, is that the underground water cannot be over-abstracted. There is a depth limit, which is the base of the shaft and the line of the tunnel. It is also economical, since there is no need for energy to drive pumps or force water along. But there is also a drawback in that the discharge is totally dependent on the level of the water table, which in turn depends on rainfall. This limits the farmer's choice to plants that can withstand long dry periods, such as date palms, and makes it impossible to grow vegetables or grain. The Saudi wheat-growing programme employs motor-driven pumps, which results in over-extraction and the lowering of the water table. Historically, local water and irrigation customs have recognized how the water table feeds the *aflaj*, and the wells and boreholes; the construction of additional wells in the vicinity of an *aflaj* has been restricted, while those depending on the *aflaj* are given the right to control the use of pumps.

Another traditional and successful method of irrigation in the Middle East has been spate irrigation schemes, improvised when the flood occurs. These schemes depend heavily on the availability of manpower to build, shift, knock down and alter small earth dams to direct floods to the cultivated farmlands. Like *aflaj* and *qanat* systems, this method is suffering from a shortage of skilled labour as workers are attracted to the towns and to the oil states. Only in Yemen has there been a revival of these traditional systems, as a result of improved knowledge and, more importantly, the return of a million people deported from Saudi Arabia. The spate system, used for thousands of years, became a natural way of recharging the underground water storage aquifers, and is now being extended in Yemen with the new labour available. The water supply to Aden and its surrounding area comes directly from underground streams fed from boreholes recharged through spate irrigation schemes north and east of the harbour.

In the Gulf, the lessons of the Gulf war are now being absorbed and acted upon. The chief one is the vulnerability of desalination plants, which has induced many countries to consider ways of storing up to a year's supply of water in case production ever has to be stopped. Saudi Arabia and Kuwait are both working on water storage in the porous rock aquifers that have been exhausted. The survival of Iraq as a result of its policy of expanding cereal production has also been noted, and is persuading new producers to go in for wheat production despite the world glut. Turkey's action in quickly closing down the Iraqi oil pipeline when asked to do so by the Americans is another factor reinforcing the determination of many states to retain control of their own resources, and not to be dependent on others for anything that would allow them to be pressured into compliance with outside demands.

The problems in the Arabian peninsula, in Libya or even in Egypt are for the future. In the Jordan Valley all the problems come together now. Given present consumption and expected population increase, there just is not enough water to go round. Water supplies per head in Israel, the Occupied Territories and Jordan are dwindling rapidly. In all areas efforts are being made to improve irrigation techniques and recycling: the cost of saving one cubic metre of water is usually lower than the cost of producing water from an alternative source. But by unhappy chance, these water-deficient countries are also the poorer ones of the region, and cannot afford the investments needed for modernization. Together, the countries of the Jordan basin, with international backing, could do a great deal; alone, they stand little chance. In the Jordan Valley, above all, cooperation is vital: the hope was that in this case the imperative of improving water supplies would transcend the political conflict, and force agreement. The events of 1992, the lack of progress in peace negotiations and the refusal of countries to take part in those sections of the peace talks devoted to water showed that in the Middle East old enmities take precedence over modern needs.

Those negotiations – or at times the lack of them – equally demonstrated that Middle Eastern countries, like those throughout the world, are well aware of the political value of water, its effect on policy and the consequences of shortages. The trouble is that there is very little many of them can do about it. For more than forty years the Middle East has been in the grip of a continuing crisis, a conflict that occasionally flares into a shooting war but never goes away. The Arab–Israeli confrontation is a fact of life of the twentieth century and may well extend into the twenty-first: it affects all aspects of life in the Middle East, and the relations of the countries of the region with powers elsewhere. The growing shortage of water in many countries, the increasingly sophisticated technology available and the better understanding of water resources by politicians have inextricably linked the problem of water to the political situation. Colonel Gaddafi, who often talks a lot of nonsense, at times talks a lot of sense. He summed up the situation: 'I am pleased', he said, 'that the Arabs have begun to realize that it is a water war. When the Arabs used to talk about political and military battles as well as guerrilla warfare, I told them the Israeli military strategy has one prime aim, that of controlling the water resources of the region.'

That does seem to have been a conscious Israeli strategic aim from the early Zionist days. It makes Israel determined to retain some control, at least, of the West Bank, though Israel would equally be delighted to get rid of the turbulent, water-consuming Gaza Strip. Jordan, driven by necessity, may in the end be forced against its will into new compromises, even an alliance with Israel. If that happens, the Palestinians will once again be driven to excess, and civil order will only be maintained at the point of a gun.

Elsewhere, the potential for armed conflict remains. Egypt has a deliberate policy of preparing for action in Central Africa, if that should prove necessary, calculating quite coldly that, given the present situation in countries that might affect its interests, the cost of military intervention would be low enough to justify its use. Iranian involvement in Sudan, and the ease with which those two countries have exploited Egypt's internal tensions, may make Cairo rethink its old doctrines.

Syria and Iraq, enemies for decades, could be forced into alliance by the actions of Turkey, as events showed when the Atatürk Dam was being filled. That could happen again if Turkey continues to pursue its chauvinistic attitude to the Tigris and the Euphrates, though Syria's support of the Kurds may have demonstrated to Turkey that overwhelming military strength is not the guarantee of success it appeared to think. Equally, Assad's use of 'liberation movements' may be the pattern for the future for countries that do not have military power or oil wealth but still need to influence their neighbours.

The West, though geographically removed, cannot dissociate itself completely, as the Americans have recognized in the studies they have commissioned. Turkey is a member of NATO, and hopes to join the European Community; if Turkey became embroiled in a shooting war with any of its neighbours, its allies would be bound to become involved. Clearly, the USA and its European friends are aware of the danger, and are trying to remove themselves. The policy of protecting the Kurds of northern Iraq and the Shia of the south is not something the allies undertook with any enthusiasm, or pursued with great vigour. Planners, if not public opinion, would like to abandon the commitments given.

For the West, the continuing concern has to be the safety of oil supplies from the Gulf, and now that Iraq has been defeated, the main dangers are from internal subversion and the continuing Iranian desire to export its Islamic revolution. In the Gulf countries, pro-vision of a steady and adequate water supply is a prime duty of government, but the only means open – desalination plants or pipe-lines to bring in supplies – are vulnerable to attack or sabotage. If the many movements pressing for either increased democracy or more fundamentalist rule in the Gulf states are not satisfied, they could well turn to violence to try to achieve their ends. That would carry the danger of an interruption to the plentiful oil supplies on which the West depends. But how could the West help? Soldiers and tanks are no defence against subversion.

In the Gulf as in the other vulnerable areas of the Middle East, the only possible policy for the West appears to be one it is reluctant to follow: to do all it can to encourage settlement of outstanding disputes, and to encourage friendly governments to settle internal discontents that might eventually lead to violent action. The trouble with such a programme is that the West in general is more fearful of what might happen if it followed that strategy than it is of what is happening now. There is always the danger that, as in the case of Iran, any relaxation of controls will allow extremists to take over.

The one certainty in the Middle East today is that water has become a commodity as important as oil: to those who possess it, it is a means of leverage and a way of projecting power; to those who lack adequate supplies, a prime concern of national security must be to increase what is available. Those two concerns must often conflict. Cooperation is the obvious answer, but cooperation depends on ami-cable relations, at least, between neighbours or groups of countries. For the foreseeable future, inter-state rivalries look likely to remain. Where and when states do reach accommodations, such pragmatic agreements are likely to spawn new groups of dissidents, and given the abundance of arms and ordnance in the Middle East, those groups will have access to everything needed for terrorist campaigns. Low-intensity operations specifically targeting water installations seem probable, with Iraq becoming the first state to sponsor such activity. The richest countries should survive without trouble by building more and more desalination plants, and a technological breakthrough enabling new forms of energy to be used would immensely benefit countries without access to vast revenues. At present, the costs are far too high for desalinated water to be used for irrigation, so that the Saudi Arabian and Libyan schemes will endure only as long as the fossil water being used. That will be something between 20 and 60 years, and in that time the likelihood is, the policy-makers believe, that the technical innovations needed will be found.

Rising populations and dwindling resources combine to make the Middle East the most vulnerable of all regions to water shortages. As we have shown, wars have already been fought to ensure adequate supplies, and the politicians have made it plain that they would be ready to use military means again to protect their national interests, while army commanders have devoted thought and effort to ensuring that the orders of the politicians, if they come, can be carried out. Inter-Arab rivalries as well as the perennial conflict between the Arabs and the Israelis have given rise to guerrilla groups, with more waiting in the wings if old opponents ever make up. The potential for violence is always present in the Middle East. When next it comes, as come it will, the areas being fought over will demonstrate that the stated cause of conflict may not be the only one. Although the battles may appear to be about land, or autonomy, or human rights, or protecting borders, every confrontation in the future will be affected by the hydrography of the region. Water wars are on the way.

References and Sources

I *Water, the Environment, Desertification and the History of the Crisis*

Adams, R. M., *Land Behind Baghdad* (Chicago and London, 1965)

Agnew, C., and Anderson, E., *Water Resources in the Arid Realm* (London, 1992)

Ahmad, A. H., *History of Eastern Arabia* (Beirut, 1965)

Ahmad, M. S., *Water Battles To Come in the Middle East* (Cairo, 1991)

Ali, K. H., *The Negotiating Warriors: Egyptian Israeli Peace Negotiations* (Cairo, 1984)

Ashtor, E., *A Social and Economic History of the Near East in the Middle Ages* (London, 1976)

Beaumont, P., Blake, G. H., and Wagstaff, J. M., *The Middle East: A Geographical Study* (London, 1988)

Berque, J., *The Arabs* (London, 1964)

Birks, S., and Sinclair, C., *Arab Manpower: The Crisis of Development* (London, 1980)

Bresheeth, H., and Yuval-Davis, N. (eds), *The Gulf War and the New World Order* (London, 1991)

Brogan, P., *World Conflicts* (London, 1989)

Bromley, S., *American Hegemony and World Oil: The Industry, the State System and the World Economy* (Cambridge, 1991)

Browne, E. G., *A Literary History of Persia* (Cambridge, 1928)

Bulloch, J., *Final Conflict* (London, 1983)

Bulloch, J., and Morris, H., *Saddam's War* (London, 1991)

Clark, Robin, *Water: The International Crisis* (London and New York, 1992)

Corm, G., *Fragmentation of the Middle East* (London, 1988)

Darwish, A., and Alexander, G., *Unholy Babylon: the Secret History of Saddam's War* (London 1991)

Darwish, A., and Raziq, E. A., *Between The Quill and the Sword: the Historical* and Political Background to the Satanic Verses Affair (London and Cairo, 1989)

Evland, W., *Ropes of Sand: America's Failure in the Middle East* (New York, 1980)

Fahmi, I., *Negotiating for Peace in the Middle East* (London, 1983)

Fawzi, General M., *Strategy for Reconciliation* (Cairo, 1988)

Gibb, H. A. R. (trans.), *The Travels of Ibn Battuta* (Cambridge, 1958)

Glubb, J. B., *A Short History of the Arab Peoples* (London, 1978)

Goldsmith, Edward, and Hildyard, Nicholas, *The Social and Environmental Effects of Large Dams* (London, 1984)

Gould, S. J. B., 'The Troubled Arab Middle East', in G. P. Chapman and K. M. Baker (eds), *The Changing Geography of Africa and the Middle East* (London, 1992)

Haykal, M. H., *Sphinx and the Commissar: The Rise and Fall of Soviet Influence in the Arab World* (London, 1978)

— *The Autumn of Fury: The Assassination of Sadat* (London, 1984)

Hirsch, Z., *The Economics of Peacemaking* (London, 1983)

Irwin, R., *The Middle East in the Middle Ages: The early Mamluk Sultanate* (London, 1986)

Kamel, M. I., *The Camp David Accords: A Testimony* (London, 1986)

Kanovsky, E., *The Economic Impact of the Six Day War* (New York, 1970)

Kerr, M., *The Arab Cold War: Gamal abd al-Nasir and his rivals 1958–1970* (Oxford, 1971)

Kerr, M. H., and Yassin, E. S. (eds), *Rich and Poor States in the Middle East* (Boulder, 1982)

Lean, G., Hinrichsen, D., and Markham, A., *Atlas of the Environment* (London, 1990)

Lindner, R. P., *Nomadism, Horses and Huns: Past and Present* (Cambridge, Mass., 1981)

— *What was a Nomadic Tribe? Comparative Studies in Society and History* (Cambridge, Mass., 1982)

— *Nomads and Ottomans in Medieval Anatolia* (Bloomington, 1983)

McLachlan, K. S., 'The Non-Arab Middle East: Iran, Turkey and Israel', in G. P. Chapman and K. M. Baker (eds), *The Changing Geography of Africa and The Middle East* (London, 1992)

McLaurin, R. D., Mughisuddin, M., and Wagner, A. R., *Foreign Policy Making in the Middle East* (New York, 1977)

Morgan, D., *The Mongols* (Massachusetts, 1987)

Naff, T., and Matson, R., *Water in the Middle East: Conflict or Cooperation?* (Westview, 1984)

Nelson, L., and Sandell, C., *Population and Water Resources* (Washington, 1992)

Quandt, W. B., *Camp David* (Washington, 1981)
Riad, M., *The Struggle for Peace in the Middle East* (London, 1981)
Spuler, B., *The Muslim World: a Historical Survey* (Leiden, Germany, 1960)
Taheri (el), H., *Water Future in the Arab World* (Cairo, 1991)
Thompson, J. H., and Reischauer, R. D. (eds), *Modernization of the Arab World* (New York, 1966)
Tibi, B., *Conflict and War in the Middle East* (London, 1992)
Watson, A. M., 'A Medieval Green Revolution: new crops and farming techniques in the early Islamic world', in Udovitch, A. L. (ed), *The Islamic Middle East, Studies in Economic and Social History* (Princeton, 1981)
Wenger, M., and Stork, J., *The Food Gap in the Middle East* (Washington, 1992)

JOURNALS, CHRONICLES, PERIODICALS AND DOCUMENTS

Allan, J. A., 'Natural Resources as National Fantasies', *Geoforum*, 4:3 (1983)
— 'Water Resources in the Middle East', *The Arab Researcher*, no. 22 (1990)
— 'Review of evolving water demands and national development options', paper presented to the Royal Geographic Society Conference, London University, May 1990
— 'Dealing with Arab food production shortages', *The Arab Researcher*, no. 29 (1992)
— 'Striking the right "price" for water: achieving harmony between basic human need, available resources and commercial viability', paper presented to conference organized by IBC Financial Focus, London University, 1992
Badieh, A. A. A., 'Water Crisis from the Nile to the Euphrates', *International Politics Journal*, vol. 104 (April 1991)
Bahiri, S., 'Comparative analysis and country profiles of Middle East economics', papers published quarterly by Middle East Economic Cooperation Project, University of Tel-Aviv, 1982
el-Fank, F., 'Realistic solution to the Arab food production gap, *The Arab Researcher*, no. 29 (1992)
Hashim, Y. A., 'Water crisis: political, legal and economic dimensions', *International Politics Journal*, vol. 104 (April 1991)
Mandoor, M., 'Strategy for Arab food security', *The Arab Researcher*, no. 29 (1992)
Mazhloum, G., 'Water and conflict in the Middle East', *The Arab Researcher*, no. 22 (1990)
Radi, M., 'Water issues in the Arab world until the year 2025', *The Arab Researcher*, no. 28 (1992)

Radwan, S., 'Agrarian reforms and rural poverty 1952–1975', International Labour Office, Geneva, 1977

Storer, D., 'The potential role of privatisation in the management of water resources in the Middle East', paper presented to conference organized by IBC Financial Focus, London University, 1992

II Ethiopia, Sudan, the Nile, Egyptian Politics in Africa, North Africa, and Gaddafi

Abate, Z., *Planned National Water Policy: A Proposed Case for Ethiopia* (Washington, 1991)

Abdel-Haiye, A., *The Nile and the Future* (Cairo, 1987)

Adloff, R., and Thompson, V., *Conflict in Chad* (California, 1981)

Ahmad, M. S., *Diplomacy Between Theory and Practice* (Cairo, 1990)

Allan, J. A., *Libya: The Experience of Oil* (London, 1981)

– 'The Changing Geography of the Lower Nile: Egypt and Sudan as Riparian States', in G. P. Chapman and K. M. Baker (eds), *The Changing Geography of Africa and The Middle East* (London, 1992)

Atsimadja, F. A., 'The Changing Geography of Central Africa', in G. P. Chapman and K. M. Baker (eds), *The Changing Geography of Africa and The Middle East* (London, 1992)

Ayubi, N., *Bureaucracy and Politics in Contemporary Egypt* (London, 1980)

Baker, R. W., *Egypt's Uncertain Revolution Under Nasser and Sadat* (Cambridge, Mass., 1978)

– *Sadat and After: Struggle for Egypt's Political Soul* (London, 1990)

Barker, G., 'Natural resource use: lessons from the past', in J. A. Allan (ed), *Libya Since Independence* (London, 1982)

Bearman, J., *Qadhafi's Libya* (London, 1986)

Bell, M., *Contemporary Africa* (London, 1986)

Berque, J., *French North Africa: The Maghreb Between Two World Wars* (London, 1967)

Berthelot, R., *The Jonglei Canal* (New York, 1976)

Blum, W., *The CIA: A Forgotten History* (London, 1986)

Butzer, K. W., *Early Hydraulic Civilisation in Egypt* (Chicago and London, 1976)

Collins, R. O., *Shadows in the Grass: Britain in the Southern Sudan, 1918–1956* (New Haven, 1983)

– *The Big Ditch: The Jonglei Canal Scheme*, M. W. Daly (ed) (London, 1985)

– *The Waters of the Nile* (Oxford, 1987)

Cooper, M. N., *The Transformation of Egypt* (London, 1982)

Craig, J. I., and Willcocks, W., *The Egyptian Irrigation* (London, 1913)

References and Sources

Craig-Harris, L. (ed), *Egypt: Internal Challenges and Regional Stability* (London and New York, 1988)

Cromer, Earl of, *Modern Egypt* (London, 1908)

Dawood, N. J. (trans.), *The Koran* (London, 1956)

Egyptian Government (author unknown), *Nile Control* (Cairo, 1921)

Eidelberg, P., *Sadat* (Quebec, 1979)

Garang, J., *The Call for Democracy in Sudan* (New York, 1987)

Haykal, M. H., *The Suez Files: Thirty Years of War* (Cairo, 1986)

Herodotus, *The Histories*, trans. Aubery de Selincourt (Harmondsworth, 1954)

Hinnebusch, R. A., *Egyptian Politics Under Sadat* (London and New York, 1985)

Holt, P. M., and Daly, M. W., *A History of the Sudan* (London, 1989)

Hopwood, D., *Egypt: Politics and Society 1945–90* (London, 1991)

Howell, P. P., Lock, J. M., and Cobb, S. M. (eds), *The Jonglei Canal: Impact and Opportunity* (Cambridge, 1988)

Hurst, H. E., *The Hydrology of the Sobat and White Nile and the Topography of the Blue Nile and Atbara* (Cairo, 1950)

— *The Nile* (London, 1952)

Hurst, H. E., and Black, P. P., *Monthly and Annual Rainfall Totals and Numbers of Rainy Days at Stations Near the Nile Basin* (Cairo, 1943)

Hurst, H. E., and Philips, P., *The Nile Basin*, Vol. I (Cairo, 1931); Vol. II (Cairo, 1932); Vol. IV (Cairo, 1932); Vol. V (Cairo, 1938) and Vols VI, X (co-authored with P. P. Black and Y. M. Simaika) (Cairo, 1966)

Hurst, H. E., and Simaika, Y. M., *The Hydrology of the Blue Nile and Atbara and of the Main Nile to Aswan* (Cairo, 1959)

Hurst, H. E., Black, P. P., and Simaika, Y. M., *Long-term Storage: an Experimental Study* (London, 1965)

al-Husseini, M. M., *Soviet Egyptian Relations 1945–85* (London, 1987)

Joffe, G., 'The changing geography of North Africa: development, migration and the demographic time bomb', in G. P. Chapman and K. M. Baker (eds), *The Changing Geography of Africa and The Middle East* (London, 1992)

Kelley, A. C., Khalifa, A. M., and El-Khorazaty, M. N., *Population and Development in Rural Egypt* (Durham, 1982)

Lloyd, S., *Suez 1956: A Personal Account* (London, 1978)

Love, K., *Suez: The Twice Fought War* (London, 1969)

Lyons, H. G., *The Physiography of the River Nile and its Basin* (Cairo, 1906)

MacDermott, A., *Egypt After Nasser* (London, 1987)

MacDonald, Sir M., and Partners, *Nile Waters Study, The Republic of Sudan Publication Organisation* (Khartoum, 1979)

Marbo, R., *The Egyptian Economy 1952–1972* (Oxford, 1974)

Naguib, M., *Egypt's Destiny: A Personal Statement* (London, 1955)

Nasser, G. A., *The Philosophy of the Revolution* (Cairo, 1954)

O'Brien, P. K., *The Revolution in Egypt's Economic System* (London, 1966)

Pasha, H. S., *Irrigation in Egypt* (Bulaq, 1937)

Rejwan, N., *Nasserist Ideology: its Exponents and Critics* (New York, 1974)

Sadat, A., *Revolt on the Nile* (London, 1957)

— *In Search of Identity* (London, 1978)

Shahin, M. M. A., *Southern Development Investigation Team: Natural Resources and Development Potential in the Southern Provinces of the Sudan* (Khartoum, 1955)

— *Hydrology of the Nile Basin: Developments in Water Science* (Amsterdam, 1985)

Shoukri, G., *Egypt: Portrait of a President, Sadat's Road to Jerusalem* (London, 1981)

Simons, G., *Libya: The Struggle For Survival* (London, 1993)

Subait, A. H., *The Story of the Peasant and the Land* (Cairo, 1965)

Sutcliffe, J. V., 'The hydrology of the Sudd region of the upper Nile', Ph.D. Thesis (Cambridge, 1957)

Sutcliffe, J. V., and Parks, Y. P., *A Hydrological Estimate of the Effects of the Jonglei Canal on Areas of Flooding* (Wallingford, Mass., 1982)

Toniolo, E., and Hill, R. (eds), *The Opening of the Nile Basin* (London, 1974)

Vatikiotis, P. J., *Nasser and His Generation* (London, 1978)

— *The History of Egypt* (Baltimore, 1986)

Warburg, G. R., *Egypt and the Sudan: Studies in History and Politics* (London, 1985)

Waterbury, J., *Hydropolitics of the Nile valley* (New York, 1979)

— *The Egypt of Nasser and Sadat: The Political Economy of Two Regimes* (Princeton, NJ, 1983)

Whittington, D., and Haynes, K. E., 'Nile water for whom? Emerging conflicts in water allocation for agriculture expansion in Egypt and Sudan', in P. Beaumont and K. S. McLachlan (eds), *Agricultural Development in the Middle East* (London, 1985)

Whittington, D., and McClelland, E., *Opportunities for Regional and International Cooperation in the Nile Basin* (Chapel Hill, North Carolina, 1991)

Woodward, P., *Nasser* (London, 1992)

Wright, J., *Libya: A Modern History* (Baltimore, 1982)

Zeid, M. A. A., and Rady, M. A., *Egypt's Water Resources Management and Policies* (Washington, 1991)

JOURNALS, CHRONICLES, PERIODICALS AND DOCUMENTS

Abate Z., 'The Integrated Development of the Nile Basin Waters', paper presented to the Royal Geographic Society Conference, London University, May 1990

Abdulla, I. H., 'The Nile waters agreement in Sudanese–Egyptian relations', *Middle East Journal*, vol. 7 (1971)

Ahmed, M. S., 'Principles and precedents in international law governing the sharing of Nile water', paper presented to the Royal Geographic Society Conference, London University, May 1990

Arab Strategic Report, Arab League Documents (Cairo, 1988)

Aramco (the Arabian American Oil Company), International Annual Report, Research Division, 1952, 1966, 1989

Bechtel report, 'Desalination in the eastern province of Saudi Arabia', prepared by the Bechtel Corporation for the UN (1966)

Beschorner, N., and Smith, A., 'Libya in the 1990s: can resources be salvaged?', Special Report no. 2134, EIU Economist Prospects Series (London, 1991)

Bishop, W. W., 'Pleistocene stratigraphy in Uganda, geological survey', Government chronicles (Entebbe, 1956)

Boutros-Ghali, B., 'Administering water in the Nile Basin', speech before the Senate in Washington, September 1989

Buren, L., 'Mauritania', *Arab Agriculture 1987 Year Book* (London, 1988)

Chesworth, P. M., 'The history of water use in Sudan and Egypt', paper presented to the Royal Geographic Society Conference, London University, May 1990

Collins, R. O., 'Nile control: myth or reality', paper presented to the Royal Geographic Society Conference, London University, May 1990

Cooper, H. H., Jr., 'A hypothesis concerning the dynamic balance of fresh water and salt in the coastal aquifer', *Journal of Geographic Research*, lxiv (1959)

Economic Bulletin, the National Bank of Egypt, 1979, 1983, 1987, 1990, 1991

Economic Trade Statistics of the UN, 1983

Egyptian government, report of the Nile Projects Commission (Cairo, 1920)

Evans, T. E., 'History of Nile flows', paper presented to the Royal Geographic Society Conference, London University, May 1990

Haddidie, A., 'Egypt's foreign policy towards Nile water', *International Politics Journal*, vol. 104 (April 1991)

Hewett, R. M. G., and Knott, D. G., 'Water resources planning in the Sudan', paper presented to the Royal Geographic Society Conference, London University, May 1990

Howell, P. P., and Allan, J. A., 'The Nile: resource evaluation, resource management, hydropolitics and legal issues', School of Oriental and African Studies special publication (London, 1990)

International Bank for Reconstruction and Development, Report of the technical mission of Sudan irrigation (1959)

International Financial Statistics Year Book

Jonglei Investigation Team Report: the Equatorial Nile Project and its effect in the Anglo-Egyptian Sudan, Government of Sudan Publications (Khartoum, 1954)

Journal of Semitic Studies, vol. 6 (1961), 145–61: 'The death of the Last Abaasis Chaliph – a contemporary Muslim account'

Keynote papers, International Conference on Water and the Environment, Dublin, 1992

Lazenby, J. B. C., and Sutcliffe, J. V., 'Hydrological data requirement for planning Nile management', paper presented to the Royal Geographic Society Conference, London University, May 1990

Ministry of Foreign Affairs, Egypt, White Paper on Egypt and the Nile, (1982)

– Papers on Egypt and the Nile (Cairo, 1984)

Ministry of Irrigation and Hydroelectric Power of Sudan, 'The Nile waters question: the case for Sudan and the case for Egypt and the Sudan's reply' (Khartoum, 1955)

Ministry of Planning, the Hashemite Kingdom of Jordan, 'Five Years 1986–1990' (Amman, 1985)

'The Multilaterals', reports on Middle East talks, BIPAC (London, 1992)

Naff, T., 'Israel and the Waters of South Lebanon', paper to Chatham House Conference on Lebanon, London, 1991

Okidi, C. O., 'History of the Nile and Lake Victoria Basins Through Treaties', paper to the Royal Geographic Society Conference, London University, May 1990

Oudah, A. M., and Rahman, H. A., 'Regional cooperation in the Horn of Africa and the Nile Basin', *International Politics Journal*, vol. 104 (Cairo, April 1991)

People's Assembly Foreign Relations Committee, report on Nile Basin states (Cairo, 1990)

People's Assembly All Party Select Committee on Water Resources, Report by Dr I. Kamel (1992)

Permanent Joint Technical Commission, data on water use by Sudan and Egypt, Royal Geographic Society (London, 1989)

'Population Concern', World Population Data Sheet

Public Affairs Committee for Shia Muslims, Dialogue (London, 1992)

Starr, J., 'A way to a water African summit', *International Politics Journal*, vol. 104 (April 1991)

Stavins, Robert, Study for green lobby group Environmental Defence Fund to examine a proposal to dam California's Tuolumne river

Stoner, R. F., 'Future Irrigation Planning in Egypt', paper presented to the Royal Geographic Society Conference, London University, May 1990

Tamrat, I., 'The Nile: A consideration of the issues – the view upstream', paper to conference organized by IBC Financial Focus, London University, 1992

Tilahun, W., 'Egypt's Imperial Aspirations Over Lake Tana and the Blue Nile' (Addis Ababa University, 1979)

UN documents (the Nile Political and Legal Issues), E/ECE/136 (1952)

UN Development Programme, Nile River Basin fact-finding mission report, RAF/86/003 and RAB/86/014 of UNDUGU Preliminary Study Mission by Paul Marc Henry (1989)

US Department of Interior, 'Land and water resources of the Blue Nile Basin: Ethiopia' (Washington, 1964)

World Bank and International Finance Corporation, *World Tables*, fourth edition (1987)

World Bank, world development report (Oxford University Press, 1990)

III *Israel, the Jordan Valley, Syria, Lebanon, the Palestinian and Arab–Israeli Water Conflict*

Depuy, T. N., *Elusive Victory: The Arab–Israeli Wars 1947–1974* (London, 1978)

Garaudy, R., *The Case of Israel* (London, 1983)

Herzog, C., *The Arab Israeli Wars: War and Peace in the Middle East from the War of Independence to Lebanon* (London, 1984)

Sharon, Ariel, *Warrior* (London, 1989)

JOURNALS, CHRONICLES, PERIODICALS AND DOCUMENTS

Alpher, J., 'Security arrangement for a Palestinian settlement', *Survival*, 34:4 (1992)

Bakr, H., 'Hydrological view of the Arab-Israeli conflict', *International Politics Journal*, vol. 104 (April 1991)

Bardawil, S., 'Israeli claims on Lebanese water: the Litani river', unpublished M.Phil. thesis (Oxford University, 1992)

Davis, U., 'Arab water resources and Israel water policies', *The Arab Researcher*, no. 22 (1990)

Kally, E., 'Extension of Israel's national water system as a function of artificial rainfall', report on water resources presented to the American Biophysical Union, 1974

– reports for the Middle East Economic Cooperation Project, Tel-Aviv University: 'Conveyance of Nile water to the Gaza Strip, the West Bank and the Negev' (1981); 'Possible Israeli–Jordanian cooperation in water utilization projects' (1981); 'Yarmuk water storage in Lake Tebrie' (1983); 'Water supply to the autonomy areas from external sources' (1984); 'Middle East cooperation in the use of energy resources under peace' (1985)

– 'Water and Peace: an Israeli perspective', Institute for Palestinian Studies (Beirut, 1991)

Kolars, J., 'The Litani River in the context of Middle Eastern water resources', report for the Centre For Middle Eastern and African Studies (University of Michigan, 1991)

Qasem (Al), A., 'The West Bank between Palestine, Israel and Jordan: law and facts in the crisis', paper presented to Conference organized by IBC Financial Focus at London University, 1992

Riad, M., 'Israel and Arab waters', *The Arab Researcher*, no. 06 (1986)

Schmida, L., 'Israeli water projects and their repercussions in the Arab–Israeli conflict', *The Arab Researcher*, no. 06 (1986)

Stauffer, T., 'Israel and Arab resources: the spoils of war', *The Arab Researcher*, no. 22 (1990)

Tahal Consulting Engineers Ltd, Israel Water Sector Review, the World Bank (Washington, 1991)

Tal, A., 'The Hashemite Kingdom of Jordan: a geographical background', Middle East Economic Cooperation Project (University of Tel-Aviv, 1983)

Taleb, M. F. A., Deason, J. P., and Salameh, E., 'Water Resources Planning and Development in Jordan', the World Bank (Washington, 1991)

World Bank report, 'Jordan–North-east Ghor Irrigation and Rural Development' (Washington, 1981)

IV *Treaties, International Law, Disputes, and Potential Conflicts*

Anderson, E. W., and Rashidian, K. H., *Iraq and the Continuing Middle East Crisis* (London, 1991)

Copenerre, A., *The Law of International Water Resources*: FAO (1977)

Dawood, N. J. (trans.), *The Koran* (London, 1956)

Gattetson, A. H., Hayton, R. D., and Olmstead, C. J., *The law of international drainage basin*, Institute of International Law (NY University, 1981)

Maktari, A. M. A., *Water Rights and Irrigation Practices in Lahj: A study of the Application of Customary Law in South-West Arabia* (Cambridge, 1971)

McLachlan, K. S., *Sovereignty, Territoriality, and International Boundaries in*

South East Asia, The Middle East and North Africa (London, 1991)

Moor (el) A., 'The Nile: The rights of downstream riparians', paper presented to conference organized by IBC Financial Focus, London University, 1992

Sanhuri, A. R. A., *A Rightful Source in Islamic Legislation* (Cairo, 1954)

JOURNALS, CHRONICLES, PERIODICALS AND DOCUMENTS

Ahmed, M. S., 'Principles and precedents in international law governing the sharing of Nile water', paper presented to the Royal Geographic Society Conference, London University, May 1990

Boyle A., 'International law of environmental rights: remedies for pollution injuries', paper presented to conference organized by IBC Financial Focus, London University, 1992

Dellapenna, J., 'Building international water management institutions: the role of treaties and other legal agreements', paper presented to conference organized by IBC Financial Focus, London University, 1992

Du Bois, F., 'Regulating the competitive use of fresh water resources: compensation and exploitation', paper presented to conference organized by IBC Financial Focus, London University, 1992

Hassan, S., 'International rules governing the exploitation of international waterways', *The Arab Researcher*, no. 24 (1990)

Khasawneh, A. A., 'The International Law Commission and the Middle East water', paper presented to conference organized by IBC Financial Focus, London University, 1992

Kinnersley, D., 'Is water an exploitable commercial product?', paper presented to conference organized by IBC Financial Focus, London University, 1992

Krishna, R., 'International watercourses: World Bank experience and policy', paper presented to conference organized by IBC Financial Focus, London University, 1992

Le Moigne, G., and Matthews, G., 'Sources of available finance: perspective from a multi-lateral lending agency', paper presented to conference organized by IBC Financial Focus, London University, 1992

Mallat, C., 'The rights that attach to water: customs and the Sharia – a legacy of principles and institutions?', paper presented to conference organized by IBC Financial Focus, London University, 1992

Teclaff, L., 'Legal and institutional resources of water demand', report by FAO, UN (Rome, 1977)

V *The Euphrates Valley, Turkey, Iraq, Syria, the Kurds and Iran*

Bulloch, J., and Morris, H., *No Friends But the Mountains* (London, 1992)

JOURNALS, CHRONICLES, PERIODICALS AND DOCUMENTS

Chalabi, H., 'Turkey and the River Euphrates: the context within international law', paper presented to conference organized by IBC Financial Focus, London University, 1992

Daoud, Z. F. A., 'The Syrian Case in the Euphrates Dispute', paper presented to the Arab Research Centre discussion on the Euphrates, London, 1990

Khalik, A. G. A., 'Euphrates Upstream States' Project and its effect on Iraqi water quota', *The Arab Researcher*, no. 24 (1990)

Mango, A., 'Turkey and the Arabs after the Gulf War', *The Arab Researcher*, no. 27 (1991)

Utkan, N., 'The Turkish case in the Euphrates dispute', paper presented to the Arab Research Centre discussion on the Euphrates, London, 1990

el-Zahawai, W., 'The Iraqi Case in the Euphrates Dispute', paper presented to the Arab Research Centre discussion on the Euphrates, London, 1990

VI *Arabian Peninsula*

Alabdel-Raziq, F. H. Y., *Water in Kuwait* (Kuwait, 1989)

McLachlan, A., and McLachlan, K. S., *Oil and Development in the Gulf* (London, 1989)

Wilkinson, J. C., *Water and Tribal Settlement in South-east Arabia* (Cambridge, 1971)

The Kingdom of Saudi Arabia (London, 1977)

JOURNALS, DOCUMENTS

el-Baz, F., 'Space research and desert development', *The Arab Researcher*, no. 06 (1986)

Evans, T. E., 'Engineering and water shortages in the Middle East', paper presented to conference organized by IBC Financial Focus, London University, 1992

Index